Following the Shore
from Boston to Brownsville

Following the Shore from Boston to Brownsville

Bill Hezlep

ISBN: 9781797903781

The two aerial photos in Chapter 9 were provided by
Bryan Carlile, **beck geodetix** Project Manager.

.

All other photos are by the author.

Parts of this book appeared previously in
POINTS EAST
The Boating Magazine for Coastal New England.

Table of Contents

Preface

Several years ago, on a summer road trip, we stopped for lunch at Schaefer's Canal House in Chesapeake City, Maryland. The restaurant sits beside the Chesapeake and Delaware Canal which, as the name says, connects the Chesapeake Bay with Delaware Bay. It was a hot afternoon so we gave the waterfront patio a pass and enjoyed the air conditioning at the bar. Through a large window we could see the canal, a few boats and the boat basin across the canal. While we were enjoying some very decent crab cakes, I asked the young bartender "where does the Intracoastal Waterway Begin?" The answer was prompt. "In Norfolk, Virginia, it goes to Florida, I helped my uncle take his boat down it."

The canal we were looking at through the window, the Chesapeake and Delaware Canal, is an integral part of the Intracoastal Waterway.

In the Rivers and Harbors Act of March 3, 1909 [House of Representatives 28243, CHAP. 268, Approved March 3, 1909], Congress ordered the United States Army Corps of Engineers to develop a set of surveys and proposals for the construction of "a continuous waterway, inland where practicable, from Boston, Massachusetts...to Point Isabel (Texas); and thence to the Rio

Grande." This Act established, as national policy, the creation of an Intracoastal Waterway from Boston to the Rio Grande.

But by March of 1909, an Intracoastal Waterway was already well underway.

As early as 1838 a coasting vessel following the "inside navigation" could travel from the east end of Long Island Sound south to the Beaufort Inlet in North Carolina without venturing out into the open ocean. By 1909, a coasting vessel entering the east end of Long Island Sound could travel south to Beaufort, N.C., then, after a coastal run to Winyah Bay (Georgetown, S.C.), could continue south on protected inside waterways to the St. Johns River in Florida. On Florida's east coast, south of the St. Johns, the Florida East Coast Canal Company was nearing completion of a navigable inside waterway connecting the St. Johns River and Jacksonville with Biscayne Bay and Miami. In the Gulf of Mexico–both on peninsular Florida's west coast and along the upper Gulf Coast, from the Florida panhandle to south Texas–segments of what would become the Intracoastal Waterway were planned, surveyed, under construction, or already in use. And, in the name of drainage and land reclamation, the seeds that would grow into a canal across Florida had been planted.

In June 1949 the segment of the waterway linking Corpus Christi, Texas to the Port of Brownsville, just a short distance from the Rio Grande and Mexico, was opened. In January 1967 the Florida Gulf Coast Waterway linking Fort Myers and the Caloosahatchee River with the Anclote River and Tarpon Springs was opened. With these openings the Intracoastal Waterway existed in its current form. Since 1967 sections of the waterway have been widened, deepened and rerouted and locks, floodgates and other navigational structures have been built, rebuilt or modified. But no significant extensions or additions have received Congressional authorization, or even serious consideration.

A journey along the Intracoastal Waterway is a trip through the United States' geography and history. As the waterway winds along the coast from Boston and the deep, cold waters and rocky shores of New England to the flat, hot, brown and seemingly endless Texas coast, it passes or runs directly through the United States': largest city, its most densely populated areas, all five of its

Urban Detritus

largest sea ports–seventeen of the twenty-five largest–its colonial dawn, its battle fields from the earliest colonial conflicts through the French and Indian Wars, and the Revolutionary War to the Civil War and through the haunts of fishermen, whale men, merchant seaman, pirates, slaves (and slavers), developers, engineers, politicians and wildcatters.

It is also a journey into the natural, less then natural and changing environment of the coast. Although two of the waterway's segments are major big ship canals, deep and broad, their banks stabilized with granite and flood lite at night, and another is a lake and some canals originally built for, and still primarily used for drainage and flood control, most of the waterway is composed of natural features–creeks, rivers, bays and sounds–linked by relatively short man-made canals and cuts. The natural and almost natural sections are often remote, wild, and lovely places teeming with coastal wildlife. But the waterway also passes through great cities, industrial areas, sprawling suburbs and coastal resorts, and in these areas the water is too often a field of fast food containers, plastic bottles, thrown away grocery bags, cigarette butts and other detritus painted in the rainbow hues of a petrochemical sheen.

From its origins deep in our Nations' history to current improvements and maintenance, the spurs that have driven the waterways development are the same engines that drive all our national transportation infrastructure: commerce, economic development, the efficient movement of commodities and equipment and national defense. Today the Intracoastal Waterway–like the Dwight D. Eisenhower National System of Interstate and Defense Highways–is an integral part of our integrated national transportation network.

The waterway connects the inland navigation network–the Mississippi, Ohio, Tennessee, Cumberland, Missouri, and Monongahela River systems and the Great Lakes–to ports along the gulf coast from Carrabelle, Florida to Brownsville, Texas. In the 2016 edition of the U.S. Army Corps of Engineer's list of American ports by tonnage handled, all five of the United States largest commercial ports and seventeen of the twenty-five largest are on, or adjacent to, the Intracoastal Waterway. In the movement of bulk commodities–such as coal, grains, crude petroleum and refined petrochemical products–that feed our industries, generate much of our power and comprise the vast majority of our exports, the inland waterways, including the Intracoastal Waterway are efficient, safe and cost effective. A standard tank barge, 195 feet long by 35 feet wide and with a loaded draft of nine feet, can transport approximately 450,000 gallons of liquid commodities. As much as 15 DOT 111 rail tank cars (30,110 gallons per), or approximately 58 large tank trucks (approximately 7,800 gallons per). And barges have a much lower cost per ton mile, a far better safety record and a lower carbon foot print than trains or trucks.

In addition to commercial freight traffic, personal pleasure vessels are heavy users of portions of the Intracoastal Waterway and contribute significantly to its economic importance. The thousands of marinas, boatyards, restaurants, parks, launch ramps and other facilities that cater to personal pleasure craft and the tens of thousands of jobs these businesses provide, are an important part of the economy and tax base of many of the communities and counties along the waterway.

The Intracoastal Waterway is not static. Like the national highway and rail systems it has and does evolve in response to: the changing national political environment, the changing needs of the cities and towns it runs past or through, the changing national economy and natural changes brought about by tides, currents, storms and a rising sea level.

Today, from north to south...Boston to the Rio Grande...the Intracoastal Waterway is composed of eight noncontiguous, relatively protected segments linked by open water routes. Relatively protected because most of the segments contain large bodies of generally shallow but open water–Long Island Sound, Chesapeake Bay, Albemarle Sound, Mississippi Sound, etc.–that under the right weather conditions can be extremely rough.

From Boston to the Cape Cod Canal across Cape Cod Bay. An open water run of approximately 61 nautical miles most of which is exposed to the North Atlantic and/or the full fetch of Cape Cod Bay in winds from southeast through north to northwest. The trip can be broken by stopping in Scituate, Plymouth, Provincetown or a number of the other harbors along the shores of Cape Cod Bay

Segment 1: The Cape Cod Canal; linking Cape Cod Bay and the approaches to Boston with Buzzards Bay. Buzzards Bay is sheltered by Martha's Vineyard and the Elizabeth Islands but is open to the southwest and in a strong summer southwester can be brutal.

Approximately 45 nautical miles across the open waters of Rhode Island Sound and Block Island Sound, exposed to the North Atlantic in winds from north of east to south-southwest. The trip can be broken at Newport or any of the other harbors in Narragansett Bay, at Point Judith or at the Great Salt Pond on Block Island.

Segment 2: Long Island Sound through one of the three northern entrances–Fishers Island Sound, The Race or Plum Gut– and on through the sprawling New York/New Jersey harbor complex to Lower Bay and Sandy Hook, New Jersey.

Around Sandy Hook, out into the Atlantic Ocean and south along the New Jersey shore for 25 nautical miles to the Manasquan, New Jersey Inlet.

Segment 3: Manasquan Inlet, New Jersey to the jetties at the Delaware Bay end of the Cape May Canal via the 118 statute miles long, convoluted, low bridge bedeviled and often shoal inside route behind the New Jersey coastal barrier islands. Mileage on the New Jersey inside route is measured north to south, Mile Mark 0 is between the outer ends of the Manasquan Inlet jetties and Mile Mark 118 (117.7) is between the outer ends of the jetties at the west, Delaware Bay, end of the Cape May Canal.

Because of fixed bridges and often thin water, vessels with an air draft (height) of more than 35 feet cannot use the New Jersey Inside Route and

6

vessels with a draft of more than five feet rarely try to use it. These vessels must keep an eye on the weather and make the 114 nautical mile Atlantic Ocean run down the New Jersey shore from Sandy Hook to the Cold Springs (Cape May) Inlet, or the longer run to the mouth of Delaware Bay.

Segment 4: The west end of the Cape May Canal to the start of the Atlantic Intracoastal Waterway on the Elizabeth River in Norfolk, Virginia via Delaware Bay, the sea level, big ship Chesapeake and Delaware Canal and the Chesapeake Bay.

Segment 5: South from Norfolk, Virginia on the Atlantic Intracoastal Waterway (the AICW) for 988 statute miles to the mouth of the St. Lucie River in Florida…if planning to cross Florida on the Okeechobee Waterway…or 1095 statute miles to Dinner Key in Miami, Florida. South of Dinner Key a 75-foot-wide by 7-foot-deep channel extends the Atlantic Intracoastal Waterway along the north side of the Florida Keys for an additional 57.5 miles, to Cross Key Bank, in Florida Bay (AICW mile 1152.5.) From Cross Key Bank, or from Biscayne Bay, vessels bound for Key West (AICW mile 1243.8) must use the Hawk Channel, on the Gulf Stream side of the Florida Keys. Mileage on the AICW is measured north to south from Mile Zero on the Elizabeth River in Norfolk, Virginia to Key West, Florida.

Vessels that continue down the Atlantic Intracoastal Waterway to Miami or the Florida Keys, if they desire to follow the Intracoastal Waterway north along Florida's west coast and then west along the upper gulf coast, must either return to the St. Lucie River and the Okeechobee Waterway, or cross the shallow, Florida Bank to Cape Sable and continue north past the Everglades and the 10,000 Islands to either Coon Key Pass or the mouth of the Caloosahatchee River, a long day for many boats, and a day that is unprotected from the Gulf of Mexico.

Segment 6: Across Florida on the Okeechobee Waterway, 154 or 165 statute miles–depending on the route followed in Lake Okeechobee–from the intersection of the Atlantic Intracoastal Waterway and the St. Lucie River (AICW mile 988) to the mouth of the Caloosahatchee River near the Gulf of Mexico. Mileage on the Okeechobee is measured east to west, Mile Mark 0 is at the intersection of the Atlantic Intracoastal Waterway and the St. Lucie River. Mile 154 (or 165) is near the mouth of the Caloosahatchee River, at the intersection of the Okeechobee Waterway and the Florida Gulf Waterway.

Segment 7: North from the mouth of the Caloosahatchee River for 150 statute miles to the Anclote Keys and the mouth of the Anclote River (which leads to Tarpon Springs) via the beautiful but in places congested and shoal, Florida Gulf Waterway (FGWW). Mileage on the Florida Gulf Waterway is measured from south to north, Mile Mark 0 is at the west end of the Okeechobee Waterway in the mouth of the Caloosahatchee River. Mile Mark 150 is at the intersection of the Florida Gulf Waterway and the Anclote River channel.

From Clearwater Pass (Inlet) or from the northern end of the Florida Gulf Waterway, Tarpon Springs or Anclote Key, to St. George Sound and the east end of the Gulf Intracoastal Waterway off the town of Carrabelle, coasting vessels following the Intracoastal Waterway must either make an approximately 145 nautical mile (166.86 statute miles or 268.54 kilometers) run across the open water of the northeastern Gulf of Mexico or they must spend two to four days following the shore line, river to river, port to port.

Segment 8: West on the heavily commercial Gulf Intracoastal Waterway (GIWW) for 1058 statute miles from: Carrabelle, Florida, to Mobile Bay, to New Orleans, across the Mississippi and on to Galveston, Texas, and finally to the turning basin in the port of

Brownsville, Texas. Mileage on the GIWW is measured in statute miles east and west from Harvey Lock, the older of the two locks that permit vessels to pass through the levee on the west bank of the Mississippi in New Orleans. The east end of the GIWW, Mile 376.2 EHL (East of Harvey Lock), is in the Carrabelle, Florida, harbor channel and the west end, Mile 681.8 WHL (West of Harvey Lock) is in the turning basin at the head of the Port of Brownsville, Texas. The annual tabulation of waterway tonnage compiled by the Corps of Engineers shows that in 2012 the Gulf Intracoastal Waterway was the third most heavily utilized commercial waterway in the United States; only the main stems of the Mississippi and Ohio Rivers carried more tonnage. By 2015 the GIWW was second in tonnage handled.

1. Boston to the Atlantic Intracoastal Waterway

etty and I first cruised down the Atlantic seaboard section of the Intracoastal Waterway in 1994. Between 1994 and 2012 we sailed or motored the Atlantic portions of the waterway twenty-one times and the whole of it…New England to Texas…five times. In the spring of 2012, we sold our boat. Life without a boat proved unsatisfactory so, in August, in Orleans, Massachusetts, out on the elbow of Cape Cod, we bought another boat. The eighth–three sail, five power–that we have owned. This one was an ageing 28-foot-long, former commercial lobster and rod and reel boat which we named *Nauset*, after the town on the Cape in which it had been built almost two decades earlier. Buying boats, like buying houses, takes time. The survey, negotiations and general paper churning took a month and it was September eighteenth before I signed the final papers and we assumed custody.

At sunrise on Saturday, September 22, 2012, after a night on the dock at the Hyannis, Massachusetts Municipal Marina and a good dinner at Tugboats Restaurant, we started south on the first leg of a long cruise. We had owned *Nauset* for three days and, except for a brief sea trial in calm, sheltered water, had never driven the boat.

Following the Shore from Boston to Brownsville

Our intention was to follow the Intracoastal Waterway from New England to somewhere near our home in Texas. To once again follow Congress's "continuous waterway, inland where practicable, from Boston, Massachusetts...to Point Isabel, Texas; and thence to the Rio Grande" for almost its entire length.

Leaving Hyannis, thick fog obscured the harbor and muffled the sounds of an incoming ferry. We motored slowly down the harbor channel in company with a pair of local lobster boats. Clear of Hyannis we turned west, passed between Cape Cod and Martha's Vineyard, rode the chart plotter and radar through Quicks Hole in pea soup fog, entered Buzzards Bay and the approach channel to the Cape Cod Canal and turned southwest, down and away from the canal.

On the morning of Tuesday, September 30, 2014 we untied *Nauset's* dock lines and left Rockport, Texas. When we reached the well-marked channel of the Gulf Intracoastal Waterway (the GIWW), we turned east and began retracing Congress's waterway, its harbors, inlets and connecting canals. On Monday, August 15, 2016, 3 years, 10 months and 23 days out of Hyannis, we picked up a Kingman Yacht Center mooring in Red Brook Harbor, on the east side of Buzzards Bay and at the west entrance to the Cape Cod Canal. *Nauset* was back on Cape Cod. The next day we moved up to Sandwich.

Between departing Hyannis and picking up that Kingman Yacht Center mooring, *Nauset* cruised:
- 2012, from Cape Cod south to Jacksonville, Florida
- 2013, in the spring and summer, from Jacksonville to Miami and the Florida Keys and then west to Houston, Texas and, in the fall, down the Texas coast
- 2014, in the fall and early winter, from south Texas back east following the gulf coast to the Florida Keys

12

- 2015, in the spring and summer, from the Florida Keys north up the east coast to the Chesapeake Bay and, in the fall, back south to Miami and the Keys
- 2016, from the Florida Keys to Cape Cod.

Leaving Hyannis, I had hoped to go through the Cape Cod Canal to Sandwich, at the east end of the canal, and perhaps on to Boston before the advancing fall and winter forced us south; although we had been to both many times. Boston, the northern end of the Intracoastal Waterway, is the 37th largest port in the United States in tonnage handled and the largest east coast port north of New York. But late September is already late in the season for driving smaller boats down the coast from Cape Cod to south of New York and NOAA's marine weather forecast for the week ahead indicated that we had a day…one good day…to cross Rhode Island and Block Island Sounds and reach the semi protected waters of Fishers Island Sound.

The Cape Cod Canal

The Wisconsin stage glacial moraines that are Cape Cod and its surrounding islands, banks, sands and shoals sit like a dam across the flow of the coastal sea lanes. A barrier to safe coastal navigation that bedeviled mariners from the dawn of European settlement to the building of the Cape Cod Canal.

The first well documented wreck on Cape Cod occurred in 1626 when the Pinnace *Sparrow-Hawk* went ashore on Nauset Beach. Three years before the wreck of the *Sparrow-Hawk*, Miles Standish of the Plymouth Colony was already considering the idea of a canal across the cape. In 1627 while trading with the Dutch at the Aptucxet Trading Post, on the Manomet River, Standish noted the proximity of the Dutch and English boats and talked about the possibility of a small canal between the Manomet and Scusset Rivers. In the seventeenth and eighteenth centuries both rivers were important trade and travel routes for the Native American tribes and the colonists. The rivers were navigable for much of their length by canoe and by the small rowing/sailing vessels used by the settlers and the portage–the land bridge between the rivers over which a boat or canoe would have to be dragged–was barely three miles.

In 1776, at the start of the Revolutionary War and a century and a half after the wreck of the *Sparrow-Hawk*, George Washington ordered Thomas Machin, a Continental Army Engineer, to investigate the possibility of a canal across the Cape which would "give greater security to navigation and against the enemy". Machin's report survives as the first known formal Cape Cod Canal survey.

Throughout the nineteenth century as the volume of coastal shipping and the number of wrecks increased—by the turn of the century wrecks were averaging close to one every two weeks—survey after survey was carried out and canal scheme after canal scheme proposed. Finally, the Boston, Cape Cod and New York Canal Company submitted a proposal that seemed both possible and financially viable and, on September 29, 1899, Massachusetts Governor Walcott signed legislation giving the company a charter to construct a canal across Cape Cod. In 1904 the New York financier August Belmont purchased the Boston, Cape Cod and New York Canal Company. Belmont re-organized the company and hired the noted Civil Engineer William Barclay Parsons as Chief Engineer.

The opening ceremony for Belmont's Canal was held on Wednesday, July 29, 1914. The next morning the canal–with a channel width of 100 feet, a project depth of 25 feet, three low opening bridges (one rail, two highway) and a small ferry–opened for business. By pre-arrangement the first vessel to transit the canal on opening day, and the first vessel to pay a canal toll was the sailing yacht *Mashantum*, owned Dr. Samuel Crowell of Dennis (on Cape Cod) and Boston and the Vice Commodore of the Boston Yacht Club. On opening day, the canal was still under construction

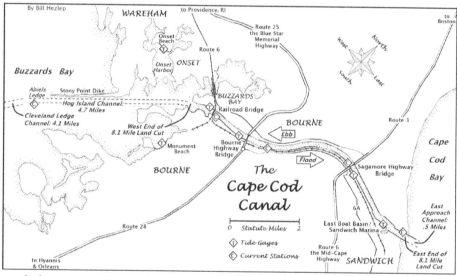

and the controlling depth in the channel was listed as 15 feet but may have been a foot less.

The canal was opened while still under construction because Belmont wanted the tolls to help finance on-going construction and maintenance and because he had publicly stated that his canal would be open before the Panama Canal. A goal he achieved by seventeen days, the Panama Canal opened August 15, 1914. The canal was finally completed in 1916.

As a profit-making business the privately-owned canal was a failure. It was doomed by the shallow water, high maintenance costs and, for the time, high transit fees. A 1915 canal toll schedule lists the toll for a 44 to 49-foot-long vessel as $8.00 and the toll for a 125 to 149-foot-long vessel as $30.00. Towing, if needed, was an additional $10.00-$15.00, depending on gross tonnage, per one-way passage. By 1915, even though the canal was still under construction, Belmont was attempting to sell it to the Federal Government.

During World War One, German submarines operated along the United States east coast. The flames of burning, torpedoed, vessels could be seen from Cape Cod and other coastal promontories. On July 22, 1918, just three miles off Cape Cod's Nauset Beach, a German U-Boat fired on the tug *Perth Amboy*. President Wilson ordered the United States Railroad Administration to assume operational control of the Belmont's Cape Cod Canal for the duration of hostilities.

On July 29, 1921 the federal government offered to buy the canal for $11,500,000 and Belmont accepted. Because of political wrangling in Washington over appropriations, first in the house and later in the senate, and problems with land titles, the government did not acquire clear title to the canal until March 30, 1928. At 12 P.M. the following day, the Corps of Engineers formally assumed control and management of the canal...now a free public waterway. Carrying out its mission, the Corps worked on the canal throughout the 1930s, providing hundreds of jobs through the depths of the Great Depression. By 1940 the canal was: 500 feet wide (the widest sea-level canal in the world), 32 feet deep, banks stabilized by heavy granite rip-rap, the highway bridges soaring works of art and the railroad bridge was the longest lift span bridge in the world, a record that stood until 1959 and the opening of the

Arthur Kill Railroad Bridge in New Jersey. Today the Cape Cod Canal is one of the world's great navigation canals, more than 20,000 vessels of all sizes and types transit the canal annually.

A trip through the canal in a small or weakly powered boat made without considering winds, tides and currents can be both interesting and educational. The mean tide range in Cape Cod Bay, east of the canal, is almost nine and a half feet. In Buzzards Bay,

The Cape Cod Canal, looking west to the Sagamore Bridge from Sandwich.

west of the canal, the mean tide range is only four feet. To complicate things, the tide phase in the two bays is also different, with high tide in Buzzards Bay three hours ahead of high tide in Cape Cod Bay. The tides in the canal flood from Buzzards Bay to Cape Cod Bay...west to east...and ebb from Cape Cod Bay to Buzzards Bay...east to west...and the tidal currents in the canal reverse every six hours.

The canal is oriented almost northeast to southwest. From late spring through to early fall the prevailing winds are from the southwest and in Buzzards Bay, at the canals west end, the southwest breeze blowing up the bays long fetch and over its shoal waters can create a rough chop; particularly if it is blowing against the ebb (west flowing) tide and is augmented by the afternoon sea breeze. In the spring and fall nor'easters blowing into Cape Cod Bay, particularly against the flood tide, can create a pattern of standing waves in the entrance to the canal that can make it difficult…and on rare occasions physically dangerous…for small craft entering or leaving the canal.

Long Island Sound & New York

From Buzzards Bay we ran southwest across Rhode Island Sound in clearing weather, to Point Judith, Rhode Island, and continued on across Block Island Sound to the Watch Hill Passage entrance to Fishers Island Sound. In Rhode Island Sound we crossed the shipping lanes leading to Providence, Rhode Island, 60th on the Corps of Engineers 2016 list of United States Ports by tonnage handled. The day ended with *Nauset* secured to a Dodson Boatyard mooring in Stonington, Connecticut.

Stonington was founded in 1649 on former Pequot Indian lands. The town, originally named Pawcatuck, was renamed "Southerton" by Massachusetts in 1658 and was then renamed "Mistick" when Connecticut received its royal charter in 1665. In 1666, renamed yet again, Stonington finally became Stonington. Throughout the eighteenth and nineteenth centuries Stonington remained a minor port, devoted primarily to fishing and whaling. Since World War I and particularly since the 1960-1980 period, Stonington like many of the towns on the Connecticut and Long

Island shores of Long Island Sound, has become a yachting center and a summer/second home community for wealthy urbanites. Although there is still a small working waterfront. Most of the 18th and 19th century buildings, commercial and residential, in the old downtown have been beautifully restored and, those that are not homes, house: art galleries, antique shops, boutiques, good restaurants and inviting pubs.

A small, easily repaired but time-consuming problem related to the shift cable on our Morse single lever engine control and a visit to Dodson's fuel dock, resulted in a mid-day departure from Stonington. In 2012 *Nauset* was 17 years old and we were the fourth owner. With an older boat that has had multiple owners, even if you had a good pre-purchase survey and have spent some time working on the boat, unexpected things will crawl up from the electrical, plumbing and mechanical systems. You never really know what gremlins may be hiding down there. That morning was our fourth day aboard *Nauset* and our first gremlin, hopefully not the first of many, had appeared. *Nauset* has a single 120-gallon diesel tank, which was, according to the fuel gage, 7/8 full when we left Hyannis. We didn't know how much fuel *Nauset's* big diesel (a 315-horse power Yanmar 6LYPA-STP) would use or how well calibrated the fuel gage was. So, we kept an eye on the fuel gage, refueled often—to the 7/8 mark on the gage—and kept track of engine hours and gallons purchased.

Long Island Sound, like the Chesapeake Bay, is a large body of water–its shores heavily dotted with old colonial towns, museums, good restaurants, marinas, inviting anchorages, rivers and creeks. The sound is oriented roughly east-northeast to west-southwest. From Fishers Island to Throgs Neck the sound is approximately 137 statute miles long, and in its mid-section it is more than 20 miles wide. Statistically westerlies are the dominant winds on the sound throughout the year: west to south-southwest from April through October and west to north-northwest from November through March. Over the course of the year, the wind strength averages 12.6 mph (11 knots): stronger in the winter, lighter in the summer, with numerous light to calm days in July and August. Daily winds tend to be light to calm from late night to morning and increase from mid-morning to night. In the fall and winter nor'easters are common, in the summer thunderstorms are frequent.

The Sounds wide, deep eastern entrance(s) and the small, almost tiny by comparison, western entrance mean that the large volume of water that enters and exits the sound during each tide cycle does so almost entirely through the east end—through: The Watch Hill Passage, The Race and Plum Gut—consequently the tide in Long Island Sound floods to the west and ebbs to the east.

The disparity in the volume of water entering and exiting the sound through the east and west entrances affects both tide and current. During the flood (westerly) water piles up in the west end of the sound and, in general, the height of the tides rise increases from east to west for the length of the sound. At Plum Gut Harbor, on Plum Island, at the east end of the sound the tidal range averages 2.5 to 3.2 feet, while at the sounds extreme west end, at Throgs Neck, the tidal range averages almost 9 feet. As with all of the semi enclosed coastal waters of the east and gulf coasts, prolonged or strong winds will affect the tides; prolonged easterlies or a strong nor'easter increase the tidal range, prolonged westerlies decrease it. In general, currents in the sound mirror the tides; while the height of the tide increases east to west, the current decreases east to west. In the Race, at the east entrance to the sound, peak ebb can reach 5.0 to 5.5 knots, peak flood 4.2 to 4.5 knots. At the currant gage on the Connecticut-New York Line between Bridgeport, Connecticut and Port Jefferson, New York, peak ebb is 1.0 to 1.2 knots while peak flood is 0.8 to 1.0 knots.

We left Stonington through the south end of Fishers Island Sound, thereby avoiding the race, and crossed to Port Jefferson, New York, mid-way down the Long Island Shore. Port Jefferson, located at the head of a two-mile-long natural, deep water harbor, is the Long Island terminus of the Bridgeport (Connecticut) to Long Island Ferry and, in part thanks to the ferry, is number 136 on the Corps of Engineers 2016 list of the 150 largest ports in the United States based on tonnage handled. Bridgeport, CT, the other end of the ferry line, is number 117, and the only Connecticut port, on the Corps of Engineers 2016 list. Port Jefferson was founded in the mid-seventeenth century and from the middle of the eighteenth century to the opening decades of the twentieth century it was a significant ship building and whaling center. The Bayles Shipyard, the last of the town's shipyards, did not close until 1923.

Overnight the wind went west-southwest and picked-up. Leaving Port Jefferson, we had 15-20+ knots pretty much on the nose, heavy going for a smaller boat. An hour out of Port Jefferson, I made the unpleasant discovery that we were taking on water somewhere up in the bow. We diverted into Oyster Bay and the Oyster Bay Marine Center, a working boatyard where help, if needed, was available. Help wasn't needed but a little bit better preparation before getting underway would have helped. Nauset has an anchor windless. The anchor windless has a hole through which the anchor rode drops down into the chain locker. When the anchor and windless are not being used a cover keeps things like waves and rain out and the cover was missing. It had been left loose and was now…missing. So, we enjoyed a day in Oyster Bay: give the boat a bath, dry out, clean up, do the laundry and enjoy an excellent dinner at Jack Halyard's American Grill—62 South Street, Oyster Bay (now called Spinnakers Restaurant and Bar).

The origin of the name Oyster Bay is unknown. But the bay was named for its oysters and the name was in use by 1639. In June of that year Captain David de Vries anchored in the bay and wrote in his journal that "there are fine oysters here, whence our nation has given it the name Oyster Bay." Oysters still form part of the local economy. Frank M. Flowers and Sons of Oyster Bay, have harvested oysters and clams from leased beds in the bay and Long Island Sound since 1937, and since the nineteen-eighties they have farmed (aquaculture) their leases by placing juvenile oysters and clams on the beds to augment the natural population.

As on the Chesapeake and Delaware Bays, oysters were a major fishery on Long Island Sound from the early nineteenth century through the middle of the twentieth century. By the 1950s the public free-to-harvest beds were in decline from over fishing and pollution and by the late 1960s there were no harvestable beds in many parts of the sound and in some formerly rich areas, oysters were nearly extinct. In response to strong public pressure to do something about water pollution, Congress passed the Clean Water Act of 1972[1] which broadly revised and strengthened the Federal Water Pollution Control Act of 1948. The Clean Water Act, in conjunction with large scale seeding of natural beds by Connecticut and New York and a rise in leased bottom aquaculture caused a resurgence in the oyster industry in the 1980s. But the industry collapsed in 1989-1990 because the MSX parasite, the organism that almost ended oystering on the Chesapeake Bay, reached Long Island Sound.

In 2002 a small resurgence began in the Long Island Sound oyster industry, brought about primarily by aquaculture but also, although to a lesser extent, by seeding of the public beds. Today possibly as many as a hundred, mostly small, oyster aquaculture operations are marketing Long Island Sound oysters, sound bay men are again oystering on some of the State seeded public beds and oysters are a $40-$50 million industry that provides a few full-time and hundreds of part-time, local jobs.

Aquaculture companies from Texas to Prince Edward Island, Canada and on the west coast are using the French concept of terroir–that the place, the environment, in which something lives and grows effects its taste and characteristics–to market oysters. Which makes sense. Oysters are filter feeders, the water in which they live and their food supply affect their taste. Crassostrea virginica, the eastern oyster, is the oyster farmed and harvested along the entire coast from Texas to Canada (there are different varieties on the west coast) and a Crassostrea virginica raised in the clear, cold, salty waters of Prince Edward Island tastes very different from one farmed in Oyster Bay, Long Island, or one from the brackish, warmer waters of the Chesapeake.

Long Island Sound aquaculturists sell their branded oysters– Blue Point, Robin's Island, Saddle Rock, Great White, Widows Hole, Peconic Pearl, Mystic, etc.–to restaurants and oyster bars all over the country. Some oyster bars and higher end restaurants offer a dozen or more name branded oysters, all of which unless they were flown in from the west coast, Europe, Japan or somewhere else, are Crassostrea virginicas. Marketing on terroir has been so successful that, as a number of recent articles in the food press have pointed out, name adjustments in the marketing chain between oyster bed and final point-of-sale are common. Many more of some popular oysters are shucked and eaten then are harvested.

During our lay day in Oyster Bay, the weather moderated and by 8:00 a.m. the next morning we were clear of Oyster Bay, out on the sound and running south. We planned to either anchor behind Sandy Hook or go down to Atlantic Highlands behind the base of the hook. From either place, if the weather and sea conditions were suitable, we could leave for Manasquan Inlet, Atlantic City or, possibly, Cape May.

Throgs Neck and the Throgs Neck Bridge mark the south end of Long Island Sound. At Throgs Neck the Intracoastal Waterway enters the sounds south entrance, the 16 statute miles long East River which links Long Island Sound to New York Harbor and separates the New York City Boroughs of Brooklyn and Queens, on Long Island, from Manhattan and the Bronx. In the river the tide floods east and ebbs west, exactly the opposite of Long Island Sound, and the tidal currents run strong, averaging better than 2 knots and reaching 5+ knots in Hell Gate.

Between Long Island Sound and Governors Island the East River passes under eight high bridges and flows through the heart of New York City, past: the Rikers Island prison and the La Guardia Airport, through Hell Gate and on past Roosevelt Island, the skyscrapers of Manhattan—including the Empire State Building and the new World Trade Center—the United Nations, the South Street Seaport Museum, the Battery, and the Manhattan Ferry Terminal. As we left the east river and entered New York Harbor we passed, possibly drove through, the site of a business argument over steam ferry routes into New York City.

A New York State law passed in 1808, granted Robert Livingston and Robert Fulton a 20-year monopoly on the operation of steam powered vessels in...and into...the navigable waters controlled by the State of New York. In 1815 Aaron Ogden, after attempting to fight the Livingston-Fulton monopoly, formed a partnership with Thomas Gibbons and purchased a New York license to operate a steam ferry service between Elizabethtown

New Jersey and New York City. The partnership ended when Gibbons tried to start a competing steam ferry line but operating under a license issued by the Federal Government. The former partners went to court in New York. In 1820, both the New York Court of Error and the Chancery Court of New York found in favor of Ogden and issued a permanent injunction barring Gibbons from operating steam vessels in, or into the waters of the State of New York.

Gibbons appealed to the United States Supreme Court.

On February 5, 1824, Gibbons vs. Ogden was finally argued before the Supreme Court. Ogden's lawyers argued the States rights position, that the various States held fully equal and concurrent power with the Federal Government in matters of commerce, including interstate commerce. Gibbons lawyers, led by Daniel Webster, argued that the Commerce Clause of the Constitution vested in Congress authority over commerce between and among the various states. On March 2, 1824, the court in a decision written by Chief Justice John Marshall decided in favor of Gibbons. The court held that the New York law…Livingston and Fulton's monopoly…was invalid because the Commerce Clause of the Constitution gave Congress, the Federal Government, absolute authority over the regulation of interstate commerce, including river and coastal navigation.

As Gibbons vs. Ogden was being argued in and decided by the Supreme Court, Federalists and States Rightists in Congress were debating the role of the Federal Government in infrastructure projects of national importance. The court's ruling settled that argument in favor of the Federal Government. And in April 1824, Congress passed the General Survey Act of 1824–the first of the long series of Congressional Acts generally referred to as the Rivers and Harbors Acts.

From the tip of Manhattan and Governors Island the waterway crosses New York Harbor to the Verrazano Narrows and the Verrazano Bridge, which spans the narrows between Brooklyn (on Long Island) and Staten Island and then continues across Lower Bay (the outer harbor,) to Sandy Hook.

New York Harbor is one of the largest natural harbors in the world and the Port of New York and New Jersey was the third

Following the *MSC Paola* under New York's Verrazano Bridge

largest port in the United States in tonnage handled and the second largest in the value of goods handled in both 2012 and 2016. The project depth for the large vessel channels within the port was 45 feet, but the Water Resources Development Act of 2000 (P.L. 106-541)–a Rivers and Harbors Act under a different name–authorized dredging to 50 feet. Now some of the channels are being cut even deeper and the clearance, the air draft, of the Bayonne Bridge is being increased so that the Port of New York and New Jersey will be able to accommodate the larger New Panamax class ships.

Along the Intracoastal Waterway, the already underway competition to serve the new larger ships is going to have an effect on ports from Boston to Brownsville, and on the rail and road nets serving the ports. The biggest impact on the Intracoastal Waterway itself will probably be increased barge traffic as bulk commodities, and possibly containers, are moved to and from ports able to handle the new, larger ships. An increase in barge traffic will probably lead to the maintenance dredging (or enlarging), straightening and stabilizing of parts of the waterway.

A problem with all of this is that wide, deeply incised, artificial channels are extremely expensive and, once cut maintenance can never end. They are forever projects. Silt and sand–from urban development, agriculture, deforestation and other causes– continually washes down into ports, harbors and channels. Tides, currents and storm waves and surges move the silt (and often the dredge spoil from creating the channels), continuously filling and altering the channels and other dredged areas.

New Jersey

As we were passing under the Verrazano Bridge and entering the South Bay, the marine weather was reporting calm, no wind, at the Sandy Hook Coast Guard Station. And small boats fishing off Sandy Hook were chattering about smooth water on the VHF radio; sometimes on channel 16, the emergency channel, which was annoying the Coast Guard.

We kept going, out around Sandy Hook and down the New Jersey shore to the Manasquan Inlet. When we reached the Inlet, we turned in and entered the New Jersey Inside Route. Mileage on the 118-statute mile long New Jersey Inside Route is counted from north to south and Mile Mark 0, is between the outer ends of the Manasquan Inlet jetties at 40°06.03′N., 74°01.55′W. On the Intracoastal Waterway, from Boston to Brownsville, mileage is counted north to south, east to west. With the exception of the portion of the Gulf Intracoastal Waterway that lies east of New Orleans, where for historical reasons mileage is counted west to east. From Mile Mark 0, we followed the inside route up the Manasquan River, and through the Point Pleasant Canal to Mantoloking, and a night in a slip at the historic Winter Yacht Basin…destroyed by Hurricane Sandy less than a month after our visit.

Leaving Mantoloking we put in a short day on the inside route, 40 miles to Beach Haven. Beach Haven is one of many very pleasant Jersey Shore beach towns along the waterway that offer: dockage and other marine services, restaurants, often very good ones, shopping and beaches. The next day we continued inside as far as Atlantic City's Absecon Inlet (inside route Mile Mark 65) where we went out into the Atlantic and followed the beach south to the Cape May (Cold Spring) Inlet[2]. As we approached the inlet several large sport fish boats returning from the edge of the Gulf Stream, 80 to 100 miles offshore, appeared on the horizon racing for the inlet. We slowed to let them pass well in front of us. A fast-moving sport fish boat makes a large wake and we knew, from experience, that we were not something they were going to slow down for.

We spent the night at Utsch's Marina, beside the waterway at the Cape May end of the Cape May Canal. By sunset the transient slips were full and most of the transients looked like south bound snowbirds, boats migrating south for the winter to the warm weather and clean, clear water of south Florida and the Bahamas.

Chapter 1

In the evening we walked over to the Lucky Bones Backwater Grill and enjoyed an excellent dinner of fresh caught Wahoo. I think the crews off half the transient boats at Utsch's were there.

Today's New Jersey coastal inside route is inside route number two…the second version. The first was the Delaware and Raritan Canal. For almost a century (1838 to 1932) the Delaware and Raritan Canal provided a safe, convenient navigable route across New Jersey from New Brunswick on the Raritan River to Bordentown, on the tidal Delaware River.

In 1676 William Penn, Proprietor of Pennsylvania, ordered a survey to determine the feasibility of a canal to connect the Delaware River with the "Bay of New York." A century and a quarter later, in 1804, the New Jersey legislature issued a charter to the New Jersey Navigation Company for the construction of a canal between the Raritan River at or near New Brunswick and the tidal Delaware River. It was twenty-six years before actual construction began; but by 1834 portions of the canal were in use and the final set of locks, connecting the canal to the Delaware River, were opened in 1838.

For the time it was a large canal: 44 miles long, 80 feet wide at the surface, with a depth of 7 to 8 feet and with 14 locks–each 220 feet long and at least 24 feet wide. There was also a navigable 60-foot-wide, 6-foot-deep feeder canal that extended up the eastern side of the Delaware River for 22 miles. The feeder canal provided water for the operation of the main canal and brought down barges carrying Pennsylvania coal, much of it destined for New York. Freight traffic on the canal peaked in the late 1880s and then declined steadily until the canals deteriorating condition and the economic downturn of the great depression brought canal operations to a close in 1932. The D&R Canal State Park in Princeton, New Jersey, in addition to interesting exhibits, has a lot of information about the history and economics of the D&R Canal.

In the early decades of the twentieth century, when power driven pleasure vessels became popular, the Delaware and Raritan Canal became a popular route for yachtsmen moving their boats up and down the east coast. The fifth edition of the <u>Inside Route</u>

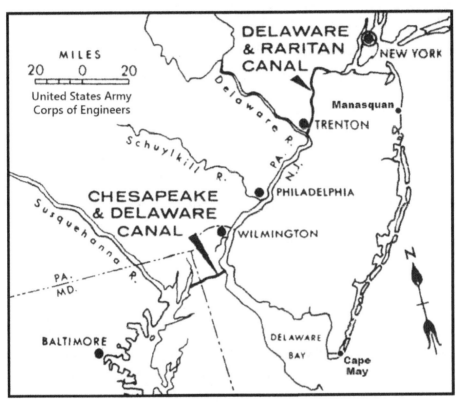

<u>Pilot, New York to Key West</u>[3] , issued in 1922, contained eight charts and chart Number 1 covered New York to Philadelphia via the: Raritan River, the Delaware and Raritan Canal and the Delaware River. In the fifth edition the Delaware and Raritan Canal (pages 6 and 7) is described as: 39 nautical/44 statute miles long, with 14 locks, a controlling depth of 7 feet, a controlling

clearance (air draft) of 50 feet set by a stone bridge in New Brunswick, a speed limit of 4½ miles per hour and a toll of 56 cents per mile travelled. In August 1926, the tolls for pleasure craft, with or without power, had changed to: $1 per lock for boats under 50 feet in length, $1.50 per lock for boats 50 to under 75 feet in length and $2.00 per lock for boats 75 feet and longer. By the late 1920s pleasure vessel use was declining for the same reasons as commercial traffic.

Before the arrival of the first European settlers, Native Americans were navigating the rivers, creeks and bays behind New Jersey's coastal barrier islands. Many, if not most, of the first settlers arrived by boat and from the beginning of European settlement the coastal waters, inlets and navigable waters behind the barrier islands were used for freight, fishing and general transportation. By the beginning of the eighteenth-century fishing and shore station whaling boats were being built and by the mid eighteenth century locally built vessels were trading up and down the Atlantic seaboard.

Within months of Congress passing the Rivers and Harbors Act of March 3, 1909, the State of New Jersey began dredging a New Jersey Intracoastal Waterway. The New Jersey State project ran from Bay Head, at the north end of Barnegat Bay, to the Cold Spring Inlet at Cape May and had a specified depth of 6 feet for a bottom width of 100 feet. By 1915 the project was substantially complete and the U.S. Coast and Geodetic Survey issued the first edition of the Inside Route Pilot, Coast of New Jersey (30 pages of text, an index and 3 charts.) That same year the State of New Jersey purchased the right-of-way for a future Bay Head-Manasquan Canal.

Construction of the Bay Head-Manasquan Canal began at the southern, Bay Head, end of the canal in 1916. Less than a mile of the canal had been dredged before the United States entered World War One and during the war work on the canal was suspended. When work resumed after the war, progress was slow and it was December 1925 before Manasquan River water flowed south into Barnegat Bay and the canal was opened to navigation in 1926.

The Bay Head-Manasquan Canal was far from an immediate success…initially it was an environmental and economic disaster. When the canal was opened the bulk of the Manasquan River's flow diverted south to Barnegat Bay through the canal, through what amounted to a new (although man made) outlet. The reduced river flow seaward of the new canal, the remaining flow out through the natural inlet, could not keep the inlet open and by 1928 Manasquan inlet was completely closed, despite several local attempts to maintain a channel. Uninterrupted ocean beach extended across the closed inlet from Point Pleasant to Manasquan and the fishing communities along the river were out of business. Early in 1930 the USACE began a project to reopen the inlet and by mid-summer 1931, the Manasquan Inlet–straightened, with new stone jetties and banks stabilized by riprap and bulkheads–was again open to navigation and looked much as it looks today.

Natural inlets in beaches and particularly inlets in and between barrier islands, are dynamic. In response to currents, winds and waves, they migrate up, or down, the beach and sand bars and shoals build and dissipate. Prior to the construction of the Manasquan River to Bay Head Canal and the subsequent closing and reopening of the Manasquan Inlet, the inlet, despite being shallow and difficult for larger vessels and despite having migrated (old charts show a number of inlet locations) had never needed dredging. Since reopening, straightening and stabilization, dredging has been an ongoing, almost annual, requirement.

Chapter 1

When the canal was opened and the river diverted south through the new outlet, the strong current quickly eroded the unreinforced sand banks of the canal; undercutting the ends of the bridges and building shoals and sandbars in and off the south end of the canal, which limited its use and at times almost closed it. In 1935 the USACE began building wooden bulkheads and riprapping parts of the canal to stabilize the banks. Today the canal has steel bulkheads and the original, narrow span bridges have been replaced with higher bridges that have a wider navigable width. But strong currents in the canal and the continuing development of shoals in the inside route channel immediately south of the canal are still problems.

Prior to the construction of the Bay Head-Manasquan Canal, the Manasquan River was tidal and ranged from saltwater near the inlet to brackish further upriver. The northern end of Barnegat Bay, with no direct connection to the Atlantic, was non-tidal freshwater. In northern Barnegat Bay the marshes were freshwater marshes. Cranberry bogs and fishing for bass, pike and other freshwater species were locally important. There was debate about the wisdom of the canal and fears that the canal would lead to: an influx of saltwater, tides and tidal currents, the transformation of the freshwater marshes to salt marsh, the loss of the freshwater fishery and the loss or decline of the cranberry bogs. All of which eventually happened.

The Bay Head-Manasquan Canal is entirely within the town limits of the town of Point Pleasant. In 1964, at the request of Point Pleasant, Congress changed the official name of the canal from Bay Head-Manasquan Canal to Point Pleasant Canal

The three-and-a-half-mile long Cape May Canal, the southern end of the New Jersey Inside Route and the link between the inside route and Delaware Bay was not built until World War II. Since their first surveys for a New Jersey coastal inside route following passage of the March 3, 1909 Rivers and Harbors Act and through repeated Congressionally mandated surveys up to the start of World War II, the Corps of Engineers had consistently reported unfavorably on the project. In 1942 the growing submarine threat in the Atlantic–ships being torpedoed and burning within sight of the Jersey shore–caused the Corps of Engineers to change course and recommend the project. But no action was taken.

In legislation passed in 1945, Congress authorized the conversion of the New Jersey inside route into a federal project which was to have a 12-foot-deep channel from Delaware Bay to the Manasquan Inlet. The project was not funded and was deferred for restudy although some work was done–the Cape May canal was built and a few improvements were made to the inside route between Cape May Harbor and the Manasquan Inlet. Neither the Cape May Canal nor the inside route between Cape May and the Manasquan Inlet was brought up to Intracoastal Waterway standards and work on the far from complete project ceased shortly after World War II. Today the New Jersey Inside Route, with the exception of the Cape May Canal, is essentially as it was originally built by the State of New Jersey.

Mile zero for the New Jersey Inside Route is between the outer ends of the Manasquan Inlet Jetties at 40°06′03″ N, 74°01′55″ W, 40 nautical miles from The Battery at the foot of Manhattan Island, New York. Distances on the waterway are measured in statute miles south from mile zero to mile 117.7, which is between the outer ends of the stone jetties at the Delaware Bay end of the Cape May Canal. The project dimensions for this section of the Intracoastal Waterway are a depth of 6 feet for a bottom width of 100 feet from mile zero to Cape May Harbor and then 12 feet deep for a bottom width of 100 to 150 feet through the Cape May Canal to Delaware Bay. The USACE's Philadelphia District Office is responsible for the waterway's maintenance and operation and, within funding limits, attempts to maintain the waterway at project specifications. The Coast Guard maintains the aids to navigation.

The New Jersey ICW's project depth is theoretical, the real, actual controlling depth in any given section is generally less than the project depth, because the soft, unconsolidated sand and marsh mud through which the waterway runs are easily eroded and moved by the tides, wind driven currents and boat wakes. Wind effects water levels in the bays as much, or more than the tides. Strong or prolonged easterly or westerly winds will blow several feet of water into or out of the bays and natural waterways through which the inside route runs. During a late spring or early fall cold front an area charted at five feet Mean Low Water can go from five feet to three feet to seven feet and back to five feet over the course of a frontal passage.

Even though they are shallow, the marsh and water areas behind New Jersey's barrier islands hold a lot of water and a large volume of water moves in and out through the relatively few and narrow inlets. Tides range from 5.5 feet in the Manasquan and Cape May Inlets through 4.4 feet in Great Bay, down to less than a foot at the top of Barnegat Bay. Currents run 2 to 2.5 knots in many of the channels and, in the major inlets, currents can reach 3 to 3.5 knots. Winds that enhance the tidal depths also enhance the currents.

The air draft on the inside route is set by several 35-foot-high fixed bridges. In addition to these bridges, the inside route is crossed by a number of hi-rise bridges and by 16 low opening bridges, most of which operate on restricted schedules.

During the boating season, the inshore route throughout its length is extremely popular with local small craft of all types. There is still a significant commercial fishing industry along New Jersey's Atlantic coast and the deeper inlets, particularly Cape May's Cold Spring Inlet and the Atlantic City Inlet are used by commercial vessels day and night. But there is very little commercial freight traffic on the waterway. In 2012, 300 net tons of commercial freight transited the Cape May Canal and that 300 tons was the 2012 total for the entire New Jersey inside route.

Delaware Bay & the Chesapeake and Delaware Canal

Monday, the first of October, waking up was not a problem. Cape May is one of the east coasts major sport and commercial fishing centers. A herd of charter sport fish boats, a couple of big head boats–group or party boats that generally take walk-ons with each person buying a ticket, paying as an individual–and a whale watching boat operate from Utsch's or from docks within hearing distance. Well before dawn the rumble of multiple diesels and the noise from charter parties, some sounding like they had already been sampling the brew, made sure we were up. By 7:45 we were clear of Cape May and the Cape May-Delaware Canal and were running up Delaware Bay.

Delaware Bay, like the Chesapeake Bay, Albemarle Sound, Mississippi Sound and some of the other larger bodies of water along the Intracoastal Waterway, is a place where the weather needs to be taken seriously. The lower Delaware River and Delaware Bay, from the Chesapeake and Delaware Canal to the 18-mile-wide mouth of the bay between Cape May and Cape Henlopen, forms a southeast to northwest oriented 60-mile-long funnel...open to the Atlantic at the big end. Within the funnel, during each tide cycle, the tide floods for six and a half to seven hours, and ebbs for five to five and a half; the compressed ebb results in strong ebb tides, which often run at 3+ knots.

At the Brandywine Shoal Light in the lower bay, the dominant winds from October to April are northerly with northwest winds of 15-16 knots blowing as much as 70% of the days in December, January and February. Southerlies dominate from May to September, but they tend to be weaker and less dominant than the winter northerlies. At the Brandywine Shoals tide gage the higher high tide reaches 6.9 feet and at Reedy Point, the east entrance to the Chesapeake and Delaware Canal, the tide is approximately the same. Up river, at the Philadelphia tide gage, the higher high reaches approximately 8 feet.

Strong or prolonged northwest to north winds will blow water out of the bay while east to south winds will blow water in; raising and lowering water levels and augmenting the currents. In a wind against tide situation a short steep wave pattern will quickly develop. In a 20-25 knot easterly wind blowing against a strong ebb tide, four to six-foot waves are not uncommon. Outside the well-marked, dredged commercial navigation channel the bay is shallow and liberally strewn with shoals, spoil banks, oyster lease stakes, crab traps and other hazards to navigation.

The Delaware Bay navigation channel, dredged to and maintained at a depth of 45-feet, runs up the bay and the lower Delaware River for 102.5 miles, to Camden, NJ. The channel is used annually by more than 2,500 large merchant vessels and numerous tugs and barges. Except in the worst weather, commercial vessels use the channel day and night and they frequently run fast. In 2016, if the data for the complex of shipping terminals along the upper end of the navigation channel was aggregated[4], the complex would be the 6th largest port complex in the United States in tonnage handled, and the largest petrochemical port complex on the east coast. As is the case with many of the east and gulf coasts larger ports, deepening of the channel to 52-55 feet, to accommodate the New Panamax class ships using the enlarged Panama Canal, has been proposed.

The Chesapeake and Delaware Canal links Delaware Bay to the Chesapeake Bay. From the traffic control signal light on Reedy Point, at the Delaware Bay entrance to the western traffic control signal light at Old Town Point Wharf, the canal is 19.7 miles (17.2 nautical miles) long. Throughout its length the canal is maintained at a width of 450 feet and a depth of 35 feet and for most of its length the banks are stabilized with granite rip-rap and lit by flood lights at night.

As far as is known, a canal to link the Chesapeake and Delaware Bays was first proposed by the Dutch cartographer Augustine Herman, who noted that a canal would cut almost 300 miles off the sea route between Philadelphia and Baltimore. In 1804 the newly formed Chesapeake and Delaware Canal Company began work on a 14-lock canal to connect the Back-Creek Branch of the Elk River, at the head of the Chesapeake, to the Christina River, a tributary stream that flows into the Delaware River near the head of Delaware Bay. Work ceased less than two years later when the company ran out of money. In 1822 the company was reorganized and refinanced, and in April 1824 construction began following a revised route recommended by the U.S. Army's Corps of Engineers. The new route linked Newbold's Landing (Delaware City) to the Back-Creek Branch of the Elk River and required only four locks.

The first vessel to pass through the new canal transited from the Chesapeake Bay to Delaware Bay on July 4, 1829. And on October 18, 1829 the canal was officially opened to general traffic.[5] On opening day the Chesapeake and Delaware Canal was: approximately 14 statute miles long, 66 feet wide at the waterline, 35 feet wide at the project depth of 10 feet and was spanned by one fixed and three swing bridges. By the 1870s more than a million tons of freight were transiting the canal annually. Over the years there were minor changes in the canal; a bridge was removed and locks and bridges were rebuilt. However, by the turn of the century, the canal company was losing money, the locks were in poor condition and it was clear that the canal needed to be rebuilt and enlarged.

In 1906 President Theodore Roosevelt appointed a commission to study converting the canal to a "free and open waterway." The federal government attempted to buy the canal but was unable to reach an agreement on price with the canal company and, in the Rivers and Harbors Act of August 4, 1917, Congress ordered the condemnation of the canal. In 1919 the Wilmington District Court awarded the canal company $2.5 million dollars in condemnation compensation and on August 13, 1919, the canal became federal property. The 2nd Edition (1913) of the Inside Route Pilot, New York to Key West, describes the canal as: 12 (nautical) miles long with a depth of 9 feet from its eastern entrance at Delaware City on Delaware Bay to its western entrance at Chesapeake City on Back Creek, with three locks 220 feet long, 24 feet wide and 9 feet deep, three opening bridges, a speed limit of 4½ statute miles per hour and adds that "no vessel shall carry sail in the canal". In the 5th Edition (1922) of the Inside Route Pilot, the physical description of the canal is unchanged but a note reading "The canal has been purchased by the Government and is maintained and operated free of toll charges" has been added.

Over the years, as the size and tonnage of the ships using the canal increased the canal was enlarged several times, reaching its present form in the mid-1970s. In 2012 more than 15,000 vessels and 9,806,025 net tons of commercial commodities (of which 3,613,113 net tons was petroleum products and 1,205,098 net tons was coal) utilized the canal. Container ships, tankers, bulkers, vehicle carriers, general cargo vessels, tugs and barges, commercial fishing vessels and personal pleasure craft utilize the canal day and night and the canal is considered to be a critical link in the eastern

Early morning on the Chesapeake and Delaware Canal

seaboard shipping routes.

In 1996 at the request of Congress, The USACE completed a study looking at the feasibility and impact of deepening the Chesapeake and Delaware Canal to 40 feet; along with the short channel connecting the Delaware Bay channel to the canal and the 40-mile-long channel from the canal to the Port of Baltimore. For economic and environmental reasons, the project was suspended in 2004. But, if the proposed dredging of the Delaware Bay channel to 52-55 feet to accommodate the New Panamax ships is carried out, the proposal to deepen the canal and the channel to Baltimore is likely to be revived. Even though vessels with a draft of over 40 feet can already reach the port of Baltimore from the south via the 50-foot channel from the Virginia Capes to Baltimore, much of which is naturally more than 50 feet deep.[6]

From the Chesapeake Bay end of the C & D Canal to the Annapolis Green 1 is approximately 40 statute miles. At 6:15 p.m., Monday, October 1st the end of a long day on the water, we picked up mooring buoy #50 in Annapolis, Maryland. Our mooring was one of a cluster just above the Spa Creek Bridge that were sized and spaced for smaller boats and it was the only remaining vacant mooring.

The Chesapeake Bay

On the Chesapeake Bay, October is boat shows and, generally, great sailing and cruising. The back-to-back Annapolis sailboat and powerboat shows would begin on Thursday and a flock of south bound cruising boats were filling up the moorings that had not been removed to make room for the boat show. Boats were crowding the anchorage off the Naval Academy sea wall and occupying what seemed like every other possible space within water taxi or dinghy distance of downtown Annapolis. Many south bound snowbird cruisers work at one or both of the boat shows and many more attend the shows and the associated rendezvous, social events and going south seminars.

Stretching 200 miles from the mouth of the Susquehanna River at Havre de Grace, Maryland, to the 17-mile-long Chesapeake Bay Bridge Tunnel spanning the mouth of the bay between Cape Charles and Cape Henry (the Virginia Capes) the Chesapeake Bay is the drowned valley of the Susquehanna River, the largest estuary

Following the Shore from Boston to Brownsville

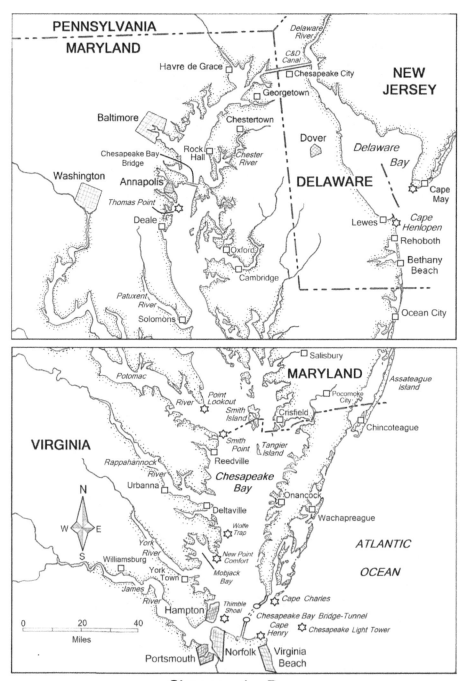

Chesapeake Bay

Chapter 1

Nine major rivers—the Susquehanna, Patapsco, Chester, Choptank, Patuxent, Potomac, Rappahannock, York and James—and more than 150 other significant rivers and streams drain into the bay. The 64,300 square miles drained by these rivers and streams includes the District of Columbia and parts of six states: New York, Pennsylvania, Delaware, Maryland, Virginia and West Virginia.

The shores of the Bay and its larger tributaries are home to: our Nations' Capital, three State capitals, two of our largest ports and hundreds of historic colonial ports, towns, settlements, plantations and Revolutionary War, War of 1812 and Civil War battle fields. More than seventeen million people live within the Bay's watershed and the run off from their farms (particularly chicken and dairy operations), over fertilized suburban lawns, septic systems, factories, city streets and highways flows into the Bay[7].

Oriented almost exactly north-south the Chesapeake Bay and its major tributaries have over 11,600 miles of shoreline and cover an area of almost 4,500 square miles. At its' widest point, south of Virginia's Tangier Island, the Bay is close to 23 miles wide. In the narrowest areas, north from Kent Island on the eastern shore and Sandy Point on the western shore, approximately where the twin spans of the Bay Bridge carry U.S. Highways 50 and 301 across the Bay, it is less than 3 miles wide and from a boat seems more a wide river than a major bay and estuary. Although depths in parts of the drowned channel of the Susquehanna River reach more than 100 feet and the deepest spot, southeast of Annapolis, reaches 174 feet, the Bays' average depth is only 21 feet and approximately 1,100 square miles–an area close to the size of Rhode Island (1,212 square miles)–is less than 6 feet deep.

For several reasons, the Bays tides are unusual. First, the Bay is longer than one full wave length of the dominant semidiurnal tide, when one higher high tide is reaching the head of the Bay, the following higher high has already entered the Bay. Second, the Bay has two distinctly different tidal regimes: the tide in the southern Bay and Tangier Sound is semidiurnal, the classic tidal cycle of two approximately equal highs and two approximately equal lows every 24 hours; the central and northern Bay have mixed tides, in each 24 hour tidal cycle there are two highs and two lows but one high is a distinctly higher high and one low a clear lower low and the difference between high and higher high, low and lower low becomes more pronounced the farther up the Bay you go. Finally, there is a small but measurable difference in the tidal range between the Bays eastern and western shores. On October 23, 2012 at the Piankatank River tide gage, on the western shore, there was a high tide of 1.4 feet above Mean Lower Low at 4:47 p.m. Across the Bay, at the tide gage at the mouth of Nassawadox Creek, a high tide of 2.0 feet above Mean Lower Low occurred an hour later, at 5:47 p.m.

The mean tidal range on the Bay decreases from: 2.8-3.0 feet at the mouth of the bay, to 2 feet at Cove Point and 1 foot at the Thomas Point Light a few miles south of Annapolis. Above the Thomas Point Light, the tide increases again until, at the head of the Bay it reaches 1.8-2.2 feet. In the Bays tributaries the tide range increases as you go up stream. At the mouth of the Potomac River the tide range is approximately 1.0-1.4 feet and 100 miles upriver, in Washington DC, the tide range is 3.0-4.2 feet. The Bays tidal currents follow the same pattern as the tide range. Decreasing from about 1 knot near the mouth of the Bay to a half knot at Cove Point and off Thomas Point and then rising again toward the head of the Bay.

As in all of the large, shallow bays, inlets and sounds along the coast, wind has a greater effect on water levels and apparent currents than the tides do. In the mid bay, from the Potomac River to above Annapolis, several days of strong northerlies can lower water levels 3-4 feet, and prolonged southerlies can raise water levels the same amount and cause coastal flooding.

Winds on the Chesapeake Bay can best be described as variable and relatively mild. The meteorological records for the mid bay Gooses Reef data buoy show no true dominant wind direction. From April to September, and again in December, the most common wind direction was south but the only month in which a south wind blew more than approximately 30 % of the time was April, with 46%. During these months the average wind speed was 9 knots, with April the windiest month at 11 knots. In October and November and in January to March north to northeast winds were common–more common than south winds in the summer–but only November had north half the time. In these months the average wind speed was 10 knots with November reaching an average of 12–the years strongest monthly average. All of which does not mean that strong winds do not blow. During fall and winter cold fronts winds of 20-30 knots, even full gale force, are not uncommon, but they rarely last more than a day or two.

As is true for the entire length of the Atlantic and Gulf coasts, fishing, oystering and crabbing on the Chesapeake Bay long pre-date the arrival of European settlers. Among the oldest Native American artifacts found along the Bays shores are fish hooks and refuse middens containing oyster shells, clam shells, and fish and crab remains. The first European colonists in the Bay area, at Jamestown, would have fared even worse than they did without the Bays bounty. And fishing, oystering and crabbing have been an important part of the bay area's culture and economy ever since.

Commercial fishing, in the sense of large-scale market fishing, appears to have begun on the Bay approximately a century after the arrival of the first colonists. By the second half of the eighteenth-century seine nets, fish weirs, fish pots (traps) and, possibly pound nets, were in use at fisheries established by a number of the large tidewater plantations and at many small bay communities. The size and value of the marine products harvested from the Bay–commercial, subsistence and recreational–grew in importance throughout the nineteenth and the first half of the twentieth centuries.

But the composition of the harvest changed as one species after another was over exploited and massive growth in population, industry and agriculture throughout the bays watershed degraded the environment and disrupted the natural life cycles of bay species. The oyster harvest peaked about 1880 and the long decline to essentially nothing began. Sturgeon, once common, were thought to have been exterminated but a small, lingering remnant population has been found in a river on the eastern shore. Shad and herring are anadromous fish, they live in the ocean but return to freshwater to spawn and they return to the river they were spawned in. Over fishing and pollution killed off the breeding stock in many streams and in others, notably the Susquehanna River, dams blocked access to the spawning areas. The vast schools of shad and herring that once migrated up the Bays tributary streams are gone.

Today on the Bay commercial fishing continues to decline and the Bays watermen, their life style dependent on exploiting the commons, are less common. Four of the more important species still fished commercially within the bay are: blue crabs (Callinectes sapidus, the Maryland State crustacean), striped bass, menhaden and oysters. And the oyster harvest, as on Long Island Sound, is heavily dependent on aquaculture.

Chapter 1

Annapolis, is the capital of Maryland, the home of the United States Naval Academy, the self-proclaimed Sailing Capital of the World, or maybe just the United States–both titles vigorously disputed by Newport, Rhode Island–and a major sailing/boating center, loaded with marinas, boatyards, marine services and yacht brokers. The historic downtown, around the Inner Harbor, is human scale, walkable and attractive, with more intact eighteenth-century buildings than any other American city, numerous good restaurants and pubs, and a lot of shops.

The city was established in 1649 when a group of Puritan exiles from Virginia settled on the south shore of the Severn River. In 1694, Francis Nicholson, the Royal Governor of Maryland made the town his capital and renamed it Annapolis–in honor of Princess Anne of Denmark and Norway, later Queen Anne of England. Governor Nicholson laid out his new capital in circles with radiating roads, in the style of the great cities of Europe, and it is claimed that Pierre L'Enfant used Annapolis as the model for his design for Washington, DC. Annapolis served as the temporary capital of the United States after the signing of the Treaty of Paris, the treaty that ended the Revolutionary War. Congress was in session in the Annapolis State House from November 1783 to June 1784, and it was there that, on December 23, 1783, George Washington resigned his commission as Commander-in-Chief of the Continental Army. On October 10, 1845, a Naval School with 50 midshipman and 7 professors was established in Annapolis–without Congressional funding or approval. In 1850 the Naval School became the United States Naval Academy.

After three days of enjoying Annapolis and after retrieving boating gear that I had stashed in a friend's basement when we parted company with our previous boat–inflatable dinghy, outboard, charts, tools, tools and tools–we set out to enjoy a few weeks of good October Bay cruising. Leaving Annapolis, we saw a couple of pelicans, the first we had seen on this cruise. DDT decimated the populations of coastal fish-eating birds that are high on the food chain, like the pelican and osprey. Forty years ago, pelicans were almost never seen on the Chesapeake and the few, rare sightings were at the south end of the bay, near its mouth. Today, thanks largely to the elimination of DDT they are not uncommon and they are occasionally seen even further north, on Delaware Bay and in southern New Jersey.

Possibly climatic warming and the accompanying slow rise in sea water temperatures, has also contributed to the pelicans' northward expansion. According to NOAA and the EPA, the average seawater temperature along the mid-Atlantic coast has increased a degree and a half, Fahrenheit, since 1900 and, in the Chesapeake the rise has been faster, two degrees since 1960. Two degrees doesn't sound like much but there has not been a freeze over of the bay, a hard freeze that brought thick ice shore to shore, since President Reagan's second inaugural in 1985. In the fresh water streams that feed into the Bay and in the Bay's quite back waters thin, skim ice is fairly common in January and February. But thick hard ice and complete freeze overs are not. They were much more common during the eighteenth, nineteenth and early twentieth centuries than they are today.

Our first stop was the old port of Deale, Maryland, at the head of Herring Bay, twenty miles down the Chesapeake's western shore from Annapolis. In Deale we spent a pleasant evening visiting with friends at the Herrington Harbour North Marina & Yacht Yard. The two Herrington Harbour Marinas, located at the north and south ends of Herring Bay, are large, clean, modern, well run and the closest Chesapeake Bay marinas to Washington, DC. We spent many years sailing from Herrington Harbour North when we both worked in the Capital area. After our afternoon and evening of nostalgia in Deale, we moved on: Chestertown, Rock Hall, St. Michaels, Oxford, a couple of favorite anchorages and, finally, Baltimore.

In Oxford we had one of those nautical adventures that, if all goes well, makes for a good sea story. But if things don't go so well…ends in an insurance claim. As is true of any ageing boat that has passed through the hands of multiple owners, there were issues with our boat. Issues is a favorite term with marine surveyors. It happens. After you have owned a few old boats, you expect it. We were in a slip at Campbell's Bachelor Point Marina/Boatyard one evening getting ready to go to the historic Robert Morris Inn for dinner, when the Chesapeake Bay decided to visit our bilge and *Nauset*, with us aboard, very nearly took a short, fast cruise straight down.

We had owned *Nauset* less than a month and I was still far from intimate familiarity with every hose and wire on the boat. When the high-water alarm went off, I raised the engine hatch and discovered that the Chesapeake Bay had come a' calling and was moving in fast. The water looked like it was up to the bottom of the engine. I turned on our automatic bilge pump. The pump was a large Rule 2000 that worked fine, or at least it did when the toggle switch controlling the pump was turned to "automatic". Why wasn't the toggle switch on auto? Uh…well…things just happen. Somewhat to my surprise the big pump did its thing and pumped out the water. But when the water level had dropped as far as the pump could take it, the pump did not go off. It kept running, slurping up a mix of water and air with occasional short time-outs. I turned the pump off and almost immediately the Chesapeake started flowing back in. That which had just been pumped out was back-siphoning through the pump that had pumped it out. With the pump running, we were OK...floating...but if the pump died or clogged, we would be exploring whatever was on the bottom under the eight feet of water we were floating in. We had to plug the bilge pumps thru-hull.

Betty remembered that Campbell's had a work float by the travel lift and with help from an acquaintance (Eric from the Swan "Black Rose") we dragged the float to *Nauset's* starboard side. Not all that easy as work floats generally lack a hydrodynamic hull shape and we had to get that thing around several rather expensive boats and under a dock. From the work float I was able to drive a soft pine plug into the bilge pump thru-hull, which stopped the water and bought us some time. But we clearly needed a haul out...sooner rather than later.

I dialed the after-hours number for the yard manager and explained the situation...that we were floating on a pine plug. He said we'd be out first thing in the morning. Then we resumed our original plan: borrowed two of the marina's courtesy bikes, rode into Oxford and enjoyed a cheeseburger in paradise at the Robert Morris Inn. At least I had a cheeseburger...and two pints of the Inn's fine Tavern Ale. Betty had one of the excellent evening specials and a glass or two of good wine. On boats, things can happen fast. From Bilge alarm to the bar at the Robert Morris Inn and that necessary first pint of ale was less than 45 minutes.

Before breakfast the next morning...ours anyway...the travel lift crew was on the job and *Nauset* went up onto dry land.

With no immediate probability of sinking, I took a look at the bilge pump and its out-put hose. The high point in the hose run was against the hull, up behind a deck beam, where it was very hard to see, I had to use a mirror and squeeze my head into a place that it wasn't designed to fit into. The output hose had no anti-siphon loop and the bilge pump thru-hull, which had neither a seacock nor a check valve, was barely above the water line. The previous night had been windy with the wind pushing small sloppy waves into the marina. The slop was hitting our starboard side, the side the bilge pump thru-hull was on, and we had been heeled slightly to starboard, pushing the thru-hull half under. While working on the boat that day I had moved our dinghy, outboard and some other stuff to the starboard side. The bilge pumps output hose had become a siphon.

Late that afternoon we were back in the water with: three new bronze thru-hulls, two new anti-siphon loops, a rerouted bilge pump output hose, a new holding tank air vent, set high in the hull, and a lot of new hose. New stuff…you expect that with old boats. The next time I had the boat up out of the water, after we reached Texas, I raised all of the near waterline thru-hulls four inches.

The day after our emergency haul out, we were on our way to Baltimore.

The Patapsco River city of Baltimore is the largest city in Maryland and the largest city on the Chesapeake Bay. Settlement in the Patapsco River area was underway by the mid-1600s, but the Port of Baltimore, as such, got its start in 1706 when Maryland's colonial General Assembly authorized development of a port at the head of the Patapsco River's northwest branch. That first port, located on the Federal Hill side of what is today Baltimore's Inner Harbor, did not do well and it was quickly superseded by the deeper and better situated ports in Baltimore Town and at Fell's Point. Today Baltimore's urban area blankets the Patapsco River, its port facilities extend from Sparrows Point, at the mouth of the river, to the Inner Harbor and the Port of Baltimore is the 16th largest port in the United States–11th in foreign tonnage and 9th in the dollar value of tonnage handled.

Even though Baltimore is 175 miles from the mouth of the Chesapeake Bay, it is one of the ports most likely to be dredged to handle the New Panamax class ships. In the Rivers and Harbors Act of 1970, Congress directed the USACE to dredge the channel from "the mouth of the Chesapeake Bay to Fort McHenry in Baltimore" to a "uniform depth of 50 feet and a width of 800 feet in Maryland and a width of 1,000 feet in Virginia." Much of the 50 Foot Channel is naturally more than 50 feet deep and, where it's not, the Corps maintenance dredging program maintains the 50-foot channel at a depth of 51 feet. Another foot or two in the relatively small sections where needed will happen.

Baltimore is far more than its port. For a visiting boater, Baltimore from the Inner Harbor tourist pavilions to Canton on the north side of the harbor and from the Inner Harbor through Federal Hill to Fort McHenry on the south, is delightful. Baltimore is one of the best, if not the best, provisioning and re-supply places anywhere along the coast from Maine to Key West. And my personal opinion is that, from Maine to Mexico, Baltimore and New Orleans share the top spot in the category of convenient provisioning and re-supply stops.

Baltimore's Inner Harbor area has half a dozen good marinas and a number of anchoring possibilities. The historic Fell's Point, Canton, and Federal Hill neighborhoods contain what not only seems like, but really is, hundreds of pubs, taverns and restaurants that range upward from grubby beer joints to some of the finest white linen dining on the east coast. A Gourmet Safeway, a Whole Foods Market, a Harris-Teeter Supermarket, the city's Broadway (small), Cross Street (large) and Lexington Markets are all within easy reach as are medical facilities, museums, marine supplies and services...and anything else a boater might need.

Chapter 1

We spent five enjoyable days at the Anchorage Marina in Fell's Point: blowing the restaurant budget at Charleston (the Chef Cindy Wolf's place at 1000 Lancaster St.) and the Black Olive, enjoying the wide selection of good craft beers at Red Sky, Max's and the Warf Rat, and breakfast at Bonaparte Breads (an excellent boulangerie on S. Ann Street), stuffing *Nauset's* frig and food lockers, stuffing me and doing a little boat work. Very little boat work…and I should have done a bit more.

In Oxford when I had my head and shoulders down in the bilge, working the bilge pump problem, I had noticed a bit of that particular odor that indicates a possible problem in the biological waste handling system, in the parts downstream from the porcelain throne. Large parts of Nauset's sewage system, probably most of it, was original vintage 1995, i.e. eighteen years old. I flushed two gallons of 10% acetic acid (pickling vinegar) through the system and then flushed it with freshwater several times. The odor cleared up…mostly…and the system was working as intended. We were good to go. Every single one of our previous seven ageing arks required waste system attention, generally extensive attention. Usually the extensive attention that works best with anything connected to sewage waste management on a boat is complete replacement and I knew that, in the end, somewhere down the road, *Nauset's* system would get the complete replacement solution.

The days were getting shorter, the nights cooler and the marine weather forecasts were starting to mention cold fronts. It was time to move on. From Baltimore we dropped down the Chesapeake Bay's western shore to Norfolk, Virginia and the start of the Atlantic Intracoastal Waterway; with in route stops in Solomons Island, Maryland and Deltaville, Virginia.

The little fishing and farming community, originally called Sandy Island, became Solomons Island in 1865 when Isaac Solomon, a Baltimore Merchant bought the island, established an oyster cannery and built workers housing and a shipyard. Once an isolated fishing community, Solomons Island today is a major yachting center and a popular stop for migrating snowbird cruisers. At Solomons Island, we anchored off Zahniser's Yachting Center, went ashore by dinghy and enjoyed an excellent dinner in the Dry Dock Restaurant. In1994, our first trip down the east coast to Florida and the Bahamas began at Zahniser's and the night before departure we ate dinner at the Dry Dock. All but one of our subsequent 20 plus trips into the land of coconut dreams has officially begun with a ritual dinner at the Dry Dock. And the one that didn't begin with dinner at the Dry Dock, was not our most pleasant cruise.

The unincorporated community of Deltaville, Virginia–located at the tip of the peninsula between the Rappahannock and Piankatank Rivers–is almost more a state of mind than a town. There is really no central there, there...no town center, town square, courthouse. The community is an area–a string of small businesses, farms and homes loosely scattered along the last ten miles of Virginia Route 33 with the numerous marinas, boatyards, boat builders and marine services down the little lanes that lead to the deep, sheltered creeks that penetrate the peninsula. Originally a fishing and wooden boat building center called Union, the community became Deltaville when a post office arrived in the early twentieth century. Today, like Solomons Island, Deltaville is a major yachting center that, also like Solomons Island, is very popular with those snowbirds. And, based on the number of crab trap floats and pound nets on the Rappahannock Spit, Stingray

Chapter 1

Point, Milford Haven Spit and some of the other shoals, there are still a fair number of working watermen in the area.

Tuesday, October twenty-third *Nauset* passed between Fort Monroe and Fort Wool, the forts that guarded the mouth of Hampton Roads, and left the Chesapeake Bay astern.

2. The Atlantic Intracoastal Waterway; Norfolk, Virginia to Beaufort, North Carolina

Hampton Roads is the broad channel through which the merged Elizabeth, James and Nansemond rivers flow into the Chesapeake Bay. Hampton Roads is also occasionally used as a name for the contiguous urban area composed of the cities of: Chesapeake, Hampton, Newport News, Norfolk, Portsmouth, Suffolk and Virginia Beach. The area was the site of the first successful English settlement in the new world. Captain Christopher Newport's three small ships–*Susan Constant*, *Godspeed* and *Discovery*–made their initial landing on Cape Henry, in what is today the City of Virginia Beach, and passed through Hampton Roads on their way to the James River and the settling of Jamestown.

Hampton Roads is home to the Naval Station, Norfolk, the largest naval complex in the world, vessels entering Hampton Roads and turning for the Elizabeth River, the Port of Norfolk and the Atlantic Intracoastal Waterway, sail past the aircraft carriers, cruisers, destroyers, frigates, submarines and amphibious ships of the Atlantic fleet. The area has been militarily important since the establishment of the Jamestown settlement. In 1610, the colonists at Jamestown built earth and log fortifications on Old Point Comfort, where Fort Monroe stands today, to defend the mouth of Hampton Roads and the water approach to Jamestown. During the Civil War the engagement between the Monitor and the Merrimack took place in Hampton Roads. And, during World War II, the Atlantic fleet was based in Norfolk and convoys bound across the Atlantic (primarily to the Mediterranean) collected in Hampton Roads–at times hundreds of ships were at anchor in the roads.

In 1767 Andrew Sprowle, a local merchant and ship owner built a shipyard on the western side of the Elizabeth River, in today's Portsmouth. During the revolutionary war Sprowle was a royalist and he left Virginia with the defeated British at the end of the war. Sprowle's shipyard, taken over by the colonists, eventually became the Norfolk Naval Shipyard and was the origin of the U.S. Navy's presence in Hampton Roads. Today the Norfolk Naval Shipyard is the navy's oldest and largest shipyard and the largest shipyard on the east coast. Despite being in Portsmouth and not Norfolk, the shipyard has never been called the Portsmouth Naval Shipyard. The shipyard was originally called the Gosport Shipyard, the name was changed to Norfolk Naval Shipyard in 1862.

The Port of Virginia, composed of the four large marine terminals on the harbor of Hampton Roads–the Norfolk International Terminal, the Portsmouth Marine Terminal, the Newport News Marine Terminal and the Virginia International Gateway–was the 13th largest port in the United States in 2016. In the competition to serve the New Panamax class ships The Port of Virginia is ahead of almost everyone else, at least with regard to east and gulf coast ports. They are only a short distance from deep water in the Atlantic, the Chesapeake channel is at or over 50 feet, the Norfolk entrance reach is at 52 feet and the channels to the Virginia International Gateway and to the Norfolk International Terminal are already at 50 feet.

In the Elizabeth River, between the Portsmouth Naval Hospital and the Waterside Shopping and Marina Complex in Norfolk, we passed the Elizabeth River Flashing Red 36, an ordinary navigation buoy, one of thousands along the waterway. But this buoy is only

Loading Coal
Norfolk, Virginia

a hundred yards or so from the otherwise unmarked start of the Atlantic Intracoastal Waterway...the AICW. AICW mile Zero is at 36°50.9′ N, 76°17.9′ W, off the foot of West Main Street, in Norfolk. The Atlantic Intracoastal Waterway extends from here to AICW mile 1243.8 at 24°33.7′N., 81°48.5′W, in Key West, Florida.

From the Flashing Red 36 we continued south down the western branch of the Elizabeth River–past the commercial cargo terminals, shipyards and naval facilities that line the river and under the high Interstate 64 Bascule Bridge (AICW mile 7.1) which clears 65 feet…closed–to the tide lock and bridge in Great Bridge Virginia. The free, bulkhead dockage, above and below the town's namesake bridge was crowded with migrating snowbirds, so we stayed at the Atlantic Yacht Basin Marina/Yacht Yard just south of the bridge (AICW mile 12).

The Atlantic Intracoastal Waterway at Great Bridge, Virginia

The docks across the AICW from the Atlantic Yacht Basin are part of the Great Bridge Battlefield Memorial Park and transient cruising boats are permitted to tie up overnight. While several skirmishes were fought in the Great Bridge area during the Civil War, the Battlefield Memorial Park at Great Bridge commemorates the Revolutionary War battle fought here on December 9, 1775. The battle, sometimes referred to as "the second Bunker Hill," was a significant early Revolutionary War engagement and was possibly the first strategically important American victory. At Great Bridge the Royalists were pushed back to Norfolk and the American Revolutionaries gained control of the southern land approaches to Norfolk, control of the bridge and control of the only road through the dismal swamp to North Carolina.

South of Norfolk, pleasure vessels cruising the waterway can choose between two routes: the Albemarle and Chesapeake Canal or the Dismal Swamp Canal. Commercial vessels must use the Albemarle and Chesapeake Canal route. Just south of the I-64 Bridge a Corps of Engineers sign giving information on the status of the Dismal Swamp Canal and Locks marks the point where the two routes diverge. Continue south on the western branch of the Elizabeth River for the tide lock, Great Bridge and the Albemarle and Chesapeake Canal. Turn west (right) immediately past the sign to reach Deep Creek and the Dismal Swamp Canal. The two routes rejoin on the south side of Albemarle Sound just north of Flashing Green 1 AR at the mouth of the Alligator River, approximately AICW mile 79.

The Chesapeake and Albemarle Canal

Generally called the "Virginia Cut," the larger and more commonly used Albemarle and Chesapeake Canal is the sum of five distinct parts. The canal begins at the 600-foot-long by 72-foot-wide tide lock in Great Bridge, VA (ICW mile 11.3.) This lock, built by the Corps of Engineers in 1931-1932 to replace an older, smaller lock, separates the tidal and brackish waters of the Elizabeth River from the non-tidal, and much less brackish waters of the Albemarle and Chesapeake Canal. Between the tide lock and Albemarle Sound the canal: follows the 13-mile-long man-made Virginia Cut, runs down the winding North Landing River to a dredged channel through broad, shallow Currituck Sound, leaves the sound through the short Carolina Cut and then follows the North River to its mouth on Albemarle Sound.

Northbound in the spring of 2016 we spent a night at the Atlantic Yacht Basin and noticed a few very small mussels on the dock pilings. Southbound in September 2017 we spent September 22nd to September 28th at the Atlantic Yacht Basin waiting while Hurricane Maria approached and then curved east. The 25-35 mile per hour northerly winds on the back side of Hurricane Maria blew a lot of water out of the Chesapeake and Albemarle Canal and at the Atlantic Yacht Basin the water level dropped to four feet below normal. For almost a full day we were so low that neither of us could physically get off the boat. Below the normal waterline the pilings were absolutely covered with little mussels. I had time to study them, photograph them and search the internet. They were invasive fresh water Quagga mussels. Quagga mussels, like the better-known Zebra mussels, reached the United States in the ballast water of coal ships and bulk freighters from Eastern Europe. I could not find any internet reports of Quagga mussels in the Albemarle and Chesapeake Canal or in that area, but there they were. Lots of them.

Although it was the second of the two routes to be built, the Chesapeake and Albemarle Canal was the first to be authorized. Originally authorized in 1772 then reauthorized, re-reauthorized, re-re-reauthorized and…between Virginia and North Carolina, the Chesapeake and Albemarle Canal was authorized at least 10 times before construction actually began in 1855. When the canal opened in 1859—completed in four years by a small fleet of barge mounted steam dredges—it was significantly wider and deeper than the Dismal Swamp Canal and was considered to be an engineering marvel. The original tide lock at Great Bridge, 220 feet long and 40 feet wide, was the second largest lock in the United States. The new canal quickly captured the bulk of the freight traffic between the Chesapeake Bay and Albemarle Sound and until the turn of the twentieth century the canal was profitable. The canal company's annual report for the fiscal year October 1, 1879 to September 30, 1880 shows $86,138.99 in toll receipts,[8] with July 1880 ($8,717.43) the peak month.

In 1910, a year after passage of the Rivers and Harbors Act of March 3, 1909, the Albemarle and Chesapeake Canal Company defaulted, went into foreclosure and was sold. Between 1910 and 1913 both the canals between the Chesapeake Bay and Albemarle Sound were considered for inclusion in the protected waterway, along with two other possible routes. The Albemarle and Chesapeake canal–already in existence, wider, deeper and with only one lock–was chosen and in 1913, acting under the authority of the 1909 Act, the Federal Government bought the Chesapeake and Albemarle Canal for $500,000.00[9] and the Corps of Engineers set about enlarging it and giving it its present form.

At AICW mile 50, 39 miles south of Great Bridge, the Waterway runs through the unincorporated North Carolina community of Coinjock founded around the middle of the eighteenth century. Today the town is a well-known rest and refueling stop on the ICW and the Coinjock Marina Restaurant (east side of the waterway) is known from Florida to Maine for its 32 once Prime Rib dinner. Beyond Coinjock the Atlantic Intracoastal Waterway follows a largely dredged channel down the North River to Albemarle Sound. From Green Can 171 in the mouth of the river and just south of AICW mile 65, the Intracoastal Waterway runs south across Albemarle Sound to the Alligator River Green 1 off the mouth of the Alligator River, where the Dismal Swamp Alternate Route rejoins.

The Dismal Swamp Canal Alternate Route

The Dismal Swamp Canal Alternate Route connects the Elizabeth River south of Norfolk, Virginia to Albemarle Sound via:

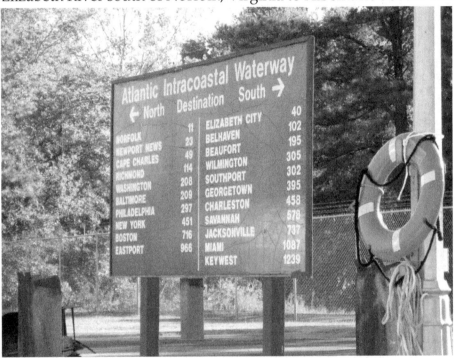

A sign at the Deep Creek Lock, Dismal Swamp Canal

Deep Creek, the Dismal Swamp Canal and the Pasquotank River. The federal project depth for the channels in Deep Creek and the Pasquotank River is 10 feet and in the Dismal Swamp Canal, 9 feet. Both Deep Creek and the Pasquotank River–which still carries limited barge traffic–are maintained at project depth but, because of water supply problems and the fact that it no longer carries any commercial traffic, the Dismal Swamp Canal is maintained at 6

64

feet. The locks at the north and south ends of the 22.6-mile-long Dismal Swamp Canal both have chambers 300 feet long and 52 feet wide, a depth over the sills of 12 feet and a lift of 12 feet. Between the locks the canal is pretty, with the look and feel of an old French barge canal in Burgundy or the Loire Valley.

A canal along the approximate route of the Dismal Swamp Canal was proposed in 1728, by Colonel William Byrd II, but it was after the Revolutionary War before anything was done—Virginia authorizing the canal in 1787, North Carolina in 1790. The Dismal Swamp Canal Company began digging from both ends in 1793, with most of the work being done by slaves rented from nearby plantations. The canal causeway road, today part of U.S. Route 17, opened in 1804 and the canal opened the next year. For the first nine years after the canal opened, traffic was limited to canoes, rafts and flat boats, because for over half its length the new canal had only a couple of feet of water.

Unfortunately for romance and elementary school history and contrary to general and popular belief, George Washington did not survey or build the Dismal Swamp Canal. Washington's only connection to the canal was financial. When the canal was authorized by Virginia (1787) and North Carolina (1790), the project was to be funded by subscription...shares. George Washington, despite doubts about the economic viability of the canal, bought 200 shares. The belief that George Washington built or surveyed the Dismal Swamp Canal may be the result of confusion between the Dismal Swamp Canal and Washington's Canal (or Ditch). Washington and a group of business associates owned approximately 50,000 acres of timber and agricultural land in and adjacent to the Dismal Swamp. George Washington surveyed and supervised the construction of Washington's Canal to help drain part of their land and, possibly, to float cut timber out. The canal ran north-northwest from Lake Drummond to the edge of the swamp at a point that may originally have been on or near a creek that was tributary to the headwaters of the Nansemond River south of Suffolk, Virginia. [10] Scattered remains of Washington's Canal can still be seen in the Dismal Swamp.[11]

Between 1812 and 1900 the canal underwent a series of improvements to widen and deepen it but continuing problems with seasonally insufficient water for lock operation, a problem to this day, and competition from the Albemarle and Chesapeake Canal rendered the Dismal Swamp Canal economically unviable as a commercial concern. In 1929 Congress purchased the canal from the nearly bankrupt Lake Drummond Canal and Water Company, the successor to the original Dismal Swamp Canal Company. In 1974 the Great Dismal Swamp National Wildlife Refuge was established, navigation on the canal was made secondary to water conservation and control and the little remaining commercial shipping was moved to the Albemarle and Chesapeake Canal. The canal is now on the National Register of Historic Places, is maintained by the U.S. Army Corps of Engineers and is operated, water levels permitting, for pleasure boat and tourist traffic.

For the 20 miles downstream from the South Mills Lock to Elizabeth City, the dismal swamp route follows Turners Cut and the winding Pasquotank River. This stretch is as pretty as any 20-mile section of the AICW. Cypress and gum trees closely hem the river, backed by cedar, pines and mixed southern hardwoods. The trees, tall as they are, are second or third growth. By the Civil War loggers had nearly shaved the area, it was cut over again, less drastically, between the turn of the century and World War I and managed, selective, sustainable cutting continues today.

Chapter 2

From late fall to early spring Bald Eagles are common, early spring to late fall Osprey are everywhere and several species of Herons and Egrets are common year-round. The water is cypress swamp black water. It's not "black" from sewage or industrial waste, its stained brown, at times almost black, by the tannins in cypress bark and leaves, and other vegetation. In the days when coasting schooners loading timber and agricultural products made Elizabeth City a significant port, the schooners water casks were often sent up the Pasquotank to be filled in the probably correct belief that the brown tannic acid infused water kept better in the wooden casks than the water available in the city.

Elizabeth City, which calls itself "The Harbor of Hospitality", sits where the river narrows, makes a tight 180° bend around Machelhe Island and passes under the Route 158 Bridge. Trading posts operated in the area as early as the mid eighteenth century and the town of Redding was incorporated on the site in 1793. In 1801 the name was changed to Elizabeth City, possibly in honor of Elizabeth Tooley, a local tavern keeper who donated a substantial part of the land on which the town was founded. From the 1805 opening of the Dismal Swamp Canal the town prospered with an economy based on canal traffic (tolls), trans-shipping of cargos to and from canal boats, agriculture and timber. The 1859 opening of the Albemarle and Chesapeake Canal and the ravages of the Civil nearly ruined the town and it was not until the opening of the Elizabeth City & Norfolk Railroad (later the Norfolk Southern Railway) in 1881 that prosperity returned. Today Elizabeth City is the heart of a thriving agricultural area and a bedroom community for the sprawling Hampton Roads military-industrial complex.

The U.S. Coast Guard Air Station, Elizabeth City, sits on the west bank of the Pasquotank a few miles downstream from the old city and the docks. This base is the Command and Control Center for all Atlantic air-sea rescue operations—from Greenland to the Azores to Barbados and the Caribbean—and it is home to many of the aircraft used in those operations. The hulking rounded building near the Coast Guard Air Station is the Navy's old Blimp hangar. Today the hanger is the manufacturing facility for TCOM, L.P. the world's largest builder of lighter-than-air aircraft. The blimps flying over sports events and cities all over the country probably came from here.

Past the Coast Guard Station, the Dismal Swamp Alternate Route continues down the Pasquotank River to its mouth on Albemarle Sound. At the river's mouth, approximately 19 miles below Elizabeth City, the alternate route rounds the 23-foot-tall flashing (white light) light structure PR (for Pasquotank River), on the tip of the Wade Point Shoal and follows a course of 188° magnetic to the Flashing Green 1 AR, off the mouth of the Alligator River, where it rejoins the primary Atlantic Intracoastal Waterway.

Albemarle Sound to the Beaufort/Morehead City Inlet

Along the Atlantic Intracoastal Waterway, from the Great Bridge lock and the Dismal Swamp Canal south to the Adams Creek Canal, the tides range from none through nominal, to about two feet at the North Carolina Rt. 101 (AICW mile 195.8) bridge which crosses Core Creek just south of the southern end of the Adams Creek Canal. Along this section of the waterway wind is the driver in the rise and fall of the water. The northerlies accompanying a strong cold front can lower water levels two to four feet and strong, or persistent, east to south winds can raise water levels by an equal amount. Hurricanes have been known to raise water levels by more than ten feet.

Since Baltimore, we had been watching the weather closely. A Tropical Storm named Sandy was not re-curving out to sea as initially predicted. Tropical Storms are a fact of life along the east and gulf coasts, particularly south and west from the Chesapeake. In the 50 years between 1960 and 2010, 89 tropical cyclones of hurricane strength came ashore between Boston and Brownsville– an average of 1.78 hurricanes per year–and 28 of those were major category 3, 4 or 5 storms. Some parts of the coast are hit more than others but there is no section of the Atlantic or gulf coasts that is immune to tropical disturbances. Between 1960 and 2010: the upper gulf coast between St. Marks, Florida and Brownsville, Texas was hit by 46 hurricanes, peninsular Florida was hit by 18, the south Atlantic coast between Jacksonville and Cape Hatteras was hit by 21 and there were only 4 north of Cape Hatteras.[12]

We decided to run for New Bern, North Carolina. New Bern is south of the big, open sounds, south of most of the outer banks and well up the Neuse River. A category 1 or 2 storm passing right offshore or even crossing the outer most part of the banks would probably have little effect on New Bern. The real danger in New Bern would be the storm surge if Sandy came ashore south of Beaufort, North Carolina. In 1999 Hurricane Floyd came ashore over Cape Fear as a strong category two storm. The strong easterly winds on the northern side of Floyd drove a storm surge up the Neuse River that destroyed the docks in New Bern. In 2018 Hurricane Florence did the same. In New Bern, the dock at which we rode out Sandy went away.

We left Great Bridge early and as we motored down the Virginia Cut, I called the New Bern Grand Marina and made a reservation for three nights. Following the AICW, Great Bridge, Virginia to Oriental, North Carolina is 170 statute miles and from Oriental it is another 21 miles up the Neuse River to New Bern…2 days…191

miles. We spent that night anchored off Tuckahoe Point (AICW mile 104), at the north end of the Alligator-Pungo Canal and reached New Bern late the next afternoon.

The anchoring spot off Tuckahoe Point, a pretty spot safe in most weather conditions, is a wide area created by the junction of the natural river and the canal. Its' one of several good anchoring places along the Alligator River, between the rivers turn to the west at Newport News Point and the north end of the Alligator-Pungo Canal. When we entered the anchorage two boats, a trawler and a large catamaran were already anchored and two more, a Canadian C&C 27 sloop and another power boat, entered after us. The power boat was interesting, a 45-foot Hatteras sport fish. A great many sport fish boats travel the ICW but you rarely see them anchored out. After sunset we could see the anchor lights of another half dozen boats camped for the night at various wide spots in the river.

After a peaceful quiet night on the hook, our alarm clock was the predawn rumble and vibration of a large vessel of some sort underway on the waterway. Sunrise was spectacular, we were inside a rainbow. The rising sun was shining through a low layer of ground fog and the sunlight through the fog was every imaginable shade of red, orange and yellow. Fifty yards away we could see the dim shape of the Hatteras sport fish. We took in our anchor and started down the Alligator-Pungo Canal, running on the chart plotter and radar. Half an hour later the rainbow effect was gone and the fog was just a gray and rapidly dissipating ground fog.

The 20-mile-long Alligator River-Pungo River Canal (the canals formal name) extends from AICW mile 104.5 to Mile 124.5 and was built between 1925 and 1928. The ceremony marking the official opening of the canal was held in Belhaven, on the Pungo River (AICW mile 136) in August 1928; although there was still some finishing work in progress. Prior to construction of the Alligator-Pungo Canal and the (constructed concurrently) short Hobucken Canal, which connects the Pamlico and Neuse Rivers via Goose Creek and the Bay River, vessels traveling the Intracoastal Waterway, Norfolk, Virginia to Beaufort Inlet, North Carolina–the original name for this segment of the AICW–had to take the longer and more exposed route through the lower part of Albemarle Sound and the whole length of Pamlico Sound.

At AICW mile 113.9 we went under the 64-foot-high Fairfield (NC Rt. 94) Bridge. On the north side of the bridge the Alligator-Pungo Canal crosses the much older Fairfield Canal. On January 29, 1849 the General Assembly of North Carolina issued a charter to the Fairfield Canal and Turnpike Company. In 1872 the company contracted with the Albemarle and Chesapeake Canal Company to use their steam dredges–the dredges originally used to dredge the Albemarle and Chesapeake Canal–to cut a canal from the town of Fairfield on Lake Mattamuskeet north to the navigable Alligator River.[13] The canal was intended to provide a steamboat route to Fairfield and help drain…improve…the surrounding land for agriculture. The Albemarle and Chesapeake Canal Company's annual report for their 1879-1880 fiscal year shows that they owned 50% of the stock of the Fairfield Canal and Turnpike Company and that their steam dredge *Albemarle* was used for maintenance dredging in the Fairfield Canal between June and December of 1879.

The Chief of Engineers Report to the Congress for 1886 contains a letter from Engineer Captain Jas. Mercur in which Capt. Mercur reports that "I passed over the river on the mail steamer *Martha E. Dickerman*, which is operated by the Norfolk Southern Railroad Company…she makes two round trips weekly to Elizabeth City, NC (from Fairfield) carrying the mails." An attachment to Capt.

Mercur's letter details commodities shipped from Fairfield and adds that "in the year ending December 31, 1885, 842 passengers traveled to Fairfield." A second letter in the report, this one from Colonel William S. Carter, President of the Fairfield Canal and Turnpike Company states that "The depth of water in the (Fairfield) canal at mean tide, by actual measurement is a little over 7 feet." And "The present year (1886) we shall ship from 100,000-125,000 bushels corn, between 15,000-20,000 bushels rice, about 12,000 bushels oats and other things in Proportion."

With construction of the Interstate Highway System and improvements in the Atlantic coast rail net, water borne freight on the AICW declined. Today the overwhelming bulk of the Atlantic Intracoastal Waterway's economic value is in the private vessels, local and transient, that use it and the thousands of marinas, boatyards, restaurants and other services that cater to them. But there is still some commercial barge traffic, particularly between Beaufort, NC and Norfolk, VA., and between Jacksonville, FL and Charleston, SC. The only published data for freight tonnage on the AICW is the figures for the USACE's check point at the Great Bridge Lock. In 2016 the Great Bridge lock handled 941,000 tons of commercial cargo. That sounds like a lot but it isn't. In 2016, the Bayou Boeuf lock on the Gulf Intracoastal Waterway at Morgan City, Louisiana, handled 23,315,000 tons of commercial cargo.

An hour and a half after getting underway and half way through the Alligator-Pungo Canal, we caught up with, and carefully passed, the large vessel that had been our early morning wakeup call. It was a three deck pushboat with a heavily loaded 10,000-barrel red flag tank barge on the head (in front, being pushed.) Barges carrying flammable, explosive or other dangerous commodities must show one or more prominently displayed, easily visible red flags or pennants.

Chapter 2

Towboats with barges are the most common non-fishing commercial vessels encountered on the Intracoastal Waterway and the term towboat is generally applied to both push boats and tugs. A push boat is a relatively shoal draft towboat with a squared off bow equipped with a pair of pushing knees (often called towing knees) that almost always pushes, rather than pulling. A tug is the traditional towing tugboat, the type seen assisting ocean going ships in every deep-water port from Maine to Texas. Traditional tugs have a boat shaped hull (a pointed bow), a relatively deep draft, generally pull rather than push and are not commonly used in the narrow, shallow parts of the ICW. In connection with tugs and barges "tow" can simply mean something being towed but it generally means everything that is being pushed or towed: one barge, a pair of fuel barges, eight hopper barges loaded with coal or, on the Mississippi and Ohio Rivers, as many as 15 to 30 or more barges. Tow can also mean the complete assembly, the pushboat or tug and all of whatever is being pushed or pulled.

Tank barges are built in a variety of sizes with the size, or capacity of the barge generally given in oil barrels–the 42-gallon barrel used in the petroleum and petrochemical industries. The most common tank barges are 30,000 and 10,000-barrel barges. 30,000-barrel barges are approximately 300 feet long, 54 feet wide and have a loaded draft of 12-13 feet and 10,000-barrel barges are generally about 195 feet long, 35 feet wide and have a loaded draft of 9 feet. The 10,000-barrel barge we passed, if fully loaded, was carrying approximately 450,000 gallons of some flammable product, as much as 15 DOT 111 rail road tank cars or approximately 58 large tank trucks.

Waterways, like many sections of the Intracoastal Waterway, that have a navigable depth of 12 feet or less, are generally considered shallow waterways and the tank barges most often seen on these waterways are the 9-foot loaded draft 10,000-barrel barges. On the deeper inland waterways and on the open water sections of the Intracoastal Waterway–the Mississippi and Ohio Rivers, the Cape Cod Canal, Long Island Sound, the Chesapeake Bay and the GIWW between Mobile Bay and New Orleans, etc.– large tank barges are common.

A push boat with a large fuel barge on the Atlantic Intracoastal Waterway

In terms of efficiency, safety and the environment, an intermodal transportation study conducted by the Texas Transportation Institute (report # 406391-7) comparing movement of freight by barge, truck and rail over the eight years from 2001 to 2009, found that barges were the safest, most efficient and least environmentally damaging. The injury rate per one million ton-miles was: 1 for barges, 95.3 for railroads and 1,609.6 for trucks. One gallon of fuel would move one ton of freight: 616 miles by barge, 478 miles by rail and only 150 miles by truck. Gallons of liquid product spilled per million ton-miles: barge 2.59 gallons, rail 4.89 gallons and truck 10.41 gallons.

On this trip through the Alligator-Pungo, parts of the canal were noticeably wider than they were when we first traveled the waterway in the early 1990s: the banks eroded, old formerly buried tree stumps standing out in the water, fallen trees littering the shore. The canal may have been wider, but mud, sand and silt had narrowed the navigable channel…despite periodic dredging by the Corps of Engineers and the State of North Carolina.

From the Chesapeake Bay south to St. Augustine, Florida, the Atlantic Intracoastal Waterway runs primarily through marshes and low soft, alluvial soils. Both the natural shorelines and the banks of the man-made canals and cuts–except where they have been stabilized with rock or something else–erode easily and are constantly being reshaped by the tides, currents, winds and the surges of winter storms and hurricanes. Shorelines and banks erode and accrete, sand and mud bars form and move, channels shift and periodically the Coast Guard adjusts the placement of the aids to navigation to compensate for the changes.

There is also an un-natural contributor to erosion and siltation in the waterway, particularly in the narrow, man-made sections…boat wakes. The wakes created by fast moving powerboats thunder ashore in waves that can be as much as three or four feet high. The large wakes sweep ashore and wash sand, silt, debris, sometimes whole trees, into the waterway. About boat wakes and the Alligator-Pungo Canal, the <u>Waterway Guide Atlantic ICW</u>, 2016 edition, page 157 says, "The canal is relatively narrow and boats dragging huge wakes have a tendency to damage the banks. Each year more and more trees topple into the water."

A recent NOAA study[14] of the impact of boat wakes on the unconsolidated, easily eroded, silts and sands through which many of the manmade segments of the AICW have been cut found that "erosion from boat wakes significantly exceeds background erosion from wind waves." The study was conducted in North

On the Alligator-Pungo Canal

A sport fish boats wake rolls ashore

Carolina, primarily in Snows Cut (AICW miles 295-297), but its conclusions are applicable to the whole of the AICW between Norfolk, Virginia and St. Augustine, Florida and also to much of the Intracoastal Waterway south and west of St. Augustine.

Chapter 2

In the spring of 2015, we were north bound on the AICW, moving the boat from the Florida Keys to the Chesapeake Bay for hurricane season.

Not long after starting through the Alligator-Pungo Canal, Betty was driving and I was out in the cockpit trying to get a good photo...any photo...of a bald eagle. Suddenly Betty yelled "hold on tight, big wake coming." I glanced astern and a large sport fish boat was coming up fast. Betty tried to call them on the VHF, to ask them to slow down. No response. They passed us at full speed, their large wake hitting us almost broadside. Betty tried to quarter into the wake, but there was neither time nor space. *Nauset* heaved, took a violent snap roll and anything loose in the cabin went airborne. The sport fish's wake rolled ashore and washed many feet up into the trees and brush. It was a classic example of what the Waterway Guide and the authors of the NOAA technical paper were talking about.

Twenty minutes after our baptism, the VHF Radio erupted with a rather graphic description of the people aboard that sport fish by someone on a boat ahead of us.

The price of boat wakes, the price of deliberately damaging parts of the waterway, is increased expensive dredging and maintenance...real monetary costs that have to be paid by someone. An insignificant portion of the cost is covered by a tax on fuel paid by commercial users of the waterway; but the great bulk of the money comes from Congress and from the coastal states to whom the waterway is an important economic asset—that is, the money comes from the taxpayers, all of them, not just boaters and marine related businesses. Because the Congress has chronically underfunded maintenance of our national transportation infrastructure, particularly since 2000, the Corps of Engineers and the coastal States have been unable to maintain large portions of the Intracoastal Waterway at project specifications.

From the beginning of federal involvement in the development of the inland and intracoastal waterways system, users had contributed very little to the systems construction and operating expenses. The 1884 tolls Act eliminated any existing fees on federal project waterways and banned the imposition of future fees. In effect users were given a free ride and the entire cost was paid from the general revenue.

In the Revenue Act of June 6, 1932, Congress, to increase federal revenue and move a little closer to balancing the federal budget, imposed a $0.01 per gallon tax on gasoline (paid at the refinery) and taxes on a number of other items. In 1956 the gasoline tax was made permanent and was allocated to the new Federal Highway Trust Fund–setting a precedent for the establishment of additional federal transportation trust funds.[15] In the Inland Waterways Revenue Act of Oct. 21, 1978 Congress established an Inland Waterways Trust Fund. The fund, modeled on the Federal Highway Trust Fund, was to be used for the construction of new locks and navigation facilities, and for major rehabilitation of existing structures, along the inland and intracoastal navigable waterways. To fund the trust, Congress placed a tax on diesel fuel sold to commercial users along 27 sections of the navigable inland and intracoastal waterways. Initially 4¢ per gallon, with collection to begin in 1981, the tax had risen to $0.20 per gallon by 1995 and it stayed at 20¢ until December 2014 when a rider on a non-waterways related act increased it to 29¢ per gallon.

Possibly because only commercial users pay the waterway tax, books and magazine articles about the Intracoastal Waterways sometimes claim that only commercial waterway traffic/tonnage is considered when the Corps of Engineers looks at the economic value of the commerce on a given waterway. Over a century ago that may have been the case. But on February 10, 1932, Congress passed an act in which the term commerce when applied to navigable waterways, including the intracoastal waterways, was specifically defined as including "...use of the waterways by seasonal passenger craft, yachts, house boats, fishing boats, motor boats and other similar water craft, whether or not operated for hire." And the change in definition was made retroactive to June 3, 1902.[16] Private vessels count as "commerce" and their economic contribution to the communities, counties and states along the waterway should be considered when the economic value of any given waterway is calculated.

The waterway fuel tax should be extended to include private, pleasure vessels. And the proceeds of the tax should be available for dredging and general maintenance as well as for new construction. The tax should also be collected on all fuels–diesel, gasoline, propane, even coal if there is a powered vessel that still uses it–sold for marine use at any refueling facility on or adjacent to any federally (tax payer) maintained waterway. If private, pleasure, vessels also paid the special purpose tax on marine fuel, there would be more money for maintenance and our waterways would be in better condition. Finally, most special purpose taxes, such as the federal gas tax, are in reality user fees and any tax on fuels sold to users of the inland and intracoastal waterways should be redefined as such.

From the south end of the Alligator-Pungo, we followed the AICW markers down the Pungo, past Belhaven, and on across the Pamlico River, up Goose Creek, through the posted "No Wake" Hobucken Canal, its banks largely intact–possibly because of there is a Coast Guard station, patrol boats parked in plain sight, on the west side of the short canal–and then down the Bay River to the

Neuse River. Transiting the Hobucken Canal, we passed the R. E. Mayo Company, a seafood processor, shrimp boats lining their dock.

In North Carolina commercial fishing, although declining in relative economic importance is still a significant industry, particularly blue crabs and shrimp. According to the North Carolina Dept. of the Environment and Natural Resources the blue crabs are harvested almost entirely in waters inside the outer banks and the bulk of the shrimp came from coastal waters. The portion of the shrimp harvest caught inside the outer banks–in Albemarle Sound, Pamlico Sound and the Neuse River–has been declining since the 1980s. The decline in the coastal shrimp harvest is primarily a result of price pressure on the shrimpers caused by the rise in fuel and other vessel costs and by the unregulated flood of cheap, imported, farm raised shrimp. In the mid-1990s marine diesel fuel was less than a dollar a gallon, sometimes much less, in August 2014 marine diesel was averaging $4.00 per gallon. And over the last several years imported, farm raised shrimp has been selling for $4.00 to $6.00 a pound, retail, while wild caught shrimp, native to the coastal United States, where available, has ranged in price from $8.00 to $14.00, or more, a pound.

The most commonly imported farm raised 'shrimp' is the Asian Tiger Prawn, *Penaeus monodon*, a native of the Indian and Pacific Oceans. Tiger Prawns may be native to the Indo-Pacific but they are widely farmed along the Caribbean shores of South and Central America, and in the Dominican Republic.[17] When coastal seafood farms are located in areas subject to hurricanes, escapes can be expected, and a sufficient number of Tiger Prawns have escaped that they have become, according to the U.S. Geological Survey's office of Nonindigenous Aquatic Species, an established invasive species in the Caribbean, in the Gulf of Mexico and along the United States southeast coast. The Tiger Prawns, large and aggressive, pray on smaller native shrimp, small crabs, juvenile oysters and anything else smaller than they are.

Shrimping inside North Carolina's outer banks–and in the large sounds in South Carolina and Georgia and behind the gulf coast barrier islands from Florida to Texas–is also under pressure from people. Over the last fifty years national demographic changes,

Shrimp boats in
Oriental, North Carolina

population growth and migration from the mid-west and northeast to the coasts and the interior south, have led to a substantial increase in the population of both the coast and the coastal watersheds. The inshore crabbing, shrimping, fishing and shell fishing grounds receive the waters, the drainage, from the coastal watersheds and all the byproducts of development, suburbanization, industry, energy production and agriculture that has been dumped into, disposed of, or incidentally drained into, them.

As soon as we were clear of the Hobucken Canal and a safe distance from other boats, we shoved *Nauset's* throttle up and used our big diesel. We rounded Maw Point and ran at 15-16 mph up the Neuse River until we were within a couple miles of the mouth of the Trent River and New Bern. While we were still in the wide lower Neuse the Hatteras sport fish from our previous nights' anchorage past us, far enough away that their wake was no problem.

New Bern was established in 1710 by Christoph von Graffenried of Bern, Switzerland, the leader of a group of Swiss and German colonists, who named the new settlement after his home town. The New Bern Grand Marina is a clean, well run marina with good, floating docks on tall pilings. The marina is right beside a Double Tree by Hilton Resort Hotel. If the forecast was wrong and Sandy strengthened and came ashore in southern North Carolina and it looked like things were going to get rough; we could grab the computer, our papers, and some clothes, kiss the boat good-by and get an upper floor interior room in the hotel. Our first two hours in New Bern were spent prepping the boat: stripping off the canvas, putting all loose gear (including the dinghy) in the cabin, putting on 11 long dock lines with chaffing gear and all the fenders. Then we went out to dinner at Persimmons Waterfront Restaurant: modern Euro-American cuisine, locally sourced fresh meat, seafood and produce, excellent wine bar and a good selection of Carolina craft beers. Life is short, when the stress level rises, eat and drink well.

Sandy was the guest who wouldn't leave. It was six days before we could comfortably move on. Sunday, the 28th the peak day, the strongest sustained winds in New Bern were about 30 mph. At the

Frying Pan Shoals data buoy, not that far away, the wind hit 53 knots (approximately 61 mph) and the waves reached 18 feet. Tuesday, October 30th the wrap-around winds from Sandy were still creating small craft warning conditions on Pamlico Sound and small craft advisory conditions on Bogue Sound. We finally pulled out of New Bern early on November first. Luckily the New Bern Grand Marina had an excellent weekly rate.

When Sandy finally moved on to her amazingly destructive landfall in New Jersey and New York and we were able to continue south, we needed diesel. The only fuel dock in New Bern was at the exposed municipal marina, out on the Neuse River, and left-over wind and chop from Sandy made going to that fuel dock in a small boat problematic. So, with an eye on our fuel gage, we resumed our trip to Florida: down the Neuse River to the Adams Creek Flashing Green 1 and the Intracoastal Waterway, through Adams Creek and the Adams Creek Canal and down the Newport River to the Morehead City Yacht Basin (AICW mile 203.5).

On August 15, 1908–eight months before passage of the March 3, 1909 Rivers and Harbors Act–the United States Army Corps of Engineers, Wilmington District, contracted with the Maryland Dredging and Contracting Company to cut and dredge a channel from the Neuse River to the Beaufort Inlet via Adams Creek, Core Creek and the Newport River. The channel was to have a bottom width of 90 feet and a depth of 10 feet in the cuts and 12 feet in the open water areas. The company began dredging simultaneously from both ends and the project was completed, to specifications, on November 15, 1910. The last section of the project to be completed was the approximately five-mile-long land cut between Adams Creek and Core Creek…the Adams Creek Canal. Today the Maryland Dredging and Contracting Company's Neuse to the Atlantic channel is a part of the Atlantic Intracoastal Waterway.

Prior to completion of the Adams Creek Canal, most vessels following the inside route south had to follow the more exposed route from Albemarle Sound, out into and down the length of Pamlico Sound to Core Sound, Down East North Carolina[18] and Beaufort. But shallow draft vessels, vessels with a draft of four feet, or less, could follow the much older Clubfoot and Harlowe Creek Canal. The Clubfoot and Harlowe Creek Canal, built between 1821 and 1827, linked the Neuse River to Beaufort, Morehead City and the Beaufort Inlet via: Clubfoot Creek, Harlowe Creek and the Newport River. In 1908, when the Maryland Dredging and Contracting Company began work, the old canal, even though it had been abandoned for seventeen years, was still navigable, and in use, by small craft.

A canal to connect the Beaufort Inlet with the Neuse River and New Bern was first considered prior to the Revolutionary War. In 1766 the General Assembly of the colony of North Carolina passed an Act authorizing the joining of the Neuse and Newport Rivers via Clubfoot and Harlowe Creeks. The route was surveyed in 1820, work on the canal began in 1821 and by 1827 the canal was in full operation. When opened the canal had a navigable depth of four feet at Mean Low Water and a tide lock to control the flow of water through the canal.

Because of financial difficulties, the deterioration of the tide lock and continuous problems with siltation, the Clubfoot and Harlowe Creek Canal was abandoned in 1856. It was re-opened in 1880 as the New Bern and Beaufort Canal. The 1885 Annual Report of the Albemarle & Chesapeake Canal Company [the company that, between 1855 and 1859, built the Albemarle & Chesapeake Canal] says that the company's dredge *Cyclops*, was used that year in maintenance dredging of the New Bern and Beaufort Canal and that the company acquired 2,500 shares in the New Bern and

Beaufort Canal. In conjunction with their 1885 annual report, the Chesapeake and Albemarle Canal Company issued a private version of the 1885 16th edition of an 1855 U.S. Coast Survey chart titled *Albemarle and Chesapeake Canal Connecting Chesapeake Bay with Currituck, Albemarle and Pamlico Sounds and Their Tributary Streams.*[19] This chart shows the earlier Clubfoot and Harlowe Creek Canal between the Neuse and Newport Rivers renamed the New Berne and Beaufort Canal. A note on the chart states that the New Berne and Beaufort Canal was 6 miles long, 5 feet deep and had no locks.[20] The Clubfoot and Harlowe Creek Canal (the New Bern and Beaufort Canal) was abandoned for a second time in 1891.

Following passage of the 1909 Rivers and Harbors Act, the Intracoastal Waterway became a hot topic in the yachting/boating press. The December 1909 issue of <u>Motor Boating Magazine</u> contained an article titled *Regarding Waterways Improvements, The Proposed Intracoastal Canal*, by Chester Wynn. In his article, Mr. Wynn stated that "From Adams Creek the going is a trifle tedious but not more than enough to add spice to the navigation of a motor boat. The course will eventually lead up Davis Creek on the line of the canal **now being built**, to the head of Core Creek and then into the Newport River. But at present the route leads from Adams Creek and Harlowe Creek to the Harlowe Creek Canal (now abandoned but navigable for motor boats) and into the Newport River which passes out to sea at Beaufort Inlet between Beaufort on the north and Morehead City on the South." Mr. Wynn's knowledge of the geography of the two canals was limited, because his implied connection between Adams Creek and Harlowe Creek did not and does not exist.

The December 1909 issue also carried an article titled *The Inland Route to Florida*, by Captain Harry Stephenson. In his piece, Capt. Stephenson reported that to reach Beaufort and the Beaufort Inlet from Pamlico Sound it was necessary to: go through Core Sound between the Core Banks and the mainland, pass between Harkers Island and the mainland through a "very crooked" channel in which some of the "pointer stakes" were missing and it was "well worth the $10.00 pilots fee to be taken through." Judging from the photos in the article, Captain Stephenson was at the helm of a substantial yacht, large enough and with a deep enough draft that he was probably unable to use the old Clubfoot and Harlowe Creek Canal.

Less than ten years later transiting the Adams Creek Canal route between the Neuse River and the Beaufort Inlet was a routine event. An article titled *Cruising South*, by Annie Carlyle, in the August 1916 issue of <u>Power Boating Magazine</u>, reported that the Adams Creek Canal was "A charming waterway. A dredged channel 10 feet deep, extends from the mouth nearly to its head, where it connects with a canal of the same depth to Core Creek, from thence to the Newport River and on to the deep water of the Beaufort Inlet. There are no charges for the canal and no locks."

The route of the old canal can still be seen on modern maps and charts (see NOAA Charts 11543 and 11545). The Adams Creek Canal, part of today's Atlantic Intracoastal Waterway, is just two miles east of the old Clubfoot and Harlowe Creek Canal. In 1985 Craven and Carteret Counties agreed to keep the Clubfoot and Harlowe Creek Canal cleaned out and flowing, primarily to mitigate drainage issues. The Craven County portion of the old canal was cleaned in 2013 and a report in the September 22, 2014 issue of the (Weekly) <u>Havelock News</u> said that a 21-foot Carolina Skiff could be taken through the old canal, end to end, Neuse River to Newport River; although at low tide both ends of the land cut had shoaled to barely a foot of water. The tide range in both the

Chapter 2

Adams Creek Canal and the Clubfoot and Harlowe Creek Canal is about two feet.

3. The Atlantic Intracoastal Waterway; Beaufort, North Carolina to Key West, Florida

Between New Bern and Morehead City the after effects of Sandy were obvious but there was less damage and debris than we had expected. There was a lot of floating debris in the Neuse River, Adams Creek and the canal but it was mostly tree limbs and pieces of what looked like cut firewood. There was only one large piece of manmade debris, most of some one's dock was floating in the canal. In the built-up residential area along the Adams Creek-Core Sound Canal a lot of trees had lost limbs, one tree was leaning at an interesting angle and a couple of the home owners were going to be buying large blue tarps to cover missing sections of roof tile.

At the Morehead City Yacht Basin, we took on 80 gallons of diesel, the most we added at one time on the Atlantic coast. The yacht basin is a short, easy run from the Beaufort/Morehead City channel and the Atlantic Ocean and it was full of sport fish boats, many of them available for charter. The 45-foot Hatteras that had been anchored near us at Tuckahoe Point, was in the Morehead City Yacht Basin and I talked briefly with the couple on board.

They rode out Sandy at the Yacht Basin and wished they had gone to New Bern instead. While Sandy caused no apparent damage in the Yacht Basin, the high storm tides and heavy rain flooded many of the low-lying roads and parking lots in town and almost all of the restaurants and stores closed. For three days they were basically marooned aboard in the rain and wind, as were the crews off several other transient cruising boats.

Morehead City, named for John Motley Morehead, the 20th governor of North Carolina, was established in the 1850s and incorporated on February 28, 1861. The city was founded to be a port. Its founders and early developers considered its location–Shepard's Point, on the south side of the inlet and on the wide, deep channel of the Newport River–a better site for a port than Beaufort, on the north side of the inlet. Beaufort, the older city and port, had a narrow, crooked channel that was prone to shoaling and often less than 12 feet deep. Morehead City became the dominant port in 1857 when the Atlantic and North Carolina Railroad reached the coast and ended on Shepard's Point and not in Beaufort. Possibly because of governor Morehead and some other influential investors.

In July 1934, the (Federal) Public Works Administration provided $1,555,000 for the USACE to dredge the Beaufort Inlet and the Newport River between deep water in the Atlantic and Morehead City's docks and turning basin to a Mean Low Water depth of 30 feet. It was a big job, when the Corps of Engineers seagoing hopper dredge *Comstock* began work on August 23, 1934, there was only 10 feet of water on the Beaufort channel bar at Mean Low Water. In addition to the dredging grant, the Public Works Administration loaned the Morehead City Port Commission $425,000 to rebuild and improve Morehead City's port facilities. Today the controlling depth of the Morehead City Channel, from the sea buoy to the terminals, is 40 feet and the commercial port at Morehead City is ranked 94th on the USACE's 2016 list of ports by tonnage. In addition to its commercial port Morehead City is still home to thriving commercial and charter fishing fleets and it is a popular stopping place for migrating snowbird yachts.

Beaufort, named for Henry Somerset, 2nd Duke of Beaufort, was initially settled in 1709, became a customs port in 1722, was incorporated in 1723 and is today the County Seat for Carteret County. The Revolutionary War and the War of 1812 essentially by-passed Beaufort and during the Civil War Union troops, almost unopposed, occupied Beaufort in 1862 and the town remained in Union hands throughout the war. Today the compact, attractive old downtown is home to numerous eighteenth and nineteenth century homes, to a great many restaurants and B&Bs and to the North Carolina Maritime Museum. In 1718 Blackbeard the pirate (Edward Teach) lost his ship, the *Queen Anne's Revenge*, on a sandbar near the Beaufort Inlet. The remains of the *Queen Anne's Revenge* were discovered in 1996 and the NC Maritime Museum houses and has a large display of artifacts recovered from the wreck.

While Beaufort lacks its south of the inlet sibling's deep-water commercial port, it is both a thriving commercial fishing port and a center for sport fishing. Because Beaufort Inlet is safely south of Cape Hatteras, Beaufort is a popular jumping off port for cruising sailing yachts bound for Florida, The Bahamas and the Caribbean. In the spring and fall the town's docks and the Taylor Creek anchorage are often crowded with migrating yachts that are leaving for or returning from the islands.

As soon as we had our fuel, we left the Morehead City Yacht Basin, went under the Beaufort to Morehead City bridges, turned south and followed the AICW through Bogue Sound, past Bogue

Inlet, Bear Inlet, and Browns Inlet to Mile Hammock Bay (AICW mile 244) where we anchored for the night. Until early in the third decade of the twentieth century there was no inside waterway channel or navigable route through the shallow sounds and marshes behind the barrier islands from Bogue Inlet (about AICW mile 228) and the Cape Fear River. And the 24 miles between Beaufort/Morehead City and Bogue Inlet had a nominal Mean Low Water depth of just 3 feet.

Captain Harry Stephenson, in his article in the December 1909 issue of <u>Motor Boating Magazine</u>, reported that "Bogue Sound is about the same as Core Sound and it is advisable to take a pilot if going through to Bogue Inlet." Annie Carlyle, writing in the December 1916 issue of <u>Power Boating Magazine</u>, had a different opinion. "Passing the bridge, a red and black stripped buoy marks the entrance to the inside route via Bogue Sound. This is a very precarious body of water with a navigable channel of three feet at low tide…it is not advisable to undertake it. Many pilots will tell you they are able to put you through and eventually they will probably succeed, but they will surely put you aground many times and consume two or three days extra in the passage."

The Rivers and Harbors Act of January 21, 1927, provided full funding for a channel with a Mean Low Water depth of 12 feet for a bottom width of 90 feet between Beaufort and the Cape Fear River. In that ACT, Congress set a precedent by requiring the State of North Carolina to furnish, without cost to the Federal Government, a 1,000-foot-wide right-of-way. To fulfill the right-of-way requirement, the state legislature gave the state's Transportation Advisory Commission the authority to acquire the land in the name of the state by purchase, donation or condemnation. Under the terms of the right-of-way, the state of North Carolina conveyed to the federal government–to the Corps of Engineers–a perpetual easement with rights to dredge, enter upon and deposit dredged material.

Snow's Cut, the two-mile-long land cut through Federal Point, that connects Myrtle Grove Sound at Carolina Beach to the Cape Fear River was the final piece of the project to be completed.[21] At the request of the citizens of Wilmington, North Carolina, Snow's Cut was named for Major William A. Snow, the USACE District Engineer at the Wilmington District who was the supervising engineer on the Beaufort to Cape Fear project and brought the project in on time and well below budget. The name was approved by the United States Board on Geographic Names in 1944.

The Beaufort to Cape Fear River section of the Intracoastal Waterway was officially opened to traffic on June 3, 1932, although the project was not actually completed until December 23, 1932. Two years later, in an article titled *Intracoastal Waterway, New York to Key West*, the October 1934 issue <u>Motor Boating Magazine</u>, informed its readers that "The new waterway from Morehead City to Cape Fear River is now open to navigation. In June 1934 there was a controlling depth of 11 feet from Beaufort Harbor to Swansboro, thence 11.5 feet to the Cape Fear River."

When we reached Mile Hammock Bay there were already a dozen transients at anchor. By late evening when the last boat arrived, there were 26 southbound snowbirds anchored in the bay: 2 large catamarans, 14 mono-hull sailboats and 10 assorted power boats. One of the sailboats was the Canadian C&C 27 that we had seen at Tuckahoe Point. It was nice having a boat in there that was smaller than us.

Mile Hammock Bay is a large dredged basin in a marsh tidal pond on the U.S. Marine Corps' Camp Lejeune. The basin was dredged to provide a boat dock and landing area for training exercises. Normally transient cruisers are allowed to anchor overnight in the basin and the transients often get close-up views of Marine Corps training exercises. We did on this visit. At 4:00 a.m. heavy artillery started firing not far from the basin and not long after sunrise, as we were eating breakfast and thinking about leaving, a short column of amphibious armored vehicles rumbled out of the woods, splashed into the basin, wove through the anchored boats and disappeared up the AICW.

From Mile Hammock Bay, we moved down to Southport, North Carolina, at the mouth of the Cape Fear River (AICW mile 309).

In 1994, during our first trip down the waterway, there was little development on the mainland side between Wrightsville Beach and Snow's Cut. Trees, mostly pine, and a few houses crowned sandy bluffs fronted by a fringe of salt marsh. Close to Snow's Cut there were a few houses, some old docks and a few, mostly old, shrimp boats. On the ocean side, from the Masonboro Inlet (Wrightsville Beach) to the Carolina Beach Inlet, spoil islands left from dredging the Intracoastal Waterway, softened, weathered and vegetated by time, wind and rain, separated the waterway from almost natural salt marsh and undeveloped Masonboro Island–part of the North Carolina National Estuarine Research Reserve and a North Carolina State Natural Area.

Twenty-two years later, in the spring of 2016, the ocean side of the waterway had not changed. But on the mainland side, development was continuous. For miles, multi-story Carolina Beach Cottages lined the crest of the once tree covered bluff. Some of the cottages were four stories high and many were up on strong pilings, which may have been a construction requirement, to get them up above any possible storm surge but were probably for nothing more than added height, to get all the floors up into the sea breeze and to give at least the upper floors a view across the waterway, the spoil islands and the marsh to Masonboro Island and the distant Atlantic. The words *ocean view*, like *water access* and *waterfront* sell real estate. The cottages looked vaguely out of place, as though they really should have been third row from the beach in Rodanthe or out in Emerald Isle.

Cape Fear River, North Carolina to the St. Johns River, Florida

The Cape Fear River is the commercial channel for the Port of Wilmington, North Carolina, ranked 73rd on the USACE's 2016 list of ports by tonnage handled. The 33.6-mile-long dredged channel up the river has a Mean Low Water controlling depth of 40 feet from deep water in the Atlantic, across the Wilmington River Bar to Southport and 38 feet from Southport upstream to the harbor basin.

Congress authorized the Cape Fear River to Georgetown, South Carolina section of the Waterway in 1930. The authorization included the same easement requirement as the Beaufort to Cape Fear River section and specified a channel 8-feet-deep, at Mean Low Water, for a width of 75 feet. Work on the project began in 1931 and the Waterway was navigable, although not complete, by 1936. In 1937 Congress authorized enlarging the Waterway from the Cape Fear River all the way to Savannah, Georgia, to the Norfolk to the Cape Fear River specifications–a depth of 12 feet for a bottom width of not less than 90 feet–and the following year Congress extended the enlargement of the Waterway to the St. Johns River, Florida. The enlarging of the Waterway to the St. Johns River was completed in 1941 and in 1947 Congress merged the various segments of the Waterway between Norfolk, Virginia and the St. Johns River, into a single federal project, "The Atlantic Intracoastal Waterway, Norfolk Virginia to St. Johns River, Florida."

On the Cape Fear River, we had an 8-10 knot southeast breeze against the ebb tide and we had a wet, bumpy, salty ride in the resulting chop. We spent the night at the South Harbor Village Marina (AICW mile 311.4) and the first order of business after we were tied up was to wash the salt off Nauset. I could have scrapped up enough sea salt to fill a salt shaker. And the bumpy, wet ride revealed a leak. It was high on the port side, near the hull to deck joint and a couple of deck fittings. That leak bedeviled us for over a year until, in Rockport, Texas, Betty found it and we were able to seal it up.

The Waterway crosses Dutchman Creek, a tidal marsh creek, less than a mile north of the South Harbor Village Marina. In 1994 and a couple of times after that, we anchored our sailboat (a 36-foot-long Mariner Ketch with a 5½ foot draft) in Dutchman Creek. Except for a few homes well up the creek, the area was undeveloped and the creek had a peaceful out in the marsh feel. Fairly large boats would anchor there, at low tide the water was over 10 feet deep and a local crabber had traps in the creek. Southport is now a popular second home and retirement community and the buildable land around Dutchman Creek…the land that's dry at high tide…is developed and the creek has silted in. The only boats in the creek now are the center console outboard powered fishing boats and the pontoon boats at the home owner's backyard docks. And some of them are in the mud at low tide.

In Holden Beach, south of the Cape Fear River, we passed an old wooden shrimp boat tied to a collapsing dock. The old boat was rotten, heeled over and down in the mud, well past it's working days. It was a sad reminder that commercial crabbing, fishing and shrimping, once economically important along the coast between the Cape Fear and Charleston, were in decline. The fishermen's catch priced out by imports. The fishermen priced out of their land and docks by beach house sprawl, gated communities and resorts. Along this part of the coast, before the lemming rush to the seashore and beach sprawl, hurricanes and great winter nor'easters were as common as they are today but tall natural dunes fronted the ocean and the storms did relatively little damage unless they hit Charleston or the Cape Fear. Now every winter brings the loss of some beach property and a strong hurricane can turn the second or third row of houses back from the beach into much more valuable beach front.

At AICW mile 347.2 we reached the Nixons Crossroads Highway Bridge, a modern 65-foot-high four lane bridge and, almost under it, the old but still in use Little River Swing Bridge. The two Bridges mark the north end of the 26-mile-long Pine Island Cut. The cut passes behind, on the land side of Myrtle Beach. Waterway travelers can motor along and watch golfers tee off while other players cross the waterway from course to course, or maybe hole to hole, on an overhead cable gondola. Boats transiting the cut need to try to stay in mid channel because when the engineers built this section of the waterway they had to drill and blast a channel through hard limestone and shale. In one notorious three-mile-long section (AICW miles 349-352), known as "The Rock Pile," the channel is narrower than usual and is rimmed by hard, sharp rock ledges at or just below water level.

At AICW mile 369, the waterway leaves Pine Island Cut and enters canalized upper Socastee Creek. Two miles further south another pair of bridges, a very low swing bridge and, immediately to its south, a new 65-foot-high four lane bridge, carry South Carolina Route 544 over the waterway. At mile 375 Socastee Creek and the waterway merge into the Waccamaw River. For the next 28 miles, to Georgetown, South Carolina (AICW mile 403), the waterway follows the broad, deep dark cypress swamp black

Waccamaw River Reflections

water Waccamaw. This is a beautiful part of the AICW, the rivers banks and the peaceful side creeks are lined with Spanish moss draped cypress and eagles, osprey, herons and egrets are common. Every time we go through this section of the waterway, I think that it ought to be protected in some way. But it's not. On every trip there is new construction: a new gated community, a new private marina, a large new home, the trees in front of it cut away because they impede the view and a quarter mile long dock reaching to deep water. Unfortunately, this lovely area future is Myrtle Beach extended.

The Waccamaw River town of Bucksport, South Carolina (AICW mile 377.5), was founded in the 1820s by Captain Henry Buck of Bucksport, Maine. Captain Buck located the town on a finger of higher, dry land that penetrated the black water cypress swamps and reached the Waccamaw River near what was, at the time, the head of navigation for ocean capable sailing vessels. The Captain built wharves and a timber mill and exported sawn pine and cypress worldwide on his own vessels. Bucksport became a major timber and forest products exporting center and it remained a significant timber port until the Civil War. In the years after the Civil War the timber business moved down the Waccamaw to the deeper, larger port of Georgetown and Bucksport faded into obscurity.

At approximately mile 403, the Waccamaw, the Great Peedee, the Black and the Sampit Rivers merge at the head of Winyah Bay. The colonial town of Georgetown, South Carolina's third oldest city, sits close to the bay on the neck between the Great Peedee and Sampit rivers. A minor seaport–unranked in the USACE's list of ports by tonnage–Georgetown is a favored stop on the snowbird migration route and during the spring and fall migration seasons the docks are crowded and the river fills with anchored and moored boats. Along Front Street restaurants range from casual cafes to fine dining and points of interest include the Rice Museum, the Georgetown branch of the South Carolina Maritime Museum and the Georgetown County Museum.

Georgetown was established in the 1720s on or near the site of an earlier Indian trading post. In 1729 Elisha Screven laid out a four by eight block rectangular grid of streets on the north bank of the Sampit River that became the heart of the town and is todays historic district–the entire four district is on the National Register of Historic Places. The low swampy, poorly drained land around the new town was not particularly well suited to cotton or tobacco, but it proved ideal for indigo and rice. Rice became the dominant crop and by the 1820s the rice plantations around Georgetown were producing almost half of the rice harvested in the United States.

The Civil War and the end of slavery put an end to large scale plantation rice cultivation. From the end of the Civil War through the great depression Georgetown was a stagnating, backwater southern town. Rice cultivation declined and finally ceased around the turn of the century and by 1910 the timber men had cut out all the local timber and had moved on. In 1936 the International Paper Company built a pulp and paper mill that utilized the regions second (and third) growth soft pine, and Georgetown began to recover. Today Georgetown's economy is based on paper, tourism, retirees, commercial fishing and shrimping and housing. Georgetown is becoming a bedroom community for nearby Charleston. In the old rice growing areas around Georgetown some rice is again being grown but it is not yet a significant factor in the local economy.[22]

The waterway follows the Georgetown shipping channel down Winyah Bay to approximately mile 410 where it turns south and enters the Estherville-Minim Creek Canal and the great low country marshes. From here to St. Augustine, Florida, the low country marshes dominate and define the waterway. At low tide the waterway is delineated by spoil banks, sand bars and shoals. At high tide the water filled marshes can give the waterway a deceptive width. From Winyah Bay to Charleston Harbor the tidal range is 5 to 6 plus feet, at Beaufort, South Carolina, 7-8 feet, at Thunderbolt, Georgia, outside Savannah, 8-9 feet, at Jekyll Island, Georgia, 7-8 feet, at Fernandina, Florida, 6-7 feet and at St. Augustine, Florida, 4-5 feet.

Crow Island (about AICW mile 417,) on the seaward side of the waterway between Minim Creek and the North Santee River, is the northern most of the Sea Islands. The Sea Islands–Sea Island cotton plantations, seafood, the Gullah/Geechee Afro-American culture and language and, today, large resorts and residential development–are a group of more than 100 tidal marsh and barrier islands that run along the southeast coast for approximately 320 miles, from Crow Island and the Santee Rivers in South Carolina to Fort George Island and the St. Johns River in Florida (AICW mile 740).

Below Crow Island and the North Santee River the waterway enters Fourmile Creek Canal, a canalized tidal creek between the North and South Santee Rivers. This area–the Santee Rivers, Fourmile Creek Canal, Minim Creek, etc.–is alligator country, alligators, some very large, are common. Several years ago, we anchored for the night in upper Minim Creek and in the early morning, when the tide changed and the boat turned, we got a crab trap float around our rudder…it happens. I could either cut the pot warp (the line between float and trap) or go swimming and take it off our rudder. I opted for a swim. Crabbing is generally not a high-income occupation and a crab trap with line and float is expensive. In addition, a lost or cut off trap becomes a long-term killing machine. Crabs and fish keep entering the trap for weeks, or months, or longer and each crab or fish that enters and dies becomes bait for the next. When our rudder was clear and I was hanging off the back of the boat, looking around and thinking that the water was warm and clean and my little swim had been rather pleasant, I noticed a couple of logs on the creek bank. A few minutes later, on the boat and wearing my classes, it was entirely too clear those logs were alligators…substantial alligators.

At mile 430 the waterway crosses Five Fathom and Jeremy Creeks. The active shrimping and fishing village of McClellanville lies a half mile up Jeremy Creek, its docks crowded with commercial vessels and a small floating dock reserved for the rare visiting yachts. Five Fathom Creek is a deep, navigable creek that connects Jeremy Creek and the fishermen of McClellanville with the Atlantic. Between miles 455 and 464, where it enters Charleston Harbor, the waterway passes the Isle of Palms and Sullivans Island, a pair of heavily developed barrier islands...Sea Islands...fronting directly on the Atlantic that are Charleston bedroom communities. Both islands suffered massive damage during Hurricane Hugo which made landfall at midnight, September 22, 1989 as a category 4 storm with maximum winds of 135-140 mph, a minimum central pressure of 934 millibars and a storm surge of 20 feet. Both islands are now more heavily developed and more populous than they were in 1989. At McClellanville, a few miles to the north and with the ocean front dune line and five miles of marsh between it and the Atlantic, the strong north side of Hurricane Hugo's eye wall still drove a 16-foot storm surge through town.

Charleston, established in 1670, is the oldest and the second largest city in South Carolina. Historic Charleston, the part everyone wants to visit, sits at the end of the peninsula between the Cooper River, on the north and the Ashley River to the south. At the tip of the peninsula the Battery looks down the harbor to the sea and Fort Sumter.

The original settlement, named Charles Town in honor of King Charles II, was on Albemarle Point on the Ashley River, at the mouth of Wappoo Creek. For defensive reasons the new settlement was moved to the peninsula in 1680. In its early years Charleston was attacked by Spain, France, Pirates and Indians and as its defenses developed in response, it became one of only two walled cities in the United States. The other was Spanish St. Augustine, less than 300 sea miles to the south. The city walls took in an area roughly a mile long by a half mile wide on the Cooper river side of the peninsula. The walls were maintained through King George's War (1744-1748), and some of the bastions and batteries were partially restored in the early years of the revolutionary war. Today almost nothing is left of the old city wall.

The Port of Charleston, along the Cooper River side of the Peninsula, was ranked 29th on the USACE's 2016 list of domestic ports by tonnage. As of the end of 2014 the Charleston entrance channel had a controlling depth of 47 feet at Mean Low Water and the various terminals and facilities that make up the Port had a Mean Low Water controlling depth of 45+ feet throughout. On October 14, 2014, the USACE released a draft Integrated Feasibility Study and Environmental Impact Statement recommending that, because of its location, infrastructure, transportation links, and short channel in from the sea, the Port of Charleston should be deepened to 52 feet; to handle the New Panamax Class ships. According to the South Carolina Port Authority the Corps of Engineers has awarded the first dredging contracts, to deepen the entrance channel to 54 feet and the channels within the port to 52 feet Mean Low Water, with work to begin in February 2018.

Charleston was historically a major shrimping and commercial fishing port. A generation ago shrimp boats, long line boats and trawlers crowded the docks in Shem Creek, off the Cooper River, and docked in other creeks and along the Ashley River. Twenty years ago, commercial boats still lined the docks behind the seafood restaurants on Shem Creek. But today Charleston is a former commercial fishing center, it's once large fleet, as in many ports to the north, done in by the flood of cheap imports, rising costs, changing land values and uses and, to some extent, over fishing. All that remains are a few charter sport fish boats and some party boats. To the north, Georgetown and McClellanville, for now, have viable fishing fleets and to the south a number of ports in Georgia and northern Florida are still active seafood centers.

The AICW crosses Charleston harbor, rounds the peninsula and ascends the Ashley River as far as the Coast Guard Station, where it turns left (south) and goes through Wappoo Creek and Elliot Cut to the Stono River and on south to: Beaufort, South Carolina, Hilton Head, Savannah, the sea isles and Florida. The famous battery from which, on April 12, 1861, General P.T.G. Beauregard, commander of the secessionist forces in Charleston, launched the attack on Fort Sumter that opened hostilities in the Civil War, sits on the tip of the peninsula and looks out over the junction of the Cooper and Ashley rivers. As boats traveling the Intracoastal Waterway round the tip of the peninsula they are motoring through the line of fire from General Beauregard's heavy artillery.

Wappoo Creek naturally connects the Ashley and Stono Rivers and from the earliest years of settlement along the North Edisto and Stono Rivers, settlers and plantation owners used the Creek to bring imported and manufactured goods from Charleston and ship agricultural products, lumber and other commodities to Charleston. But Wappoo Creek was a convoluted, salt marsh tidal creek that at low tide was almost dry, navigation was possible only because of the creek's 4.0 to 5.5-foot tide.

Prior to 1777 the General Assembly provided for the digging of Wappoo Cut, which straightened parts of Wappoo Creek, and the dredging of other sections, to "facilitate boat traffic between Charles Town and the islands." The Stono River end of Wappoo Cut became known as Elliot Cut–it may have been named for Thomas Elliot, a local land owner.[23] Although Gen. Wilmot G. DeSaussure, writing in 1884, said the cut was named for William Elliot who had "opened this Elliot's Cut prior to 1777[24]."

In Wappoo Creek and Elliot Cut the flood tide is north to south, from the Ashley River and Charleston Harbor to the Stono River, and the ebb tide is south to north. The tidal currents in Elliot Cut can reach 4-4.5 knots at peak ebb, a bit less at peak flood. As we rounded the Battery and started up the Ashly River a current arrow on our chart plotter indicated that if we wanted to go a little further, we had a fair tide, a flood tide, through creek and cut. We gave up Charleston, turned left, went through to the Stono River and docked for the night at the St. Johns Yacht Harbor Marina (AICW mile 472.5.)

The next day, November 5th we moved on, to Beaufort, South Carolina, and the Beaufort Downtown Marina (AICW mile 536.2.) This Beaufort was founded in 1711, just two years after that other Beaufort and, like it was named for Henry Somerset, 2nd Duke of Beaufort. Beaufort is the second oldest city in South Carolina, the County Seat of Beaufort County and the heart of the Carolina Low Country. Beaufort, again like the other Beaufort, suffered relatively little physical damage during the Civil War. In November, 1861, early in the war, a federal amphibious attack captured Beaufort, adjacent Port Royal and a number of the nearby islands. The area remained under federal control throughout the war.

From Beaufort, we continued down the waterway to the Isle of Hope, outside Savannah, Georgia (AICW mile 595.) At mile 576 we crossed the Savannah River, the South Carolina-Georgia state line and the shipping channel to the Port of Savannah. Savannah, the first settlement in Georgia, was established in 1733 by James Oglethorpe. Throughout its history Savannah has been an important seaport. In 2016 it was ranked 18th on the USACE's list of domestic ports by tonnage and was the largest Atlantic coast port south of the Chesapeake Bay. The 31-mile-long channel from the sea buoy to the Georgia Port Authority terminals has a maintained project depth of 42 feet at Mean Low Water.

Leaving the Isle of Hope, we continued south to St. Simons Island, the largest of Georgia's Sea Islands. We anchored for the night in the Frederica River (on the west side of the island,) and off the Fort Frederica National Monument. In route near mile 595, we passed a tidal creek inlet named "Moon River." Johnny Mercer, who wrote the Lyrics for the hit song *Moon River* was from Savannah and the creek inlet was named in honor of Mercer and the song. The Moon River is actual just one end...the southern end...of the meandering tidal creek that makes the Isle of Hope an island. The other end of the creek is called the Herb River and opens off the Wilmington River in Thunderbolt, Georgia, which like Isle of Hope, is a Savannah suburb.

Fort Frederica and the adjacent town, were established by James Oglethorpe in 1736 to protect the southern approaches to Savannah from the Spanish in St. Augustine. The fort was named for Frederick Louis Hanover, Prince of Wales, the eldest son of King George II and Queen Caroline of Ansbach, and the father of King George III. The name was feminized (changed to Frederica) to distinguish the fort from Fort Frederick in South Carolina...named for the same Frederick. In 1742, during the War of the Austrian Succession, a Spanish invasion was turned back...defeated...in a battle fought near the fort. The unsuccessful invasion was Spain's final attempt at asserting control over any territory east of the Mississippi and north of the St. Marys River.

Leaving the Frederica River, we motored south past the heavily developed, resort end of St. Simons Island, crossed St. Simons Sound and the Brunswick channel, passed through Jekyll Creek and entered St. Andrew Sound. St. Simons Island, the largest of Georgia's Sea Islands, along with Little St. Simons Island, Sea Island, Jekyll Island (all Sea Islands) and the town of Brunswick comprise Georgia's fabled Golden Isles coastal resort area. The unofficial but widely advertised motto of Brunswick and the Golden Isles is "where we live life as it should be lived."

Brunswick, the seat of Glynn County and the capital of the Golden Isles, is a sea port and transportation hub. The Port of Brunswick was ranked 102nd on the USACE's 2016 list of domestic ports by tonnage. The Brunswick channel extends 31.5 miles from the sea buoy to the terminals in Brunswick and the controlling depth is 38 feet from the sea buoy over the bar and into St. Simons Sound and 36 feet from there to the automobile, freight and tanker terminals. Brunswick, and a number of the small out ports associated with it, such as Darian and St. Marys, are still home to a large commercial fishing fleet. Shrimp boats working in the sounds and along the coast are a common sight and, during the season, excellent local, wild caught shrimp is on the menu at all the good restaurants. Sidney Lanier, Georgia's greatest poet, wrote *The Marshes of Glynn*, his long, lyrical poem about the mysteries and beauty of Georgia's coastal salt marshes while visiting Brunswick and Glynn County in the 1870s.

Jekyll Island was named by James Oglethorpe for Sir Joseph Jekyll, a friend who provided much of the financing for the Georgia colony. The island played an important part in the opening years of Georgia's history and then became one of the greatest and largest of the Sea Island cotton plantations. On Nov. 28, 1858, more than 40 years after Congress outlawed the importation of slaves, the schooner *Wanderer* landed 409 enslaved Africans–purchased from Portuguese slave traders in Benguela, Angola–on Jekyll Island. It was the last well documented cargo of slaves landed in the United States[25]. There is a memorial to the Slaves landed on Jekyll Island in the St. Andrews Picnic area on the islands south end.

Jekyll Island is best known as a Georgia park and the home of the Jekyll Island Club. The club was established in 1886 when a group of wealthy, powerful financiers and business men–John P.

Morgan, William Rockefeller, William Vanderbilt, Vincent Astor and Joseph Pulitzer among them–purchased the island for use as a private club. From 1888 through 1942 the club was, for the brief winter social season, a virtual Newport of the south. Georgia bought the island and the club's buildings in 1947. The club became a historic landmark in 1978 and, after extensive restoration, was reopened as a resort in 1985. The old Jekyll Island Club wharf, the landing for ferries from Brunswick and the tenders from the member's yachts (anchored in St. Simons Sound and Jekyll Creek), is now the resorts marina (AICW mile 683.6.) Two miles further south the larger and better equipped Jekyll Harbor Marina provides transient dockage and is a favored stop on the waterway.

Below Jekyll Island the AICW crosses St. Andrews Sound and continues south behind the Cumberland Island National Seashore. From St. Andrews Sound, the waterway ascends the Cumberland River to the Cumberland Dividing and then runs down Cumberland Sound to the St. Marys Inlet, the Florida-Georgia state line, and Fernandina Florida. Cumberland Dividing marks the change in tides between St. Andrews Sound and the Cumberland River, to the north, and Cumberland Sound, the St. Marys River and St. Marys Inlet to the south. North of the Dividing the tide floods and ebbs through the St. Andrews Inlet while south of the Dividing the tide floods and ebbs through the St. Marys Inlet. Tidal currents can reach 2.5 knots in the Dividing and on a full moon the tide range often exceeds 8 feet.

At approximately AICW mile 708, the waterway passes the U.S. Navy's Kings Bay ballistic missile submarine base. From there to the Flashing Green 25, just inside the St. Marys Inlet, the waterway follows the dredged 45-foot-deep Kings Bay Channel. At the Flashing Green 25, the AICW–now almost on the Georgia-Florida state line–turns south into the 36-foot-deep dredged channel to the minor Port of Fernandina and the Amelia River while the Kings Bay submarine channel continues out through the inlet to deep water in the Atlantic.

Amelia Island was temporarily occupied by France, Spain and England at various times during the 16th, 17th and 18th centuries. The first real settlement on the island was a Spanish town established in what is now Fernandina Beach in 1685 and destroyed by British buccaneers in 1702. James Oglethorpe visited the island and gave it the name Amelia Island (after the Princess Amelia, second daughter of King George II). Oglethorpe built a short lived (1736? -1742) fort on the northern tip of the Island to protect the St. Marys River entrance, a back door to his newly established colony of Georgia. The first permanent settlement on the island was the Spanish town of Fernandina, today Fernandina Beach. Fernandina, named for Ferdinand II, King of Spain, was established and named on January 1, 1811, by Enrique White, governor of Spanish East Florida. The new settlement was incorporated May 10, 1811 and was the last Spanish town in the western hemisphere incorporated under the 1573 Spanish Laws of The Indies. The island, along with the rest of Florida, became part of the United States following the signing of the Adams-Onis Treaty in 1819.

The 50 square block historic district contains: the Florida House Inn, opened in 1857 and arguably the oldest hotel in Florida, the Atlantic terminus of the first Trans-Florida railroad–which ran from Fernandina to Cedar Key and began operating on March 1, 1861–Florida's oldest continuously operating watering hole, the Palace Saloon, opened in 1903 and said to be haunted by the ghost of its first bar tender, and more than 400 structures that are listed on the National Register of Historic Places. The towns name was officially changed from Fernandina to Fernandina Beach in

January 1952. Today Fernandina Beach, in fact all of Amelia Island, is primarily a beach and golf resort, a retirement mecca and a commuters' bedroom community for Jacksonville.

The Amelia River leads the AICW south past Fernandina Beach and behind Amelia Island. South of Amelia Island, the waterway continues through a maze of creeks to Nassau Sound, Sisters Creek and the St. Johns River. In his article, *The Inland Route to Florida* (<u>Motor Boating Magazine</u>, Dec. 1909) Captain Harry Stephenson, advised Yachtsmen to travel outside from Fernandina to the St. Johns River, or to hire a pilot. "If the weather is fine, go outside twenty miles from bar to bar. If going through inside, get a pilot at Fernandina. The creeks are so crooked and there are so many of them that it is impossible to give directions for going through."

For deep draft sailboats the Captain's advice to consider a short river-to-river ocean cruise is still worth thinking about. Although pilots are no longer available or needed, the Coast Guard keeps the route well marked. Throughout the low country marshes, from Winyah Bay to St. Augustine the 4 to 9-foot tide range and strong currents create a dynamic, active erosional environment and this short stretch is one of the more dynamic areas, constant erosion and accretion result in a continuously changing navigation channel.

Early in the afternoon on November 9th we passed under the Sisters Creek Bridge (AICW mile 739.2) and crossed the St. Johns River.

One of the few north flowing rivers in the United States, the St. Johns, from its head in a nameless marsh in Indian River County, to its Atlantic jetties is 310 miles long, the longest river in Florida and in economic and recreational terms, its most important river. According to the United States Bureau of the Census, in 2013, 19.55 million people called Florida home and 3.5 million of them–

approximately 18% or almost 1 out of 5 Floridians–lived within the watershed of the St. Johns.

The AICW crosses the St. Johns, and the shipping channel to Jacksonville five miles above the jetties at its mouth and 14 miles below the center city. The port facilities along the river in Jacksonville were ranked 35th on the USACE's 2016 list of domestic ports by tonnage. The big ship channel to Jacksonville is 26.8 miles long and is maintained at 36 feet from the sea buoy to channel mile 20 and 34 feet to the head-of-channel. From the head of the big ship channel a 12-foot-deep barge channel continues upstream for 129 more miles, through Green Cove Springs and Palatka, to the Port of Sanford. Downstream from the AICW crossing are shipyards, the Mayport Naval Station and, pinched between the river and the naval station, the fishing village of Mayport, still a significant center for commercial shrimping. The USACE Jacksonville District is studying the feasibility of dredging the commercial channel in the St. Johns River to a minimum depth of 50 feet.

Once past the St. Johns, we continued south for eight miles to the Palm Cove Marina (AICW mile 747) in Jacksonville Beach. The first leg of the trip to Texas was over. We would fly to Texas for the Holidays and some house time and *Nauset* would await our return. It had been an interesting and enjoyable trip and we now felt like *Nauset* was becoming our boat.

The Palm Cove Marina is a clean, well-run full-service marina with floating docks, clean heads, a good laundry and an easy on/off fuel dock. The excellent Marker 32 restaurant is on site and a Publix supermarket, a West Marine and a lot of other shopping are within reasonable walking distance. The marina is also safely below the winter freeze line and a short shuttle or Uber ride from the Jacksonville Airport. Our first stop in the marina was the fuel dock where we added 65.2 gallons of diesel which brought the fuel gage to 7/8, its level when we left Hyannis.

Between leaving Hyannis, Massachusetts on September twenty-second and reaching the Palm Cove Marina in Jacksonville Beach, Florida, on November ninth, we were underway all or part of 23 days and we covered approximately 1,480 nautical miles/1,702 statute miles. We put 167.1 hours on the engine and used 545 gallons of diesel, costing a total of $2,168 (average $4.00 per gallon). That equals: 3.26 gallons of fuel per engine hour, 8.85 Nautical Miles/10.1 Statute Miles per engine hour and 2.71 Nautical Miles/3.12 Statute Miles per gallon of fuel used.

When we reached the Palm Cove Marina in Jacksonville Beach, FL., there were…umm…olfactory hints that perhaps all was not well in the waste management department. Flushing the sewage system with vinegar and copious amounts of freshwater in Baltimore had clearly not cured whatever the problem was. Something less than ideal was lurking down there below the cabin sole.

Procrastination is one of the things that I do well. We had planned to leave the boat at the Palm Cove Marina and fly to the house for the holidays. Says I to Betty "I can just flush the system well with freshwater and vinegar and it will be fine until we get back and then, further down the road, we'll…I'll…take care of it…down there. Besides these things take time, you have to: think about it, plan everything out, research parts, measure and re-measure and all that." Right. And off to the house for the holidays.

The St. Johns River to Key West

The 340 miles of Florida's east coast between the St. Johns River (AICW mile 739.5) and the top of Biscayne Bay (AICW mile 1079),

Chapter

The Atlantic Intracoastal Waterway at
Jacksonville Beach, Florida

is composed primarily of narrow, linear barrier islands separated from the mainland by salt lagoons and shallow, brackish tidal rivers. Early settlers and the Florida Territorial and–after March 3, 1845–State Legislature, looked at the coastal lagoons and rivers and imagined a watery highway crowded with flatboats, steamboats, tugs and barges…commerce. But a continuous, protected inshore navigation route, usable by more than very shallow draft vessels, did not become a reality until the third decade of the twentieth century.

On May 23, 1881, after a number of attempts at getting the Federal Government to build a protected inshore channel south from the St. Johns River along the approximate route of today's Intracoastal Waterway, the Florida State Legislature issued a charter to the Florida Coast Line Canal and Transportation Company for the construction of a fifty-foot-wide by three feet deep canal or channel, connecting the St. Augustine Inlet with the Indian River. The following year, at the company's request, the charter was modified to permit a fifty foot by three-foot canal from the St. Johns River to Biscayne Bay. Work on the canal began in 1883. In 1889 the Florida Legislature directed the company to deepen the project to five feet, Mean Low Water, for its entire length and, as an aid in financing the canal, granted the company approximately one million acres of public land.[26] By the middle of 1891, Coast Line Company steamboats were maintaining a service between the Indian River and New Smyrna and a year later they were operating a scheduled service between Daytona and Stuart, on the St. Lucie River.

In 1920, Congress directed the Secretary of War to have the Corps of Engineers carry out a new survey for "An Intracoastal Waterway from Jacksonville, Florida, to Miami, Florida." World War I was over and Florida's first great real estate bubble (1920-1925) was beginning. The Corps of Engineers did not report back to Congress until 1926. In their report the Corps concluded that, although the speculative real estate bubble had ended the year before, the population of Florida, particularly along the east coast, had increased substantially during the boom and that a free and open federal waterway was now justified. The Corps recommended that Congress authorize acquisition of the Florida Coast Line Canal and Transportation Company's canal and the enlargement of the canal to a width of 75 feet and a Mean Low Water depth of 8 feet, from Jacksonville to Miami. Provided that local interests acquire the assets and rights of the canal company and transfer them, along with land for dredge spoils and other necessary work to the United States Government free of charge, the same conditions that applied in North and South Carolina.

A year after the Corps submitted its report, Congress authorized the project. Within months the Florida Legislature created the Florida Inland Navigation District and authorized the issuance of bonds to raise the money to buy the Florida Coast Line Canal and transfer it and other necessary land to the federal government, free of charge, to fulfill the local interests' obligations.[27]

In an editorial in the October 1934, issue of <u>Motor Boating Magazine</u>, titled *Intracoastal Waterway, New York to Key West*, the magazine informed its readers that: "The controlling depth for this section (the St. Johns River to Miami) is 5 feet. From St. Johns River to St. Augustine the depth is 8 feet. From New River Inlet (Ft. Lauderdale) to Miami the depth is 9 feet. There are by-passes at Matanzas Inlet and Ponce de Leon Inlet. The U.S. Lighthouse Service has established channel markers and buoys to indicate the dredged channels. Apply to the United States Engineer Office, Dyle-Upchurch Building, 4 east Bay Street, Jacksonville, Florida, for the latest pamphlet on information concerning the condition of the section of the Intracoastal Waterway from St. Johns River to Miami."

The 75 by 8-foot project was completed in 1935, and the Intracoastal Waterway between the St. Johns River and Miami was a reality. In 1945, in response to requests from the State of Florida and commercial waterway interests, Congress authorized the USACE to enlarge the waterway to a width of 125 feet and a depth of 12 feet from the St. Johns River to Miami, but an economic impact study of this project reduced the depth between Fort Pierce and Miami to 10 feet. Work on enlarging the waterway was completed in 1965.

We returned to *Nauset* on Tuesday, March 19, 2013. In north Florida March is spring and generally pretty nice, but when we moved back aboard, it was unusually cold, windy and wet, more like a Florida mid-winter than spring. Definitely not good weather for camping aboard a small boat. Even with the reverse cycle heat and air unit running, it was somewhere between chilly and cold.

Following the Shore from Boston to Brownsville

Weather, boat work and shopping delayed our departure and it was nine days before we left for the Florida Keys.

Not far south of Jacksonville Beach we entered the straight, narrow and occasionally shallow, Palm Valley Cut (AICW miles 747-759.) In the cut, we saw a few small clumps of mangroves, clear proof that we were getting further south. From Winyah Bay, South Carolina, to the St. Johns River, the great low country salt marshes dominate the coastal wetlands. From the St. Johns to St. Augustine, the salt marshes thin to almost nothing and between St. Augustine and Daytona Beach, mangroves appear and the wet land vegetation along the waterway becomes mixed. South of Daytona Beach, mangroves fill-in until they dominate the shores.

Satellite imagery with a resolution fine enough to discriminate between vegetation assemblages is less than fifty years old. A study[28] comparing imagery obtained in 1984 with imagery obtained in 2011, showed that during that twenty-seven-year period, along the coast between Daytona Beach and St. Augustine, the wet land area covered by mangroves doubled, and the salt marsh decreased accordingly. A hard freeze, a freeze in which the temperature falls into the mid-twenties and stays there for twelve or more hours, will kill most of the mangrove seedlings. Hard freezes have occurred inland but along the coast...along the Intracoastal Waterway...between St. Augustine and Daytona Beach, there has not been a hard freeze in more than twenty years. Mangroves and salt marshes are both important nurseries for a wide variety of marine species, but the assemblages of species in them is different. The change from salt marsh to mangrove probably won't cause a decrease in the quantity of marine life. But the species will change, some will become more common, others less common and a few will be able to spread into new areas.

Ecological change, driven by climatic warming and the warming of the sea, is visibly taking place.

At the end of our first day out of Jacksonville Beach, we spent a cold night anchored in Daytona Beach. The next day we continued south down the AICW to Melbourne, where we again spent the night at anchor. But we were much further south and Melbourne was nowhere near as cold. In route to Melbourne we went through the Haulover Canal and passed the Cape Canaveral Space Center.

The Haulover Canal, less than 2 miles long, is cut through the narrow ribbon of rock and sand that separates the Mosquito Lagoon from the Indian River. The bascule bridge that carries Florida State Route 3, the Courtney Parkway, across the canal is at AICW mile 869.2. South of the bridge a Florida historic marker says that Indians and the Spanish used a narrow spot in the ribbon of rock less than a mile south of the current canal to haul canoes and small boats across. Early Anglo settlers continued the practice but used rollers and wooden skidways to haul larger vessels across and during the 2nd Seminole War (1835-1842) a small fort, Fort Ann, was built to protect the Haulover. Facing the possibility of a third Seminole War, Congress included $5,000 in the Rivers and Harbors Act of August 30, 1852 for "Connecting the waters of the Indian River and Mosquito Lagoon at the Haulover, Florida." A second appropriation, for $1,500, was included in the June 15, 1854 "Act for Certain Improvements in Florida." The canal, built at the site of the Haulover by a contractor using a construction crew of slaves, was 3 feet deep, 14 feet wide and was completed before the start of the 3rd Seminole War (1856-1858.) In 1885 the Florida Coastline Canal and Transportation Company built a deeper, wider canal at the site of the present canal. Following the 1927 acquisition of the company's assets by the federal government this canal was incorporated into the Intracoastal Waterway and was enlarged to waterway dimensions by the Corps of Engineers.

At AICW mile 894, the lateral barge canal that connects the Intracoastal Waterway to Port Canaveral. Port Canaveral Harbor is best known as a cruise ship port but it is also a commercial freight port and it was ranked 77th in the USACE's 2016 list of domestic ports by tonnage. And it still hosts a viable commercial fishing, mainly shrimping, fleet. The controlling depth in the Outer Reach, part of the long entrance channel, was 40.6 feet in 2014. In the port's multiple basins, depths ranged from 31 feet to 41 feet.

Saturday the 30th was a short day, a bit over thirty-three miles from Melbourne to Vero Beach (AICW mile 952.) The Varo Beach Municipal Marina has a large mooring field, a secure dinghy dock and nice shower and laundry facilities. We spent the night on a mooring, did a load of laundry and on Sunday morning we walked over to the beach for breakfast. After breakfast we took a short walk along the beach. It was near high tide and the beach was narrow. To get to the beach we had to descend a seawall on a short flight of steep wooden steps. Most of the section of beach we walked was backed by seawalls of various heights and materials. During strong northeasterly and easterly winds, there is no beach at high tide...the waves reach the seawalls.

The beautiful sandy beaches and clear water along Florida's long, thin and frequently hurricane swept barrier islands are a magnet for locals, tourists, retirees and the second home crowd. Except for parks, wildlife refuges, military bases and other protected areas, there are almost no natural areas or protective sand dunes remaining. Beach houses, condos, restaurants, motels, resorts and shopping centers stand shoulder-to-shoulder, inlet-to-inlet, facing the sea. Development fostered by federal, state and local political policies and tax dollars: subsidized flood insurance, beach and inlet stabilization structures and beach nourishment. On June 26, 1936, Congress passed "An Act For the improvement and protection of the beaches along the shores of the United States" This Act made it the "...policy of the United States...to prevent erosion due to the action of waves, tides and currents, with the purpose of preventing damage to property along the shores of the United States and promoting and encouraging the healthful recreation of the people."

The National Flood Insurance Program (NFIP)—managed by the Federal Emergency Management Agency (FEMA)—provides federally subsidized flood insurance to people who choose to live and run businesses in flood prone areas, including beaches and back-beach coastal areas subject to the storm surges and waves of cyclonic storms and powerful winter nor'easters. In theory the NFIP, like the Post Office, is supposed to be self-supporting...collected premiums balancing claims. However, FEMA is also operating under a political mandate to keep premiums affordable. The emphasis on affordability has led to substantial losses and FEMA has had to borrow from the treasury to cover the losses: $17.5 billion in 2005 (for Katrina, Rita and Wilma), $6.25 billion in 2012 (for Sandy), etc. In March of 2017 FEMA's NFIP debt to the treasury equaled $24.5 billion. In October of 2017, with additional losses from Harvey, Irma, Maria and other natural disasters looming, Congress passed the "Additional Supplemental Appropriations for Disaster Relief Requirements Act" [signed by the President and became Public Law No. 115-72 on October 26, 2017] which forgave (wrote off) $16.0 billion of the NFIP debt. Less than five months later, at the end of February 2018, the NFIP's treasury debt was again over $20 billion and FEMA's NFIP exposure, the dollar value of policy obligations, was in excess of $1.25 trillion. [29] 2018's hurricanes Florence and Michael, the California wild fires and the years other disasters will add to that.

Looking out from the shore, the beach and sea seem eternal, but the only eternal elements are the waves and the winds that drive them. Beach sand moves. The endless waves sweep it ashore, along the shore and back to sea. Waves always strike the shore at some degree of an angle. As they wash in, they pick up and carry sand, most which is re-deposited further up or down the beach or carried out to near shore bars. The gentle wavelets of a warm, calm summer day may move a few grains of sand a fraction of an inch, but wave after wave, day after day, year after year over decades and centuries, a lot of sand moves.

To see sand movement, at least its effects, fly over or look down from a hi-rise building at any developed beach on which groins have been constructed. A groin is a man-made barrier...a sand dam...built perpendicular to a beach to trap and hold the moving sands. The up side of each groin, the side that faces the prevailing current and wind, traps and holds sand while the down side loses sand. Instead of a long smooth beach line, the beach becomes a scalloped series of arcs. Once a barrier island beach is developed, maintaining the value of that real estate dictates that the beach and its sand, the source of the value, must be stabilized and, if necessary, replaced. Stabilization generally translates to engineered structures: groins, geo-tubes, seawalls, etc.[30] Replacement means beach nourishment, feeding the beach by putting sand from somewhere else on it. The sand used in beach nourishment is not new sand, it did not magically appear and it was not manufactured in a factory in China. The sand is often dredged from the nearby sea floor. The dredging of sand from the nearby sea floor alters the slope of the nearshore area–by, for example, removing nearshore sand bars–which changes the dynamics of incoming waves and can lead to increased beach erosion. If the sand isn't dredged from a nearby source it is brought in by truck, train or barge from open pit sand mines or some other beach. Or it may even be brought in by ship from a foreign source—although not into the United States. In the U.S. special interest laws prevent the use of foreign sand on beaches and the importation of sand in foreign flag vessels.

Beach nourishment, pumping or trucking sand onto an eroding, disappearing beach is very expensive and the bulk of the cost is almost always born by the national tax payers. It can also be an environmental disaster. But properly done, and in the right places, it can maintain or restore, even add, economic value. By the mid-1970s, the long, wide expanse of sand that was Miami Beach had eroded to almost nothing. As in Vero Beach, at high tide, there was no beach. Between 1976 and 1981, ten miles of Miami Beach was rebuilt...nourished...at a cost of almost sixty-four million dollars, and the local economy rebounded. Given the ongoing closure of the shore–the limiting of public access points and parking areas, the spread of private beaches and gated beach communities and restrictive "residents only" town ordinances, federal and state, tax funded, beach nourishment is probably justified at major, public beach resort areas such as: Miami Beach, Myrtle Beach and Galveston Island. Elsewhere...not so much...if at all. On beaches closed to the public, the owners and/or local residents should pay the total cost.

From Vero Beach we continued down the Indian River past the minor commercial port of Fort Pierce and the Fort Pierce Inlet, to the St. Lucie River and Inlet (AICW mile 988.) The junction of the St. Lucie River and the AICW, sometimes called "the crossroads" is where the Okeechobee Waterway, the navigable waterway across Florida, meets the Atlantic Intracoastal Waterway.

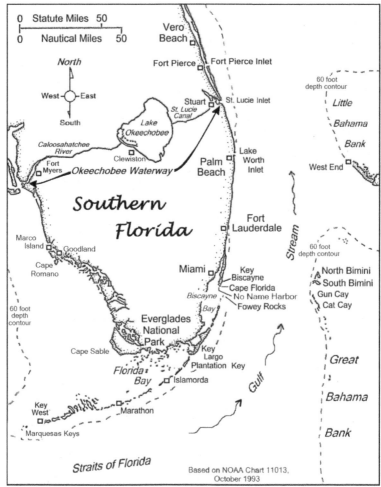

Based on NOAA Chart 11013, October 1993

Okeechobee Waterway Mile Zero is in the AICW channel at 27°9.99′N., 080°10.79′W., about a quarter mile south of the 16-foot high AICW flashing red 240. We turned right and went up the St. Lucie to Stuart and the Sunset Bay Marina.

We detoured to Stuart because we had had a quality of life aboard issue, *Nauset's* hot water heater had ceased producing hot water and I knew, from previous experience, that there was an excellent plumbing supply store near the Sunset Bay Marina. The small four and six-gallon marine hot water heaters fail fairly regularly and the problem is generally the heating element or the thermostat.

The morning after we reached Stuart, I drained the hot water heater and removed the heating element, it looked good and there was electrical continuity through it. That meant that the thermostat had probably failed. When we bought *Nauset* there were several thick folders of manuals, parts lists, brochures, etc. but the only information on the hot water heater was a sales receipt. The water heater had been purchased in 2006 from a recreational vehicle supply company in California and the receipt had the company's name, address and phone number...and the water heaters model and serial numbers. I called and was told that our water heater was no longer manufactured but they could email me a manual and parts list. The parts list showed that the thermostat was a standard household type. That evening, we had hot water. Works better when you do the dishes.

Leaving Stuart, we returned to the AICW, turned right and motored down the waterway to the Lantana Ocean Avenue Bridge (AICW mile 1031), where we anchored on the west side of the waterway south of the bridge. On the way we motored through Lake Worth, past: the commercial port of Palm Beach Harbor (101st on the USACE's 2016 list of domestic ports by tonnage) and past dozens...many dozens...of large, opulent yachts docked at the: Rybovich Superyacht Marina, the Palm Harbor Marina and Yacht Club and the Palm Beach Town Docks. The short channel through the Lake Worth Inlet, just 1.7 miles from sea buoy to turning basin and maintained at a depth of 34 feet, is a good, deep, almost all-weather inlet with a decent anchorage just inside the inlet. The inlet is popular with boats going to and returning from the Bahamas, Palm Beach is one of the easiest places in Florida for the crew off a yacht to clear into or, if necessary, out of the United States. The offices of the Customs Bureau and Immigration and Naturalization (Homeland Security) are in the commercial port, not out at a remote suburban airport.

From the Lantana Ocean Avenue Bridge through Fort Lauderdale to Miami's Dodge Island Highway and Railroad Bridges and southern Biscayne Bay is only 58.4 statute miles. But in that short distance there are 33 bridges, only four of which are fixed hi-rise bridges. All the rest open and most operate on restricted opening schedules.

A mile or two south of the Lantana Bridge, the banks of the waterway begin to narrow. At the Ocean Avenue/Boynton Beach Bridge (AICW mile 1035) the waterway closes in and for the next forty-five miles–through: Delray Beach, Highland Beach, Boca Raton, Deerfield Beach, Pompano Beach, Fort Lauderdale, Hollywood, and Aventura–the waterway is a man-made canal bordered by concrete, stone or steel bulkheads and closely hemmed in by houses, apartments, condominiums, and hotels; all of which, because they are on the AICW, are considered waterfront property. Most of the buildings are individual homes or low-rise, two to four or six story apartments and condominiums, but in some section's strings of high-rise buildings loom over the waterway. Throughout this stretch numerous lateral canals intersect the waterway, the concrete canal sides lined with docks and boats, the banks packed with closely set houses and condominiums…more low-lying waterfront property. Local speed boats and sport fish boats often ignoring speed and wake limits, churn through the canals and up and down the waterway. Their wakes ricochet off the bulkheads creating what seems like a perpetual heavy chop and larger wakes splash up onto patios, parking lots and lawns. In mid-week it can be bad, on weekends it is often maritime madness.

At AICW mile 1067 the waterway enters Port Everglades, Fort Lauderdale's commercial port, and passes the Port Everglades Inlet. Port Everglades, 27th on the USACE's 2016 list of domestic ports by tonnage, is the second largest port in Florida, behind only Tampa. The entry channel, short and direct with no bridges or obstructions, is dredged to 45 feet, the turning basin and main docks have a depth of 42 feet and there is a minimum of 31 feet throughout the port. The USACE Jacksonville District, Broward County and the State of Florida have been studying the feasibility of dredging and widening the channels into and within Port Everglades.

In south Florida most of the land through which the AICW runs has an average elevation above the Mean High Tide level of less than six feet. From Palm Beach south much of it is less than three feet above Mean High Tide and any change in sea level has serious consequences and costs. Hurricane Sandy was a major storm in New Jersey and New York. Along south Florida's coast it was a strong, prolonged cyclonic gale, a nor'easter. Nevertheless, it caused damage. In Fort Lauderdale a quarter mile of State Route A1A, the coast road that plays a role in some of Jimmy Buffett's songs, washed out. In particularly low areas localized flooding during spring (or King) tides, the higher high tides caused by alignment of the earth, sun and moon, is not only no longer unusual, it's the norm. Because the substrate is mostly porous coral rock and pumping of ground water has lowered the water table permitting seawater intrusion, during high tides and storms the ocean not only emerges from storm drains, it percolates up through the very soil and spreads over lawns, gardens, streets and parking lots well inland from the shore.

The Venetian Causeway (AICW mile 1088.6) and the adjacent MacArthur Causeway are just to the north of Government Cut,

Dodge Island and the Port of Miami. On the south side of Government Cut, the Dodge Island Highway and Railroad Bridges (AICW mile 1089.3) connect Dodge Island and the Port to the mainland. Government Cut and the Port of Miami are the divide between upper and lower Biscayne Bay and they mark the end of St. Marys Inlet to Miami Florida and the beginning of the tropical, almost Bahamas/Caribbean Florida of the snowbird boater's dreams. The land of clear water and warm winters.

On September 18, 2015 the USACE Jacksonville District announced that the third and final phase of the project to dredge the Port of Miami to a controlling depth of 52 feet in the entrance channel and 50 feet in the inner channel and turning basin to accommodate the New Panamax ships and the new generation of very large cruise ships, was complete. The inner harbor (in the Miami River) remains at a Mean Low Water controlling depth of 15 feet. The Port of Miami was ranked 61st on the USACE's 2016 list of domestic ports by tonnage. Miami may be 61st on the tonnage list but it is, by a substantial margin, the largest cruise ship port in the United States. In 2016 Miami handled 972 cruise ship port visits and almost 5 million passengers. Like the Port of Palm Beach and Port Everglades, the channel into the Port of Miami is short and straight. The tide range throughout the Port of Miami is three feet.

Below Miami, the tail of the Atlantic Intracoastal Waterway, the Miami to Key West section specified in the Rivers and Harbors Act of March 3, 1909 and in other Acts, was never completed. A protected waterway on the north side of the Keys with a channel 75-feet wide and 7-feet deep (Mean Low Water) from Miami south to Cross Key Bank, in Florida Bay, via: Biscayne Bay, Card Sound, Barnes Sound, Jewfish Creek, Blackwater Sound, Tarpon Basin and Button Wood Sound was completed in 1939. In 1945 Congress authorized but did not appropriate funds for a project to extend this channel along the north, the Florida Bay, side of the Keys from Cross Key Bank to Key West and to expand the entire channel, from Miami to Key West to a width of 90 feet. This project, which would have been an environmental disaster, was never completed. Instead the Hawk Channel, the natural 12 to 20+ foot-deep strip of navigable water between the ocean side of the Keys and the Florida Reef, was marked with Intracoastal Waterway markers all the way from Miami to Key West.

A seabreeze shower over Biscayne Bay

We ended Tuesday, April 9th anchored in No Name Harbor, a small basin in Bill Baggs Cape Florida State Park, which occupies the south end of Key Biscayne. Bill Baggs Cape Florida State Park is one of Florida's many excellent state parks. In addition to No Name Harbor, the park contains the Cape Florida Lighthouse, the Lighthouse Museum, two good restaurants, camping and picnicking areas, and more than a mile of broad, white sand beach. No name Harbor, popular with both cruising and local boaters, is home to one of the parks restaurants, the Boaters Grill, which is a very good Cuban style seafood restaurant. No Name Harbor also has: toilets, a washer and dryer and a sewage waste pump-out. And it is a short walk, or bike ride, from the shops, restaurants and supermarket on Key Biscayne.

Biscayne Bay National Park lies to the south of Key Biscayne. Boca Chita Key, Sands Key, Elliott Key and the rest of the park are what people make the long trek south for: clean, clear, warm water, good snorkeling and, except on weekends, peaceful anchorages. Further south the Florida Keys, the Marquesas, the Dry Tortugas, the Everglades and the back country of Florida Bay offer a whole winter of exploring and fishing.

Wednesday, April 10th we followed the protected Intracoastal Waterway route along the north side of the Keys to the Coral Bay Boatyard, at approximately Overseas Highway Mile 81.5 on Upper Matecumbe Key, in the village of Islamorada. Islamorada, incorporated as a separate village within Monroe County in 1997, calls itself a Village of Islands and The Sport Fishing Capital of the World. The local Chamber of Commerce claims that the name Islamorada originated with the early Spanish explorers and means "Purple Isles." But "morada" can also be translated as dwelling or abode, and the name may simply reflect the fact that Upper Matecumbe Key was inhabited by Native Americans when the early Spanish explorers first visited.

The Coral Bay Boatyard is a nice little Keys kind of place, a good place to relax and do a little boat work. The famous Lorelei Beach Cafe & Bar is an easy walk up the road and the Islamorada Seafood Company, the Zane Gray Lounge, the Morada Bay Beach Café and Florida Keys Brewing are a short walk the other way. The Trading Post, a very good little market is right next door. Coral Bay is a working boat yard, UPS, FedEx, Lewis Off-Shore, Port Supply, etc. deliver daily; if you need something you can get it.

By the time we reached Coral Bay, that odor was again wafting up from below the cabin sole and it was becoming more assertive by the day. Betty was developing an attitude. Vinegar and procrastination were no longer an option, I had to do something. Replacing the entire system was on the "after we get to Texas" work list. But it was clear, even to me, that the Texas work list needed to be shortened by one major item.

I broke out the tape measure, opened the starboard hatch, the one over the source of that olfactory unpleasantness, and began measuring, sketching and checking. Then a day searching the marine supply catalogs and the internet, collecting data and details. A day planning, thinking and re-measuring. And the orders went out. Four days later UPS delivered a small mountain of stuff. We unpacked it all and made sure everything I needed was there. The next day would be in-and-out day.

Take-it-out and put-it-in day began before sunrise with a pot of good coffee and pumping the offending system as dry as possible. Then as the sun rose, the boat was opened up for maximum ventilation, anything that might absorb any unfortunate drips was stashed in the bow or taken ashore, the hatch came up and work began. Even with a heat gun old, thick walled, wire reinforced hose that has had seventeen years to lock itself in place on PVC fittings is hard to remove. So, with a hack saw I cut each hose and, as they were cut, plugged each cut section with rags and paper towels.

Fifteen minutes after the first hose was cut, the old holding tank with its' attached pump and cut off hoses rose up from its parking space, passed through the cabin door, across the cockpit and up onto the dock, with only a couple of stray drips. So far, so good. I then removed several of the remaining cut off hose sections, the ones I could reach from above. With the old tank out, it was clear that we had had a leak or two in the system. The shelf the tank had been mounted on and some of the area behind it had rather a lot of brown stuff, green stuff and wet stuff that had to be removed. Once the area had been scrubbed and disinfected and was mostly dry, I slithered down there and removed the remaining cut off hose sections.

Except for the small tank, the system was very similar to the one I installed in *S/V Walkabout* in 1994 when we first moved aboard. But most of the system, if not all of it, was seventeen years old. Effluent had permeated the rubber and plastic parts and the tank itself was no bouquet. There were three leaks in the system: one where the hose from the toilet entered the tank, one where the output fitting joined the tank and...most unusual...there was a crack along the bottom seam of the tank itself, below the output fitting. The end of the tank that the input and output fittings were mounted on, the end with the cracked seam, was slightly concave. I suspect that modern, high pressure, vacuum pump-out systems may have been causing the tank to flex during pump-outs. Once all the components of the old system were out and the mess cleaned up, it was time to install the new system: a new, larger tank, all new hoses, new electric macerator pump, new everything. New works best.

By 5:00 p.m. on in-and-out day the new system was in and flushable and it was time for a shower, happy hour and dinner. After I'd had a long, hot shower, Betty and I walked down to the Lorelei: conch fritters, burgers and Key West Sunset Ale...health food...paradise style.

Most boats, like RVs, have a black water (sewage) holding tank. On older boats large enough to spend days or weeks on, if there is an environmentally legal black water system at all, it is probably

130

too small for more than overnight or weekend use. Many new boats also have holding tanks that are much too small. Betty and I lived, full time, on boats for 14 years. We know many full-time cruising people and we have discussed the holding tank thing with a number of them. The consensus opinion seems to be that in full time use, even with careful, minimal flushing, a forty to fifty gallon holding tank is necessary. Each adult on a boat will put about three gallons of stuff into the tank per twenty-four-hour day (based on a standard manual marine toilet). For a couple that's six plus gallons per day or more than forty gallons per week.

The release of raw (untreated) human waste is illegal on any inland waters and within three miles of the coast. Waste must be stored (type three Marine Sanitation Device) or, where their use is legal, processed by an onboard treat and release system (type one or two MSD). Well maintained treat and release systems kill bacteria, but they do not remove the nutrients that feed algae blooms, so in "No Discharge" areas boats fitted with treat and release systems must also have a holding tank. On a boat capable of going to Florida for the winter or making a Great Loop cruise, a large black water holding tank is a necessary investment. While availability of waste pump-out stations and pump-out boats along the coast and on the inland waters is improving every year, there are still areas where they are hard to find or, particularly for deep draft sailboats, hard to get to.

Does all of this really help anything? Does it have a genuine environmental benefit? In some areas the answer is an unequivocal yes. Since the use of black water holding tanks, type three MSDs, became the law, the water in areas where large numbers of occupied boats congregate–such as the Great Salt Pond on Block Island–is in many cases significantly cleaner than it was. Boats are a small point source from which pollution can be and should be controlled.

4. Across Florida

The dream of a navigable waterway across the Florida peninsula is as old as European settlement in what is today the United States. An order to explore the Florida peninsula, examine possible routes across it and determine if a navigable waterway across it existed, was included in the instructions Pedro Menendez de Aviles, the founder of St. Augustine–the first permanent European settlement in the United States–received from King Philip II of Spain. Aviles never found a natural cross Florida waterway, but the Trans-Florida route he recommended largely anticipated later proposals for a Trans-Florida canal. Throughout the 19th and the early 20th centuries Congress repeatedly ordered surveys of possible navigable routes across Florida.

The Rivers and Harbors Act of March 3, 1909 included a requirement for a "Survey for the construction of a continuous inland waterway across the State of Florida..." The Engineers who carried out the 1909 survey requirement looked at five routes for a Trans-Florida waterway and their report, submitted to Congress in 1913, did not give a positive recommendation to any of the five routes. In 1921, in response to a request from the Senate Commerce Committee, the Board of Engineers reviewed the 1913 report and confirmed its original negative recommendations.[31] Subsequent surveys, through the start of the Great Depression, also received negative reports.

The Great Depression began with the stock market crash of October 1929 and did not end until the industrial ramp-up for World War II was well underway. Actions taken by Congress and the Roosevelt Administration to aid recovery from the depression and prosecute the war effort led to an almost two-decade long surge in Intracoastal Waterway proposals and projects. From Boston to Brownsville hundreds of surveys were requested and projects authorized. And the long dreamed of Trans-Florida barge and/or ship canal was well represented.

In the early 1930s a Special Board of USACE Engineers was convened and tasked with reviewing and reporting on the various surveys for a trans-Florida canal. Secretary of the Interior Herald Ickes, who controlled the Public Works Administration and was a close associate of President Roosevelt, appointed his own Board of Review, composed of P.W.A. engineers, and gave them the same task. Political and business supporters of a Trans-Florida canal, led by the Mayor and the Chamber of Commerce of Jacksonville, Florida, formed the *National Gulf-Atlantic Ship Canal Association*, headed by former Army Chief of Staff General Charles Summerall to pressure both boards and lobby Congress in favor of a ship canal. Opponents of a canal also organized, lobbied Congress and testified before the boards. And the opponents, for the first time, raised the possibility that a canal might damage the shallow limestone aquafers of central Florida.

The P.W.A. Board submitted their report on October 19, 1933. They concluded that a ship canal, with locks, was: physically possible, economically justified, would not cause excessive damage and was a public necessity. And they estimated the cost of a canal at no more than $115,000,000. The Special Board submitted its report on December 30, 1933. The Special Board had considered twenty-eight possible routes and had studied seven in detail. They concluded that a route that followed the St. Johns River, the Ocklawaha River and the Withlacoochee River, referred to as Route 13-B in their report, would work for either a barge or a ship canal and that, to protect the aquafers, any canal built should be a lock canal, without deep cuts. The Special Board also stated that a commercial grade Trans-Florida canal would cost approximately $190,000,000, was not economically justified and that a canal should not be constructed.

The *National Gulf-Atlantic Canal Association* would not accept the Special Boards report and put intense political pressure on the President and Congress. The 10 Senators from the Gulf States requested that President Roosevelt appoint an Interdepartmental Board to review and rectify the conflicting reports. In April 1934, the President established a five-man board. To avoid the appearance of political favoritism the Department of the Interior (Mr. Ickes) was to appoint two P.W.A. engineers and the USACE was to appoint two of their engineers, the four appointed engineers were to select the fifth member of the board. The Interdepartmental Board submitted their findings on June 28, 1934. The report recommended that a 30-foot-deep sea level canal, on the model of the Cape Cod Canal, be built: a sea level ship canal would be easier and cheaper to build, cheaper to maintain and operate, would cause no damage to the water supply of any part of Florida and the economic benefits to the nation as a whole justified the canal. The cost of the recommended canal was estimated at approximately $142, 700,000.

On August 28, 1935 the President signed an executive order allocating $5,000,000 from the W.P.A. Emergency Relief Fund to the Trans-Florida sea level ship canal project and he directed that the USACE begin work. In September the President announced that he would allocate no more emergency relief money to the canal–Congress would have to fund it through the normal appropriations process. Congress declined to appropriate additional funds and in September 1936, work ceased.

It was 1942 before Congress returned to the Trans-Florida Canal. Early that year, with German Submarines sinking coasting vessels within sight of American beaches, Congress asked the USACE to review the project and in June 1942, both the Chief of Engineers and the Board of Engineers for Rivers and Harbors recommended that, in view of the war situation, a lock canal for barges, 12 feet deep and 150 feet wide, following the preferred B-13 Route was justified. In an Act passed on July 23, 1942, Congress authorized the enlargement and extension of the Gulf Intracoastal Waterway and included an authorization for the B-13 barge canal in the Act. But, the $93,000,000 appropriation that accompanied the Act was applied entirely to the Gulf Intracoastal Waterway.

The trans-Florida Barge Canal is described on page 9 in the 1951 edition of The Intracoastal Waterway, Part I, Atlantic Section, published by the USACE. The canal is shown on a map of the Intracoastal Waterway system inserted behind the table of contents and Chart No. 8, in the chart folio in the back of the publication, shows the canal in detail:

> "*Authorized barge canal across northern Florida.*–An act of Congress approved July 23, 1942, authorized the construction of a barge canal 12 feet deep and 150 feet wide across Florida as a connecting link of the Intracoastal Waterway. The route follows the St. Johns River to above Palatka, up the valley of the Ocklawaha River, across the divide and down the valley of the Withlacoochee River. The authorized project will provide a high-level lock canal, with three locks on the Atlantic side and two on the

Gulf side of the summit. Locks will be 75 feet wide and 600 feet long, with a 14-foot depth over the sills. Start of construction depends on provision of the necessary funds."

A 1958 economic restudy of the inactive Trans-Florida barge canal project concluded that conditions had changed and there was economic justification for the canal. In 1960 John F. Kennedy while campaigning in Florida supported the canal. With Kennedy, and later Johnson, in office, Congressional interest revived and in 1962 Congress appropriated sufficient funds to restart the canal. The USAC revised the canal plans and on February 24, 1964, with President Lyndon Johnson in attendance, construction resumed.

But national attitudes were changing, the natural environment, clean air and clean water were rising to the top of the public priority list. In 1969 Marjorie Harris Carr, a zoologist and Florida environmentalist, led the creation of Florida Defenders of the Environment. The group, many of whom were trained earth and biological science professionals, wrote a carefully researched paper titled <u>The Environmental Impact of the Cross-Florida Barge Canal with Special Emphasis on the Ocklawaha River</u>. In 1969 the Florida Defenders of the Environment joined the Legal Defense Fund and other organizations in a law suit to stop the Cross-Florida Barge Canal.

On January 15, 1971 U.S. District Judge Barrington Parker ruled that the Corps of Engineers had not complied with the 1969

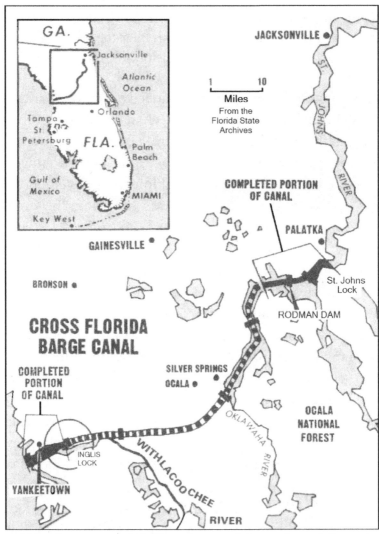

National Environmental Policy Act and issued an injunction that stopped work on the canal. Four days later President Richard Nixon, acting on the advice of the Council on Environmental Quality, stopped the project. The Trans-Florida Barge Canal, a congressionally authorized project on which $50,000,000 of federal money and $12,000,000 of Florida State money had been expended was one third complete.

138

Chapter 4

The Trans-Florida barge canal's final demise, a play in four acts, began on May 22, 1990:

- On that date Senators Bob Graham and Connie Mack of Florida, introduced legislation to convert the canal right-of-way into a greenway corridor.
- On October 27, 1990 Senate Bill 2740, which de-authorized the barge canal passed Congress and was sent to the President.
- On November 28, 1990, the President signed the bill into law.
- On January 22, 1991, The Governor and Cabinet of the State of Florida signed a resolution agreeing to the terms of the de-authorization bill.

In 1998 the Cross Florida Greenway was officially renamed the Marjorie Harris Carr Cross Florida Greenway.

The Okeechobee Waterway

While Congress, Florida, the President, the courts, environmentalists and various business interests were playing political football with the Trans-Florida barge canal, a navigable waterway across south Florida...the Okeechobee Waterway...was quietly taking shape. The Okeechobee Waterway (the OWW) crosses Florida through its name sake lake and links the Atlantic Ocean with the Gulf of Mexico. Unlike the coastal waterways and the never built Trans-Florida canal, the origin of the OWW is rooted in drainage and land reclamation, not navigation.

The structural basement underlying Lake Okeechobee (the Big Water) is a large, shallow, natural, rain and sediment filled depression in the limestone of central Florida. The southern rim of the depression is marginally lower than the rest and when heavy rains fill the depression most of the runoff flows south in the form of a shallow freshwater river 50 miles wide...the river of grass...the Everglades. But some goes west giving rise to the Caloosahatchee and east where it forms the Loxahatchee and the swamps that back Florida's east coast from Stuart south to Miami and the Everglades.

A report by Buckingham Smith, published by Congress in 1848, suggested the possibility of draining the wet lands of south Florida, particularly the Everglades. In 1850 Congress passed the Swamp and Overflow Land Grant Act which provided for the states to drain and reclaim wet lands and in 1855 Florida created a Board of Internal Improvements that was given the power to apply for the federal grants and handle the disposition of Florida's swamps. Little happened until 1878 when unusually heavy and prolonged rains caused the Caloosahatchee to flood for much of the year driving people from their farms, ranches and tropical fruit plantations. The displaced residents asked the state to investigate draining the Caloosahatchee valley and lowering the water level in Lake Okeechobee. By 1915, local interests had constructed mud and sand levees around most of Lake Okeechobee.

While the perceived economic benefits of draining and developing the wet lands provided the driving force and political muscle behind the work, navigation benefitted. A 14-mile-long, 7-foot-deep navigation canal linking Fort Myers to the Gulf of Mexico was completed in 1885. By 1887 intermittent steamboat service was beginning on a 300-mile route into the heart of Florida: up the dredged for drainage Caloosahatchee River to Lake Okeechobee, across the lake and then north up the Kissimmee River.

Chapter 4

The 1922 (5th Ed.) of <u>The Inside Route Pilot, New York to Key West</u> does not use the name Okeechobee Waterway but a section on pages 80 and 81 titled *Route Across Florida Via Drainage Canals, Lake Okeechobee, and Caloosahatchee River* states that:

> "The opening of the State drainage canals from Lake Okeechobee to the Atlantic Coast has created a waterway, navigable for vessels of 3-foot draft between the Atlantic Ocean…and the Gulf of Mexico at San Carlos Bay."

In 1930 Congress authorized the construction of 67.8 miles of levee along the south shore of Lake Okeechobee and 15.7 miles along the north shore. The project authorization included a 6-foot-deep navigable channel inside the south shore levee for the transportation of equipment and material needed in the construction of the levee and stated that dredge spoil from cutting the canal was to be used in levee construction. Work on the project began in 1930 and it was completed in 1938. A modification to the project authorized in 1935 gave the federal government responsibility for maintaining, operating and (except for $500,000 to be raised locally) paying for the navigation channel.

By 1937 a navigable channel a minimum of 80 feet wide and 6 feet deep connected the Atlantic Ocean and the Gulf of Mexico. The precursor of today's Okeechobee Waterway was officially opened on March 27, 1937.

A major Hurricane–now called the Fort Lauderdale Hurricane–crossed the northern Bahamas on September 15, 1947 and came ashore at Fort Lauderdale on September 17. Winds of 160 mph were recorded at Hopetown on Abaco Island in the Bahamas and peak winds of 155 mph were recorded at Hillsboro Inlet north of Fort Lauderdale. The storm tracked directly over Lake Okeechobee, the levees held but the very heavy rains associated with the storm caused extensive flooding and created concerns about the integrity of the levees.[32]

The year after the Fort Lauderdale Hurricane Congress passed a Flood Control Act in which they authorized the first phase of the Central and South Florida Project. The project was a comprehensive plan to reduce flood and storm damage and provide improved water control for navigation and irrigation in central and south Florida. The Herbert Hoover Dike, the largest project within the plan, is a 143-mile-long earthen levee system that completely encircles Lake Okeechobee, with the exception of a channel lined with levees that leads Fisheating Creek into the lake. As originally planned the dike had 19 culverts, hurricane gates and other water control structures. Additional water control structures, notably the Port Mayaca Lock, have been constructed since the dike was completed in the late 1960s, and portions of the dike have been raised and strengthened. Today the top of the dike ranges from 32 to 46 feet in elevation above Mean Sea Level. The elevation above Mean Sea Level of the TOP of the dike shows clearly just how low and flat south Florida is and how little sea level would have to rise for the sea to completely alter the environment and drown major portions of the area.

Vessel counts and freight tonnage figures for the Okeechobee Waterway indicate that, as a navigational waterway, its economic value lies in its heavy use by private pleasure vessels, not commercial freight. The OWW carries essentially no commercial traffic. During 2013 the Port Mayaca Lock, at OWW Mile 38.9 locked through 4,232 vessels of all types, but only 2,000 tons of commercial cargo and the W. P. Franklin Lock, at OWW Mile 121.4, locked through 4,982 vessels of all types, but only 3,000 tons of commercial cargo. In 2016 the Port Mayaca Lock handled 5,000 tons of commercial cargo and the W. P. Franklin Lock handled

6,000 tons.[33] For private pleasure vessels the waterway provides a safe, convenient, scenic and interesting east-west shortcut, enabling them to by-pass the long, expensive and potentially hazardous run around the tip of Florida and through or around the Keys. The recreational facilities and opportunities along the waterway and the facilities that dock, store and service private pleasure vessels contribute substantially to the economy of the area through which the waterway passes.

From Ocean to Gulf the OWW is either 154 or 165 miles long, depending on which of two routes across Lake Okeechobee is followed. Route 1, which crosses the lake, is 154 miles long and is the most commonly used route. Route 2 (the Rim Route), which follows the original navigation channel behind the levee around the south rim of the lake, is 165 miles long. Mileage on the Okeechobee is counted from east to west and, as on all the coastal waterways, is given in statute miles. The beginning of the Okeechobee Waterway, the mile Zero marker, is in the AICW channel at 27°9.99'N., 080°10.79'W. A point in the St. Lucie Cross Roads, where the Atlantic Intracoastal Waterway crosses the St. Lucie River, and about a quarter mile south of the 16-foot high AICW Flashing Red 240. The western terminus of the Okeechobee Waterway is at 26°30.6'N., 082°01.1'W., near the mouth of the Caloosahatchee River. The western end of the Okeechobee Waterway is also the origin point, Mile Mark Zero, on the Florida Gulf Intracoastal Waterway.

East to West through the Okeechobee

Betty and I have transited and enjoyed the Okeechobee Waterway, in both sail and power boats, over a dozen times. From Okeechobee Waterway Mile Zero, vessels going through to

At the St. Lucie Lock on the Okeechobee Waterway

Florida's west coast, follow the St. Lucie River west, upstream to the St. Lucie Lock and Dam, mile 15.1, passing through Stuart on the way. Up river to the lock and dam, the St. Lucie is a tidal river with a salt/brackish estuarine environment. The tide range at the lock is 1 to 2 feet from Mean Low Water. Above the lock transient vessels enter the freshwater, non-tidal, Everglades/Lake Okeechobee environment. The first lock and dam on the site was built by the Everglades Drainage District in 1925. The current lock and dam were constructed in 1941 and the lock chamber is 250 feet long and 50 feet wide with depth over the gate sills of 10 feet. Depending on the tide level in the St. Lucie River, the lock normally raises, or lowers, vessels between 13 and 14.5 feet.

Immediately upstream from the St. Lucie Lock, the Corps of Engineers maintains and operates a recreational facility. The facility is primarily an RV Park but it also has a launch ramp and 8 boat slips, with power and water, for boats up to 35 feet in length and a draft of 6 feet or less.

144

Chapter 4

At mile 29, the waterway passes the Indiantown Marina. The marina, which has a large land area, is a popular haul out and boat storage facility. Hundreds of boats, primarily from Canada and the northern United States, are brought here to be stored on land through the hot Florida summer and, because it is considered safely inland, through Hurricane season. The marina does have transient dockage and it's a popular overnight stop for boats crossing Florida.

The town of Indiantown, about a mile from the marina, is an unincorporated community within the Port St. Lucie Metropolitan Statistical Area. It was originally a Seminole trading post, white ranchers and farmers began to arrive in the 1880s and 90s and during the Florida land boom of the 1920s the railroad reached Indiantown and some development took place. But the land boom died in 1926, development ceased and several subsequent Hurricanes destroyed much of what had been built–so much for safe from Hurricanes boat storage. Today the town is a quiet farming and residential community with a few restaurants and limited shopping. The one tourist attraction is the Seminole Inn, built during the land boom and now on the National Register of Historic Places. The restaurant and bar at the Inn are nice and the walls of the second story hallways are painted with murals that depict the regions history.

At mile 38, the waterway passes under the Port Mayaca RR Lift Bridge. With a clearance of just 49 (or 48 depending on the source) feet in the raised position, the bridge has set the controlling air draft for the waterway since the beginning of cross-Florida navigation. Most power boats have no problem but sailors need to know their mast height. In 1998 we took our Mariner ketch, which had a 52-foot-high main mast, through with the help of a service based in Indiantown. They set empty 55-gallon plastic drums on one side of our boat, pumped them full of water and heeled the boat over enough that we were able to get under. But it was close, the tri-color masthead light cleared by what looked like inches, the VHF antenna…ping…ping…pinged on the bridge girders.

The Port Mayaca Lock, at waterway mile 38.9, is the west end of the St. Lucie Canal and the lock's west gates open onto Lake Okeechobee. The lock, which carries the waterway through the Herbert Hoover Dike, was built in 1977 so that the water level in Lake Okeechobee could rise and be better controlled during

About to float the Port Mayaca Lock
Okeechobee Waterway

periods of high water. The lock limits the effects of high lake levels on the St. Lucie Canal and helps to control flooding in the communities that were, and are still, developing on the low, swampy, flood prone land along the St. Lucie River. The lock chamber is 400 feet long and 56 feet wide with a depth over the gate sills of 14 feet. When the lock is operating, the water level in the St. Lucie Canal is normally only ½ to 2 feet below lake level. When the canal and lake are at the same level, the lock gates stand open and passing vessels, in the terminology of the gulf coast

Lock Operation Basics

A navigation lock is used as a sort of "water elevator" to get from one water level or "pool" to another. Water always seeks a lower level, so valves and tunnels are used to raise and lower the water in the Lock.

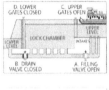

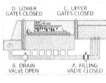

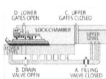

United States Army Corps of Engineers diagram

For a boat going from a higher level to a lower level (e.g. from the river into the canal), the lock is filled by opening the filling valve. The upper and lower gates are closed. The water level of the chamber rises to the upstream level. The upper gate then opens and the boat moves in.

To lower the boat, the gates are closed behind it. Then the filling valve is closed and the emptying valve is opened. The pressure of the higher water in the lock drains to downstream level in minutes.

The lower gates are then opened and the boat moves out on the lower water level.

waterways "float the lock" they drive through at idle speed. From the Port Mayaca Lock across Lake Okeechobee to the Moore Haven Lock is 39.1 miles on route 1, the open lake route, and 50 miles if route 2 (the rim route), along the south shore of the lake is followed.

NOAA and the USACE,[34] give a low water surface elevation of 12.56 feet above mean sea level for Lake Okeechobee. At that level the lake: is approximately 36 miles north-south and 29 miles east-west, has a surface area of approximately 451,000 acres (705 square miles), an average depth of approximately 9 feet, a maximum depth of almost 12 feet…barely above Mean Sea Level.

Although the lake is shallow, the twenty plus mile fetch across the lake permits short steep 4 to 5-foot waves that can develop very quickly. Rough conditions on the lake are not uncommon during winter cold fronts and strong thunderstorms at any time of year. In the fall and winter in particular, it is often easiest to cross the lake in the early morning, as soon as it is light enough to see. The winds over the lake tend to increase as the day warms up and die down, or at least decrease overnight.

Clewiston, on the west side of the lake is at waterway mile 65.0 on route 1, the across the lake route, and at mile 75.7 on route 2, the rim route. Clewiston is where the routes merge and route 2 ends. From there to the end of the waterway official mileage figures are route 1 mileage. The town of Clewiston is entered through a small lock–the lock chamber is only 60 feet long by 50 feet wide–that separates Lake Okeechobee from the Clewiston drainage canal. As with the Port Mayaca Lock, depending on the level of the lake, boats may go up, down or float the lock. Vessels too long for the lock chamber visit Clewiston only when the lock is standing open but the crew needs to be aware of lake levels and weather conditions, if the lock closes, they can be trapped. Clewiston was founded by Alonzo Clewis of Tampa and Philadelphian John O'Brien and was incorporated in 1925. The town calls itself "The Sweetest Town in America" and its economy was originally sugar based. Sugar was so dominant that Clewiston was sometimes said to be a U.S. Sugar Corporation company town. Today, although sugar remains important and the U.S. Sugar Corporation is still the largest business and largest employer, the town is also a center for winter vegetables, fruit, cattle and sport fishing for Large Mouth Bass.

In early spring 2012, on an east bound trip through the Okeechobee Waterway, we spent two days in Clewiston; at Rolland and Mary Martin's "World-Famous" Bass Fishing Resort. In addition to hotel accommodations and small boat launch ramps, the resort has both an RV park and a small marina. When we arrived the marina harbor master was refueling an impressive, too big for the lock, sport fish boat while the three-man crew stood around looking as though they had been to better places and had better things to do. They ignored us...didn't say a word.

After lunch we walked into town to see what there was to see and to buy some bread, orange juice and few other things. During our walk we passed a couple of small Latino stores and a gas station convenience store and I noticed that all of them had prominent signs advertising "Coke Cola Hecho en Mexico" (made in Mexico). We live in Texas where coke made and bottled in Mexico is available if you look for it. It tastes different from...better than...coke made and bottled in the United States. In 2012 Mexican produced Coca Cola was still made with natural cane sugar (Sucrose) while coke manufactured in the U.S., like almost everything else requiring large amounts of sweeting, was made with Corn Syrup and High Fructose Corn Syrup. The Sugar Cane workers, most of whom come from Central America, Mexico and Haiti, prefer the cane sugar sweetened coke.

When we returned to the resort the big sport fish was gone. One of the crew told the dock master that the boat's owner wanted it in Gulf Shores, Alabama. They still had a long way to go and they were on a tight schedule. That night we ate dinner in the resorts Tiki Bar and then spent an hour eves-dropping on a group of RV'ers, all of whom seemed to be preparing for long drives north. They were having a fine time, knocking back pitchers of brew and catching up on each other's comings, goings, summer plans and the road conditions in Montana.

At the Moore Haven Lock, waterway mile 78, the OWW leaves Lake Okeechobee and enters the Caloosahatchee Canal. The Moore Haven Lock and Dam, was built in 1935, under the authority of the Rivers and Harbors Act of 1930, as a flood control and navigation structure. The lock chamber is 250 feet long and 50 feet wide with a depth of 10 feet over the gate sills. The average drop, or lift, in the lock is between 1 and 2 feet. The incorporated City of Moore Haven, founded in 1915 by James A. Moore, is the county seat for Glades County, Florida. Moore Haven was the first real town in this part of Florida and, like Clewiston, was initially a sugar town. The sugar industry is still an important part of the local economy but, as in Clewiston, winter vegetables, fruit, ranching, sport fishing for Large Mouth Bass and RV Parks for northern snowbirds have rounded out the economy. A mile down the Caloosahatchee Canal from the lock, the City of Moore Haven has dockage with power and water for transient boats.

The 15.5-mile-long Caloosahatchee Canal—a canalized section of the Caloosahatchee River—carries the Okeechobee waterway west from the Moore Haven Lock and Dam to the Ortona Lock and Dam at waterway mile 93.5. Constructed in 1937, primarily for navigational purposes, the Ortona Lock has a chamber 250 feet long and 50 feet wide with a depth of 12 feet over the gate sills. The average drop or lift in the lock is 7.5-8.5 feet.

Below the Ortona Lock and Dam the waterway follows the un-canalized but still controlled Caloosahatchee River for 27.9 miles to waterway mile 121.4 and the Franklin Lock and Dam. The Franklin Lock and Dam was built in 1965, primarily for flood control and to control saltwater intrusion into the upper Caloosahatchee. The lock is, effectively, the western edge of the freshwater, non-tidal the Everglades environmental area. Below the lock the Caloosahatchee is a tidal, sea level river, a brackish, estuarine environment. The Franklin Lock has a chamber 400 feet long and 56 feet wide with a depth of 14 feet over the gate sills. The drop, or rise, in the lock is seldom more than 3 feet. From the Franklin Lock and Dam, it is 33.2 miles downstream, through the greater Fort Myers urban area, to the west end of the Okeechobee Waterway and Mile Zero of the Florida Gulf Intracoastal Waterway.

5. Florida's Gulf Coast, from Key West to St. Marks

Friday, May 17, 2013, we slipped out of Coral Bay and left Islamorada. We ran down the Florida Bay side of the Keys to Marathon and then across Florida Bay to the Everglades National Park and the National Park Service's marina at Flamingo.

We had last visited Flamingo in 2008. During that visit, the large lodge that had formerly stood near the marina was gone, destroyed in 2005 by hurricanes Katrina and Wilma. The park restaurant, also destroyed by the hurricanes, was being rebuilt, but everything else was open: a small café, the marina, the RV park looked full, the store was crowded and well-stocked, the restrooms behind the store were clean and the launch ramps were busy. At the marina, where we were far from alone, the overnight dockage fee was $20 (per night), which included electrical power and heads and showers for the visiting boaters. Except for the Everglade's large population of resident insects, it was pretty nice.

This time Flamingo was a sad reminder of political games and budgets cut the wrong way and in the wrong places. We stayed one night. The restaurant, still closed, looked exactly as it had looked in 2008: saw dust and scrap wood lying around, wires hanging from ceiling conduit, scaffolding still in place. The café was closed. The park store was poorly stocked, none too clean and its restrooms were filthy. The RV Park was almost empty. There were few trailerable boats using the launch ramps. In the marina, the overnight dockage fee had risen to $50 (per night) and we were the only boat. The docks were in good condition but there was no electrical power and the water was turned off...the taps locked. The heads and showers for visiting boaters were locked.

The afternoon we arrived we met a German couple who had honeymooned at Flamingo in the early 1990's. They had wanted to stay at the park lodge for a few days but were staying in Miami instead. They had driven down for the day and could not believe how far Flamingo had been allowed to deteriorate. They told us, several times, how lovely everything had been and how much they had enjoyed it.

At 9:45 a.m. the next morning we rounded Northwest Cape Sable, turned north, set a course for Cape Romano, turned on the auto pilot and sat back to enjoy a long day on the water. It was a lovely day to be out on the Florida Bank, sunny, warm and a light morning breeze.

While the foundational geology of southern Florida is not identical to that of the Bahamas it is very similar. The south tip of the Florida Peninsula, the Cay Sal Bank, The Bahamas, the Turks and Caicos and the still further east Silver and Navidad Banks can be thought of as a single geo-region. The portion of southern peninsular Florida that lies south of a line from Palm Beach, to Coral Springs, to 26° North/81° West, to Fort Myers, to Gasparilla Island, along with Florida Bay and the Keys, down to somewhere in the vicinity of Bahia Honda Key, is essentially a large Andros Island, while the outer Keys, from approximately Little Pine and No Name Keys through Key West and the Marquesas to the Dry Tortugas are Florida's Exuma Islands.

Chapter 5

Aboard a boat running from the outer Keys north past Cape Sable and along the shore past Cape Romano to roughly the mouth of the Caloosahatchee River and Sanibel Island, the feeling is similar to crossing one of the Bahama's banks. Through the shallow clean, clear water sea fans, soft corals, other bottom flora and fauna and the occasional fish are visible.

Six miles off Highland Point in the Everglades, the engine temperature began to rise rapidly...shut the engine down...open the engine hatch. Engine coolant, a 50/50 blend of distilled water and antifreeze was everywhere. The hose that carried coolant from the engine to *Nauset's* hot water heater was hanging loose between the engine and the forward bulkhead. It had been attached to an engine block coolant port, now there was a hole in the block with the remains of a brass pipe nipple visible inside. Whoever installed the hot water heater had used a short, thin walled, brass pipe nipple to connect stiff, wire reinforced hose, a couple of heavy bronze pipe fittings, and a bronze shut-off valve to the engine. And left them unsupported. Six years of engine vibration and the weight of all that stuff was a bit more than that poor little brass pipe nipple could take. I had the tools to fix the problem, knew how to do it and we carried spare coolant. But parts: a new pipe nipple, a threaded bronze street L or a threaded plug to simply plug up the engine block coolant port. Not on the boat.

We were adrift in twelve to fifteen feet of water with an 8-10 knot southwest wind and about a foot of chop. It was six miles to shore, about 30 miles to Coon Key Pass and Goodland and significantly farther than that to Capri Pass and Marco Island. When the afternoon sea breeze kicked in, wind and sea would pick-up. We had been carrying Tow Boat/US's unlimited on-the-water towing for years and now it was going to be very helpful.

Out there off the Everglades, our cell phone claimed it had No Service. I called Tow Boat/US three times on the VHF radio...no reply. I tried the Colusa Island Marina in Goodland a couple times, again...no reply. Reluctantly, I called the Coast Guard. On the third call, Coast Guard Station Fort Myers Beach responded with a loud clear signal. I explained the situation and asked them to call Tow Boat/US. Ten minutes later the Coast Guard called back and told us that Tow Boat/US, Naples, Florida, was dispatching a boat and that their ETA at our location was four hours. I lowered the anchor. We couldn't set it but the weight of the anchor and 75 feet of anchor chain would keep us from drifting very far. Then...lunch and wait. Every fifteen minutes or so the Coast Guard called to make sure we were OK.

The tow boat arrived a little before 3:30 p.m., a half hour ahead of their estimate. By then the afternoon sea breeze had come up, the wind, still southwest, had increased to twelve to fifteen knots and the seas were about two feet. By 7:00 p.m. we were safely tied up at the Colusa Island Marina in Goodland. Before he left, the tow boat operator made sure that we knew where the heads and showers were and that we knew about several restaurants that were within an easy walk of the marina.

That evening I called some friends from our sailboat cruising days who live in Fort Myers. The next day, Sunday, they drove down to Goodland, ran me to the Ace Hardware in Marco Island and helped with repairs. By mid-afternoon Sunday repairs were complete, with more appropriate fittings and proper support. An investment in an old, hard used boat equals repairs and up-grades.

From Goodland, we continued north on the natural inside route up the Big Marco River to Marco Island and Capri Pass. Just inside Capri Pass, the Calhoun Channel leads north to the inside route to Gordon Pass and Naples. In 1938 Congress authorized improvements to the "inside route from Naples Harbor to Big Marco Pass to be prosecuted by the war department under the direction of the secretary of war and the supervision of the chief of engineers." The USACE completed a 6-foot-deep by 70-foot-wide channel in 1940. The channel was cleaned out and partially relocated in 1945 because of storm damage. Congress never designated this inside route–by definition an intracoastal waterway because it runs behind the coastal islands–a federal project and it is not considered a part of The Intracoastal Waterway. The channel is maintained by the Florida West Coast Navigation District, although the United States Coast Guard does maintain the aids to navigation.

We followed the Calhoun Channel to Naples, went out into the gulf through Gordon Pass and followed the coast north to San Carlos Bay. At the head of San Carlos Bay, we entered the Caloosahatchee River and a half mile up the river we turned left, rounded the end of Sanibel Island, passed under the western span of the Sanibel Island Causeway and entered the Florida Gulf Intracoastal Waterway (FGWW) at approximately waterway mile 3. We continued up the FGWW to Gasparilla Sound and ended the day at the Gasparilla Marina in Placida, Florida (FGWW mile 34.2).

If we had continued up the Caloosahatchee River, through the main, 70-foot-high, east span of the Sanibel Island Causeway, to a hundred yards or so past the Caloosahatchee Flashing Green 15, we would have been very close to 26°30.6'N., 82°01.1'W., the point at which the Okeechobee Waterway meets the Florida Gulf Waterway. At that point a right turn would have taken us up the Caloosahatchee River and on to Florida's Atlantic coast via the Okeechobee Waterway and a left turn would have started us up the Florida Gulf Waterway.

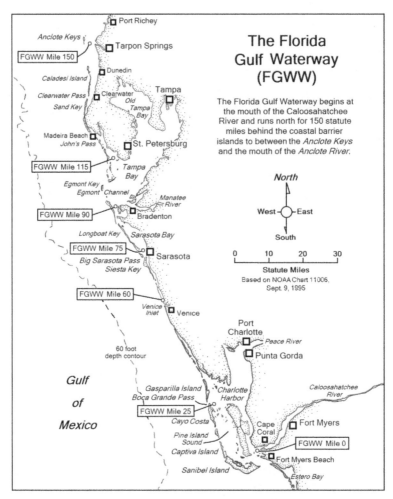

The Florida
Gulf Waterway
(FGWW)

The Florida Gulf Waterway begins at
the mouth of the Caloosahatchee
River and runs north for 150 statute
miles behind the coastal barrier
islands to between the *Anclote Keys*
and the mouth of the *Anclote River.*

The Florida Gulf Waterway (FGWW), which the United States Coast Pilot describes as a "toll free canal between the Caloosahatchee River and the Anclote River," runs north in the sheltered waters behind Florida's west coast barrier islands for 150 miles from its origin in the mouth of the Caloosahatchee River to the Anclote River Flashing Green 1 (approximately 28°10.4′N., 082°49.5′W.) The FGWW is a Federal project and is part of the Intracoastal Waterway with construction and maintenance managed by the USACE's Jacksonville, Florida District. The project depth for the waterway's channel is 9 feet for a width of 100 feet, but lack of consistent funding, strong currents in the numerous inlets and the soft sands and silts of Florida's gulf coast have hampered the USACE's efforts to maintain the channel. Mileage on the FGWW is measured in statute miles from south to north and twenty-five bridges, only five of which are high bridges, span the waterway.

Between 1890 and the early 1930s Congress authorized and funded a number of small projects along the route of the Florida Gulf Waterway. Then, in the Rivers and Harbors Act of November 3, 1935, Congress called for a survey of "the Intracoastal Waterway from the Caloosahatchee River to the Withlacoochee River with a view to securing a waterway of suitable dimensions for the purpose of affording exit to the north for craft using Okeechobee Cross-Florida Canal." The Withlacoochee was the western, Gulf of Mexico, end of the Trans-Florida Barge Canal. In 1939, in a report on this survey requirement, the Board of Engineers for Rivers and Harbors recommended an Intracoastal Waterway 9 feet deep and 100 feet wide for the full 150 statute miles from the mouth of the Caloosahatchee River north to the mouth of the Anclote River, which incorporated all of the improvements already made. In the 50 statute miles between the Anclote River and the Withlacoochee River, the Board recommended simply placing waterway markers along the 12-foot depth contour in the Gulf of Mexico and providing channels into two harbors of refuge, the Homosassa and Crystal Rivers.

In 1945, after World War II, Congress acting on the Board of Engineers recommendation, consolidated the various small projects between the Caloosahatchee and Anclote Rivers and authorized the Florida West Coast Waterway project. The authorization contained the same local cost sharing and right-of-way provisions that had been applied along the Atlantic Intracoastal Waterway. In 1947, in order to full fill the local participation requirements, the Florida Legislature, following their earlier east coast model, created the Florida West Coast Inland Navigation District; with the powers of taxation, land acquisition and, where necessary, eminent domain.

Between 1935 and the years following World War II, extensive real estate development and population growth had taken place in and around Venice. Because the planned waterway route would have cut most of the newly developed areas off from the beaches, strong local opposition to the waterway plan developed. The Corps of Engineers proposed several alternative routes but the local opposition was not overcome until 1962 when the Venice City Council ratified the route known as the C-1 route. The Florida Gulf Coast Intracoastal Waterway was finally completed in January 1967 and formally opened at a ceremony in Venice on February 25, 1967[35].

There are two large seaports on Tampa Bay and while crossing the bay the FGWW follows the main shipping channel for several miles. The Port of Tampa, the largest port in Florida and 19th on the USACE's 2016 list of domestic ports by tonnage, is in Tampa and Port Manatee, 90th on the 2016 tonnage list is on the south side of Tampa Bay near Bradenton. The shipping channel from the sea buoy in the Gulf of Mexico to the Port of Tampa is 49.9 miles long with controlling depths of 45 ft. in the entrance channel and 43 ft. in the Tampa Bay channels. The tides in Tampa Bay are mixed semidiurnal, with clear high and higher high and low and lower low tides and the tide range, from higher high to lower low, is less than two feet.

Almost the entire Tampa channel is dredged and maintenance dredging is constant. In 1823 when Fort Brooke was established in what is today downtown Tampa the small vessels of the time were able to able to reach upper Tampa Bay with relative ease. Once port facilities are established, they rarely move and with the passage of time and growth in vessel size, dredging became the order of the day. Along the gulf coast from the Florida Keys to the Mexican border, there are no ports naturally deep enough for modern ships. Most of the gulf ports were not deep enough for the vessels of the time when they were founded; consequently, many of the very early Congressional appropriations for rivers and harbors were for improving harbors on the gulf coast by: clearing or cutting bars, dredging channels and turning basins and clearing snags from rivers and channels.

On Monday, May 20th during our run from Goodland to Placida and the Gasparilla Marina, I noticed that our alternator, which had been soaked with engine coolant, was not charging our batteries. At the Gasparilla Marina a little checking with the volt meter confirmed that our alternator was not alternating, there was no output.

It didn't take me long to discover that a new Yanmar alternator, of the type we have, costs more than $1,000 and the only place anywhere near Placida, Florida that stocked Yanmar alternators was Mastry Marine Engine in St. Petersburg. Mastry is owned by Yanmar and it's the southeastern distributor of Yanmar marine diesels. I called Mastry's parts department, explained our problem, and asked about a new alternator. The parts man I talked to told me that they did have a new alternator in stock, however he suggested that I talk to their service department first because our alternator was probably repairable and repair would cost less than replacement.

We decided to move the boat to a marina in St. Petersburg, we could be there by late afternoon. If we ran the shore power battery charger overnight and left with fully charged batteries, we should have no problems.

As soon as we were docked in St. Petersburg, I called Mastry's service department. Their service people were booked for several days, they didn't have a technician they could send to our boat but they let me talk to one of their top people. He said that oily residue from the coolant might very well be the cause of our alternators problem and he suggested that before I bought a new one, I should give ours a bath. He then gave me very detailed instructions on how to bathe an alternator.

Bathe the alternator...? I'm not a diesel mechanic but all our boats have had diesel engines and before we took our first long cruise, I took a hands-on marine diesel maintenance course. We carry a good set of tools and we're not afraid to use them and try things. So, following our instructions, Betty and I bathed that poor alternator...while it was on the engine...and the engine was running. When we were finished giving the alternator its bath, we tested it under various rpms and battery loads and it did its thing exactly the way it was supposed to.

Spending time with the volt meter, checking things and tracing wiring turned up several problems that I fixed and caused me to decide that, down in Texas...assuming we got there...a lot of quality boat time was going to be devoted to the electrical system. Over the years and owners since *Nauset* was built, stuff had been added, deleted, modified, changed, and moved. Old unused wire was left behind and thin wire was re-used where heavier wire was needed. *Nauset* was built with a gasoline engine. When the gas engine was removed and our big Yanmar installed, ninety percent of the gas engine wiring harness was left in place. Nothing unusual in the life of a boat.

Chapter 5

From St. Petersburg we moved a few miles north to Florida's Caladesi State Park. Located on Caladesi Island, north of Clearwater, and reachable only by boat, Caladesi State Park is one of Florida's best state parks and the tourist industry consistently rates the ocean side beach on Caladesi Island one of America's best beaches. It really is a lovely place, the sort of place that makes our preferred mode of travel worthwhile.

Between the Caloosahatchee River and Caladesi State Park, we had followed the Florida Gulf Intracoastal Waterway. Now we had to either make the open water run across the northern Gulf to East Pass and St George Sound, or follow the coast around Florida's Big Bend. Leaving Caladesi we had what looked like a good forecast for following the coast up and around the Big Bend...a 10-knot northeast to east wind and 2-foot seas. The forecast was significantly less than correct. When we reached the north end of Anclote Key and open water, what we found was a 15-knot north-northwest wind and a 3 to 4-foot sea. Definitely not our thing. So, we went up the Anclote River to Tarpon Springs, tied up at the Turtle Cove Marina and waited two days for the wind to clock and the seas to drop.

The first settlers in the Tarpon Springs area arrived in the 1840s. Turtle fishermen from the Keys and the Bahamas discovered sponges along Florida's west coast in the early 1870s and sponge fishermen from the Keys, many of them Bahamians, moved to the area over the next decade. Rail service arrived and the city was incorporated in 1887. The railroad made getting to Tarpon Springs relatively easy and from the end of the 1880s through World War I the city was a popular winter destination for wealthy Americans.

By 1890 enough sponges were being harvested that local business man John Cheyney was able to establish a sponge company. In the decade between 1895 and 1905 John Corcoris, an associate of Cheyney's, introduced mechanization to the sponge industry and in 1905 he brought in the first Greek sponge divers. Sponge fishing flourished and by the end of World War II 180 sponge boats were working out of Tarpon Springs. In 1948 a toxic algal bloom…a red tide…decimated the over fished sponge beds and the sponge industry collapsed. Today the sponge beds have largely recovered and a regulated, sustainable fishery supplies natural sponges to the medical and cosmetics industries.

Despite the fact that we had been up and down Florida's west coast a dozen times, we had never been to Tarpon Springs. We enjoyed our visit but the area we could walk to from the Turtle Cove Marina–the sponge docks, Dodecanese Blvd, the historic downtown–was mostly a make-believe tourist land. The working waterfront and the Long-line, sponge, shrimp and stone crab boats along the river side were real and very interesting. But the land side was crowded with Greek restaurants, a few of which were very good, and: shops selling Genuine Greek imports, cigar roller stands, a pet-the-shark private aquarium, t-shirt shops, street side barkers hawking trips on a Real Sponge Boat and See Live Dolphin cruises and a shop selling Authentic Sea Shells and Sponges. Authentic sea shells?

A lot of the Authentic Sea Shells sold in shell and beach shops along the Atlantic and Gulf coasts of the United States are imported shells. Most come from Indonesia, the Philippines or the Indian Ocean and many are from species native to Indo-Pacific waters, species not found naturally along the Atlantic or Gulf Coasts. Living marine organisms are stripped from local beaches, lagoons and reefs by desperately poor native divers who kill the animals, clean the shells and sell them for pennies. The shells are exported, through a chain of middle men to the U.S. and elsewhere so that tourists and vacationers can buy pretty shells. For pennies

Chapter 5

and tourists, the life-web of the reefs is destroyed and the natural environment impoverished.

There was a very good seafood market on the working docks. The market was clean and bright, it did not smell of ageing fish and it had a nice display of fresh, local seafood. A couple of small, probably local, long-line boats were on the dock behind the seafood market. Local boats are rarely out more than two days and their catch tends to be iced and sold fresh, not frozen. In the U.S. large deep water long-liners and trawlers typically stay out from a week to several weeks and deliver their catch to the buyers frozen. But in most markets the majority of the seafood displayed on ice was imported, primarily from Indonesia, Thailand, China, India and a couple other places. Vessels from these countries often stay out several months or longer, sometimes much longer, and many of them utilize miles long drift nets that catch, and kill, everything that swims in the sea: fish of all types, edible and otherwise, sea turtles, dolphins, even whales. The marketable fish are gutted–sometimes filleted or completely dressed–and then frozen on the catching vessel. The rest, the euphemistic "by-catch," may be converted to fish meal for animal feed or industrial uses but often its simply thrown back into the sea. By the time a fish that was caught by one of these vessels reaches the dinner table it is often two or three months old and it may have been thawed or partially thawed and refrozen several times.

We left Tarpon Springs the Sunday of Memorial Day weekend, the wind had gone easterly and the seas were leveling out. Sunday ended with a peaceful night anchored several miles up a piece of wide deep canal that would have been the west end of the Trans-Florida Barge Canal. Today the western stub of the canal provides a nice place to anchor, fish and swim. And the spoil islands created when the miles long canal approach channel was dredged, have weathered and naturalized. They are now an archipelago of protected mangrove, shell and sand islets and islands that supports a large and varied bird population and is dotted with attractive small beaches.

Monday May 27, 2013, Memorial Day, we moved up the coast to Deadman Bay, the Steinhatchee River and the end-of-the-road river mouth community of Steinhatchee/Jena. The Steinhatchee River was dredged by the USACE to serve as a harbor of refuge for small craft following the coast between the Anclote River and the east end of the Gulf Intracoastal Waterway (Rivers and Harbors Act of August 26, 1937.) The Flashing Green 1 (29°30.4'N., 83°27.4'W.) at the mouth of the Steinhatchee River is approximately 104 nautical miles north of Anclote Key and the north end of the Florida Gulf Waterway. And it is 70 nautical miles from the East Pass entrance to St. George Sound and the east end of the Gulf Intracoastal Waterway. Because of budget constraints the river has not been maintained at the authorized depth of 9 feet. In 2013, the Steinhatchee channel had a controlling depth of 4 feet at mean lower low water, a channel width of 75 feet and the tide range was 3 to 4½ feet. Except for the strong current, it was not a problem for a small boat like *Nauset*.

We tied up at the Good Times Motel & Marina on the south bank of the river. A Tarpon Springs sponge boat with a deck load of fresh sponges was on the end of the dock, out from us, and we glad the wind was not blowing directly from him to us. As it was, we occasionally got more than a casual whiff of not quite fresh sponge. Sponges, even though they live attached to the sea floor, are animals (phylum Porifera.) The sponge, the part of the living sponge valued by the medical, cosmetics and bath products industries, is the animal's skeleton, a matrix of cartilaginous tissue that supports the soft parts of the animal. Like all harvested animals, sponges must be cleaned and processed before use. Ageing, not quit freshly harvested sponges, like the ones on the boat at the end of the dock, smell like what they are...dead, decaying marine organisms...think really dead fish.

There was only one other transient boat at the marina, a 36-foot trawler with Port Clinton, Ohio as a hailing port. At the land end of the dock, up on pilings and hopefully above the next storm surge, was the Who Dat Bar and Grill. The Who Dat had: nice views up and down the Steinhatchee, a good bar with half a dozen Florida craft beers on draft, good food with a menu that went beyond Gulf Coast fried, and interesting people. The happy hour and dinner crowd was mostly local families, fisherman and fishing guides, unwinding after the long Memorial Day weekend.

Originally called Deadman Bay and dating to the Seminole wars if not earlier, the community at the mouth of the Steinhatchee River is composed of two towns; Steinhatchee on the north bank, in Taylor County, and Jena, on the south bank, in Dixie County. The north and south sides of the river may be two towns, separated by a river and a county line, but they are one community; a lingering piece of an older, quieter Florida, that is not yet a boutique, art gallery and linen napkin restaurant kind of place. The economy is commercial fishing–stone crabs, shrimp, oysters, sponges, scallops and fin fish–along with limited small-scale sport fishing and tourism, particularly during Florida's short scallop season. Some low-key motels, a few B&Bs, some restaurants, a couple of seafood packing plants, a small boatyard, three modest marinas and a few signs for fishing guides are Steinhatchee.

Every time we visit Steinhatchee we think, and talk about, a February 2002 visit. We had come down to Steinhatchee from St. Marks on the last calm day before a strong cold front. The front stalled over northwestern Florida, bringing rain, fog, rain, wind and more rain with intermittent thunderstorms. We were on the end of an L shaped floating dock, bow pointing upstream into the river's current. A sport fish boat and a couple small boats in slips were on the upstream side of the dock and a large offshore stone crab boat that was chartered to the University of Florida for

Nauset and a sponge boat on a dock in
Steinhatchee, Florida

oceanographic research took up most of the downstream side.

At 2:00 a.m. Betty woke me up and said that the water did not sound right, meaning that the water passing the hull did not sound the way it did when we went to bed. She went up to the main cabin and reported that it looked as though we were closer to the next dock downstream then we had been. I got up, dressed and stepped off the boat onto the dock to see what was going on. Betty was right, more than right, we were much closer to the downstream dock then we had been and we could hear what sounded like something cracking and breaking. I walked up the dock and found that the cracking/breaking noises were the shore end of our dock twisting and breaking. The galvanized steel frame was twisting, its welds breaking and the dock's deck was breaking up. The dock was breaking loose.

January and February 2003 had been wet months in North Florida, and the rain accompanying the stalled front had raised the Steinhatchee River to near flood stage. In addition, there was an astronomical low tide that night. The result was an extremely strong ebb tide. The large, deep draft crab boat/research vessel on the downstream side of the dock was broadside to the river current and the ebb tide. It and was acting like a dam and it was putting a tremendous strain on the dock. The dock, along with all the boats tied to it, including us, seemed to be about to go down the river and out to sea.

I unplugged and retrieved our shore power cable. Betty started the motor and I removed and retrieved dock lines until only the forward spring line remained. At that point: the starboard edge of our transom was against the dock; the bow was six feet off the dock and the five-eighths inch nylon spring line resembled an iron bar. Betty pushed the throttle up, I cut that spring line and we were out of there. We moved to midstream, above the marina and anchored, just in time for the wind gust on the leading edge of a major thunderstorm. Worried about dragging anchor, we kept the engine running and took turns at the helm until sunrise. When it was light enough to see, we raised the anchor and moved to a marina on the north bank where we sat out another five days of rain, fog and wind, before the stalled front dissipated and we could continue south.

The dock we had been on, had been secured to the shore by four heavy steel cables, two upstream and two downstream. The upstream cables tore loose but the downstream cables held. As the outboard end of the dock pivoted downstream, the large research vessel, no longer broadside to the current, ceased acting like a dam. In fact, it became an excellent anchor, as it swung into shoal water near shore it went hard aground in the falling tide. The day after our long night of adventure, the research vessel was untied, the other boats moved and the almost loose dock was swung back into place. By the time we left Steinhatchee it looked like nothing had happened. Cats and sailors have nine lives, sometimes I think Betty and I have used 30 of ours.

Tuesday May 28th leaving Steinhatchee we had a light east-southeast wind and barely a foot of chop. By the time we reached the mouth of the St. Marks river the wind was southeast at 10-15 knots and we had a 2 to 4-foot following sea. The forecast for the next several days called for increasing southerly winds and seas. The forecast was correct and we stayed at Shields Marina in St. Marks until June 1st waiting for the wind to clock around to the west or, even better, north of west. Shields Marina had an excellent ships store and we took advantage of our wait-on-weather to make and run new, heavier gage power and ground cables between the batteries and the 12-volt circuit panel and to rework some of the wiring behind the panel.

The town of St. Marks is approximately 9 nautical miles, or 10.3 statute miles, up the river from the St. Marks Flashing Green 1. The channel up to St. Marks is well marked and, primarily because of a little used commercial barge terminal on the north bank just upstream from the town, the channel is a federal project, maintained by the Corps of Engineers. The project specifications for the entire channel call for a width of 125 feet and a depth of 12 feet, but because of lack of funding and limited commercial traffic, the channel has not been maintained at specifications. In March

2014, the controlling depth for the middle half of the channel was 8.8 feet at mean lower low water (NOAA Chart 11406, Jan. 2015.) The tide range in the river is 3-4 feet and the current rarely exceeds one mile per hour.

For tourism promotional purposes, the Florida State Government's Department of Tourism and the Florida Chamber of Commerce have divided Florida's coast into a series of loosely defined tourist coasts. Steinhatchee was in the middle of the Nature Coast. The St. Marks River is more or less where the Nature Coast (Port Richey west to Wakulla Beach) meets the Forgotten Coast (St. Marks west to Mexico Beach.)

The little riverside town of St. Marks is about 20 miles from Florida's capital city, Tallahassee. In town there are: several restaurants, a small but complete grocery, a couple of fresh seafood markets and a very nice State Historic Park. An improved biking and hiking trail follows an old rail line that more or less parallels Florida State Route 363 from St. Marks to the edge of Tallahassee. There has been a settlement of some sort at St Marks since at least 1676. Despite the town's long history and proximity to Tallahassee, the St. Marks and Wakulla Rivers are still surprisingly natural: birds are everywhere, large alligator gar swim through the marina and along the water front and alligators, some very large, are numerous. Scenes for several of the Tarzan movies were filmed in the area and guided kayak tours through the bayous and marsh creeks are popular.

Panfilo de Narvaez, the first Spanish explorer to visit the area of St. Marks, arrived in 1528 and Hernando De Soto visited in 1539. In 1676 the Spanish built a log fort on the point at the confluence of the Wakulla and St. Marks Rivers—today called Tucker's Point. A small settlement may have already existed on the point. Three years later the fort and settlement were looted and burned by

Buccaneers from the Caribbean. In 1718 the Spanish tried again, building a second wooden fort and in 1739 they began a stone fort. The stone fort was not yet complete when Spain lost West Florida to England in 1763. Between 1763 and 1821, when Spain ceded Florida to the United States, the fort and settlement at St. Marks changed hands several times. The Federal government began construction of a hospital next to the old fort in 1857 and used some of the stone from the fort in building the hospital. The final military action at the site occurred in 1861, at the start of the Civil War when Confederate troops seized the hospital and what was left of the old fort. The Confederates changed the fort's name to Fort Ward, and constructed earthwork batteries and a magazine.

Today the site of the old fort(s) and hospital is the San Marcos de Apalache Historic State Park. The park, a short drive or reasonable bike ride or walk from St. Marks, has: an interesting museum, an easily walked interpretive history and nature trail, picnic grounds and restrooms.

6. St. Marks, Florida to Gulfport, Mississippi

Saturday, June 1st we left St. Marks as soon as it was light enough to see the aids to navigation on the river. The wind in the early morning was westerly at between 5 and 10 knots at most of the reporting stations. As the day progressed and the land warmed up, the sea breeze would kick in, increasing the wind speed by 5 or more knots and backing the apparent wind direction to southwest or even south-southwest. Wave direction, the direction the waves are coming from, generally lags behind wind direction and when we left the St. Marks River the seas were south-southwest at about two feet. Our course from the St. Marks River would be south-southwest, into the wind and seas, until we were far enough south to round the long and dangerous shoals that extend south from Lighthouse Point at the east end of St. George Sound. East Pass, between Dog Island and St. George Island, is the best entrance to St. George Sound and we wanted to get south, around the shoals and inside, through East Pass, before the wind and seas increased and a heavy sea built in East Pass.

The Gulf Intracoastal Waterway actual begins at a seemingly arbitrary point in the dredged channel to the harbor in the town of Carrabelle and not at or just inside East Pass. In the Rivers and Harbors Act of August 26, 1937, Congress ordered an extension of the Gulf Intracoastal Waterway east from Carrabelle, Florida to St. Marks. If that project had been completed, we would have left the St. Marks River channel well before its end and we would have: followed dredged channels southwest across (and behind most of)

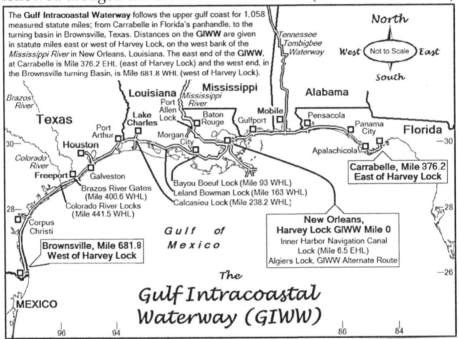

The **Gulf Intracoastal Waterway** follows the upper gulf coast for 1,058 measured statute miles; from Carrabelle in Florida's panhandle, to the turning basin in Brownsville, Texas. Distances on the GIWW are given in statute miles east or west of Harvey Lock, on the west bank of the *Mississippi River* in New Orleans, Louisiana. The east end of the GIWW, at Carrabelle is Mile 376.2 EHL (east of Harvey Lock) and the west end, in the Brownsville turning Basin, is Mile 681.8 WHL (west of Harvey Lock).

North

West (Not to Scale) East

South

Tennessee Tombigbee Waterway

Brazos River

Texas

Louisiana

Mississippi River

Mississippi

Alabama

Port Allen Lock

Lake Charles

Baton Rouge

Mobile

Gulfport

Pensacola

Panama City

Florida

Port Arthur

Morgan City

30—

Houston

—30

Colorado River

Apalachicola

Freeport

Galveston

Bayou Boeuf Lock (Mile 93 WHL)

Carrabelle, Mile 376.2 East of Harvey Lock

Brazos River Gates (Mile 400.6 WHL)

Leland Bowman Lock (Mile 163 WHL)

Colorado River Locks (Mile 441.5 WHL)

Calcasieu Lock (Mile 238.2 WHL)

28—

—28

Corpus Christi

Gulf of

Mexico

New Orleans, Harvey Lock GIWW Mile 0

Brownsville, Mile 681.8 West of Harvey Lock

Inner Harbor Navigation Canal Lock (Mile 6.5 EHL)

Algiers Lock, GIWW Alternate Route

—26

MEXICO

The

Gulf Intracoastal Waterway (GIWW)

96   94   86   84

the shoals to Ochlockonee Bay, gone up the bay to the Ochlockonee River, then upstream on the Ochlockonee to the Crooked River and down the Crooked River to Carrabelle and St. George Sound.

If the Carrabelle-to-St. Marks project had been completed, the Ochlockonee and Crooked Rivers would have been straightened and dredged to a depth of at least 9 feet. The straightening, dredging and spoil islands resulting from the dredging, would have altered the regional drainage and the fresh-saltwater balance,

174

degrading the regional environment. It would also have encouraged real estate development and everything that goes with waterfront subdivisions. The extension was never funded and, except for surveys, no work was ever done. But the dormant project, never de-authorized, remains on the books.

We reached the East Pass Green 3 at about 11:40 a.m. and by noon we were in St. George Sound and headed west on the Gulf Intracoastal Waterway (the GIWW.) We followed the Waterway through St. George Sound to Apalachicola, passed under the U.S. Route 98/319 Bridge (GIWW mile 351.4 EHL) and continued west to Gulf County Florida's White City Park (GIWW mile 329.3 EHL.) Gulf County allows transient boats to tie up for the night in the park. It was a long day, one of the longer days on the trip to Texas; over 100 statute miles, with much of the day spent in the open waters of the Gulf of Mexico.

When we tied up at the White City Park two boats were already there: a large trawler type yacht with some rather unfriendly people and their paid captain aboard and a former stone crab boat that was being used as a dive boat by several young men, professional divers, who were log diving. The great Longleaf pine forest that spread over the southeastern United States from Virginia to Texas was one of the largest forest systems in North America. All of the ports along the gulf coast from Florida's panhandle to Houston were timber ports. The ports were at the mouths of rivers and whole logs, squared and partially squared (two sides) timbers and rough-cut planks were floated down to the coast and loaded onto waiting ships for export to the rapidly growing cities of the east coast and to ports all over the world. In part because of their high resin content, large, mature longleaf logs are heavy, barely float and sometimes sink. The log divers worked for a company that recovered old, sunken longleaf pine (and other) logs for the specialty wood products industry. The divers would locate logs worth salvaging, attach a float and record their location. Later a work barge would recover the logs.

The Gulf Intracoastal Waterway (GIWW) follows the upper Gulf Coast for 1,057 statute miles, from the Carrabelle, Florida, harbor channel to the middle of the turning basin in the port of Brownsville, Texas. Distances on the GIWW are measured in statute miles east or west of the Harvey Lock, one of the two locks that pass vessels through the Mississippi River's west bank levee in New Orleans. When we tied up for the night at White City Park, we were 329.3 miles EHL...East of Harvey Lock. We were also almost exactly on the divide between Eastern and Central Time. From Hyannis, Massachusetts, to the dock in the White City Park, we had been on Eastern Time, in the morning, when we started west, we'd be on Central Time...Texas Time.

The east end of the GIWW, Mile 376.2 EHL (East of Harvey Lock), is in the Carrabelle, Florida, harbor channel at 29°47.5'N., 84°40.4'W., approximately 3.7 miles from the head of the dredged channel in the town of Carrabelle and 3.3 miles from the open waters of the Gulf of Mexico via East Pass. GIWW Mile Mark Zero is at 29°54.5'N., 90°5.0'W., the center of the chamber of the Harvey Lock in New Orleans. And the west end of the GIWW, Mile 681.8 WHL (West of Harvey Lock), is in the center of the turning basin at the head of the Port of Brownsville, Texas, at approximately 25°57.07'N., 97°24.0'W.

The waterway crosses the shipping channel in Mobile Bay at GIWW mile 133.6 EHL. East of the crossing the Gulf Intracoastal Waterway is similar to the Atlantic Intracoastal Waterway between Norfolk, Virginia, and Morehead City, North Carolina; predominantly a beach resort and pleasure vessel waterway but with a noticeable commercial fishing presence and, after years of decline, increasing commercial freight traffic. From Mobile Bay west to the Mississippi River the GIWW carries a large volume of commercial traffic. But because it is moving on the open waters of Mobile Bay, Mississippi Sound and Lake Borgne, and the principle barge terminals are also big ship ports, the volume of barge traffic is not as noticeable as it would be on a narrow, hemmed in canal. From the Mississippi River west to Corpus Christi, Texas, many of the inlets, bays, rivers and lateral channels are heavily used by pleasure vessels and commercial fishing vessels are abundant, but the GIWW channel is first and foremost a commercial, freight waterway. From Corpus Christi west to Port Isabel, the GIWW runs through the remote Laguna Madre and, compared to sections further east, is relatively little used. Port Isabel, the South Padre Island resort area and the Port of Brownsville are clustered along the GIWWs final twenty-five miles.

A Rivers and Harbors Act in 1930 authorized, and funded, the construction of a 9-foot-deep by 100-foot-wide Intracoastal Waterway channel from Pensacola to New Orleans and the Mississippi River. A second Act, passed in 1935, extended the 9-foot channel east from Pensacola to St. Georges Sound. At its western end the waterway was routed through the Rigolets to Lake Pontchartrain and it connected to the Mississippi River through the Port of New Orleans's Inner Harbor Navigation Canal and Lock, a toll canal constructed by the Port of New Orleans between 1918 and 1923.[36] The Inner Harbor Navigation Canal and Lock remained under the control of and were operated by the Port of New Orleans. With the completion of these projects in September 1936 a continuous channel at least 9 feet deep by 100 feet wide was open from St. George Sound to the Mississippi River.

On July 23, 1942, as part of the war effort during World War II, Congress authorized enlarging the GIWW between its east end in

St. George Sound, Florida and Bon Secour Bay on the east side of Mobile Bay and between the Rigolets and Corpus Christi, Texas from a depth of 9 feet for a width of 100 feet to a depth of 12 feet for a width of 125 feet. In Mobile Bay, through the Pass au Herons and in the open waters of Mississippi Sound, the authorized project width was increased to 150 feet. As part of this project, the GIWW in New Orleans was re-routed to its present alignment, by-passing the Rigolets and Lake Pontchartrain. And in 1944, the USACE was authorized to lease the Inner Harbor Navigation Canal Lock and the section of the Inner Harbor Navigation Canal between the Lock and the re-aligned GIWWs junction with the canal from the Port of New Orleans. As part of the lease agreement, the toll charged commercial vessels was eliminated.

In White City, Florida, on the line between eastern and central time, sunrise came early. By 6:00 am, we were off the White City Park dock and headed west through the land cut that carries the GIWW behind Port St. Joe, St. Joseph Bay and Cape San Blass. At mile 328 EHL we passed the Gulf County Canal, a six-mile-long lateral extension of the GIWW that connects the waterway to Port St. Joe and St. Joseph Bay.[37] At approximately mile 310 EHL, the land cut and dredged channel through South Wetappo Creek merges almost imperceptibly into East St. Andrews Bay. Twenty miles further west the GIWW passes: Panama City, St. Andrew (with its large and well protected commercial and charter fishing basin) and, on Dyer's Point at the entrance to West St. Andrews Bay, the Port facilities of Panama City Harbor. Panama City Harbor was 105th on the USACE's 2016 list of domestic ports by tonnage. The approach channel from the Gulf of Mexico through the New Cut is maintained at 34 feet. St. Andrews Bay from the approach channel to the Panama City Harbor docks is naturally deeper than

34 feet. The tide gages in the New Cut and at Panama City show a diurnal tide with a daily range of less than half a foot.

Originally St. Andrews Bay had two natural entrances, known as the East Channel and the West Channel, which were separated by a small island named Hurricane Island. The wide shoal area at the east end of today's Shell Island, identified on modern charts as the St. Andrew Bay East Entrance Channel, is what is left of the former West Channel, Hurricane Island and East Channel. The West channel was essentially unnavigable but the broader, deeper East Channel, although it had a dangerous, breaking bar and numerous shifting shoals, was used by the early Spanish, French and British and was used by American residents until the second decade of the twentieth century.

In 1910, Congress authorized and funded a project to dredge a 22-foot-deep channel through the East Channel. In September 1926 the area was hit by a major hurricane, Hurricane Island was largely washed away and the 22-foot channel partially filled in. The channel was restored, but by 1934 the remnants of Hurricane Island had subsided into a series of shoals and the constantly shifting sands were making the 22-foot channel almost impossible to maintain. The New Cut, the current straight, rock-jettied, deep entrance to St. Andrews Bay was created between 1935 and 1938 when the USACE cut a channel through the peninsula west of the Bay's natural entrance. The seven-mile-long section of cut off peninsula became today's Shell Island.

Eleven miles past the Port of Panama City we left the deep waters of West St. Andrews Bay and entered the dredged channel to and up West Bay Creek. At mile 267 EHL we entered the thirteen-mile-long "Little Grand Canyon" land cut that connects West Bay Creek and West Bay to Peach Creek and Choctawhatchee Bay. The Little Grand Canyon Cut was the most difficult land cut on the GIWW. The banks of the cut reach a height of 40 feet above mean sea level. With the current GIWW project depth of 12 feet, the banks of the cut, from project depth to 40 feet above mean sea level are 52 feet high and the entire cut is through nearly pure sand...unconsolidated, easily eroded beach deposits and relic dunes. Wind, waves and boat wakes are constantly chewing at the unconsolidated sand. Small sand slides and slumps are common and large land slumps can completely close the waterway.

Choctawhatchee Bay is approximately 35 miles in length, east to west, and between 3 and 6 miles wide. Except for the dredged channels at each end, the bay is deep along the charted GIWW route. Choctawhatchee Bay's only natural inlet from the Gulf of Mexico, East Pass (locally known as Destin Pass), is toward the bay's west end, between the major beach resort cities of Destin, on the east side and Fort Walton Beach, to the west. East Pass, plagued by shifting sand bars and shoals that had, at times, closed the pass, was dredged in 1929 to provide a deeper, more permanent small craft[38] navigation channel.

Florida's Emerald Coast, as defined by the Florida State Department of Tourism and the Florida Chamber of Commerce begins at the small resort town of Mexico Beach, located at the entrance to St. Joseph Bay just a few miles from port St. Joe, and extends west through Panama City to Destin, Fort Walton Beach and Pensacola, to the Alabama-Florida State Line. Mexico Beach is an outlier, really a part of the "Forgotten Coast." The true beginning of the Emerald Coast–also known as Floribama, south Alabama (or South Georgia) and/or The Redneck Riviera–is the west side of the St. Andrews Bay Inlet and it does not magically end at the state line; Orange Beach, Gulf Shores and Fort Morgan Alabama are very much a part of it.

Chapter 6

This section of the coast receives its fair share of tropical cyclones. While the eye of a particular storm may not have made landfall on the Emerald Coast, since 1995 the waves and storm surges of at least 13 named storms have swept ashore on the soft, fine grain, easily eroded and transported sands of the Emerald Coast's beaches: hurricanes Opel and Erin (1995), hurricanes Earl and Georges (1998), tropical storm Isidore (2002), hurricane Ivan (2004), hurricanes Dennis, Katrina and Rita (2005), tropical storm Ida (2009), hurricane Gustav, tropical storm Debby (2012) and, in 2018 major hurricane Michael. With the exception of military facilities, parks and a few, small, protected natural areas the Emerald Coasts beaches are heavily developed and vulnerable. All of the resorts built on sand along this low, easily eroded shore have been damaged by, and rebuilt after, named storms and their beaches have been nourished...rebuilt...often multiple times. Panama City Beach, at the east end of the Emerald Coast, was rebuilt by the USACE, in 1998, 2005 and 2011 at a cumulative cost in excess of fifty million dollars. Michael guaranteed the need to rebuild...again.

At approximately mile 224 EHL, the GIWW enters Fort Walton Beach and the narrows between Santa Rosa Island and the mainland. At 4:00 p.m., after yet another over 100-mile day, we tied up at the public dock in Fort Walton Beach's Landing Park (GIWW mile 223 EHL.) Landing Park is popular with transient boats because there is a large supermarket less than a quarter mile from the dock and, a couple hundred feet from the dock there's an Irish themed tap room with a large bank of beer taps...all good craft beers...and decent sandwiches and burgers.

From Fort Walton Beach we continued west through the narrows between Santa Rosa Island and the mainland to GIWW mile 205 EHL where we entered Santa Rosa Sound. At the west end of the sound, we crossed the entrance to Pensacola Bay, once guarded by Fort Pickens (on the west end of Santa Rosa Island, built 1829-1834) and Fort McRee (on the east end of Perdido Key, built 1834-1839) and entered the narrow, shoal prone entrance to Big Lagoon.

Pensacola Pass, naturally navigable, was used from the earliest days of European exploration and settlement. The first known explorer was the Spaniard Diego Miruelo, who sailed into Pensacola Bay in 1516, just twenty-four years after Columbus's first voyage to the new world. Today the Caucus Channel and the Caucus Cut, dredged to and maintained at a controlling depth of 44 feet[39] for modern naval vessels, runs through the pass that Miruelo sailed through almost half a millennium ago. The small commercial port of Pensacola Harbor was ranked 136th on the USACE's 2012 list of domestic ports by tonnage. In 2016, although still an internationally connected sea port, tonnage had dropped and Pensacola was unranked.

From mile 175 EHL to mile 171 EHL the GIWW is a channel dredged through the narrow, winding and shoal waterway that connects the Big Lagoon to Perdido Bay. When we rounded the second bend in the narrows, we found ourselves looking at the front end of a large tow. We pulled over into thin water as far from the dredged channel as we could get and watched as the tow went by...8 coal filled open hopper barges and a large pushboat. An 8-barge tow is over 1,000 feet long. To swing around the bends in the channel, he needed the entire channel and then some. The water behind him was brown, so clouded with sand and silt that our depth sounder's emergency alarm went off and the display screen went blank.

At approximately GIWW mile 167 EHL the waterway reaches, and for several miles follows, the Alabama-Florida state line, which runs down the center of Perdido Bay to Perdido Pass and the Gulf of Mexico. We continued west through: Perdido Bay, Wolf Bay, Portage Creek and the land cut to Bon Secour Bay. In the land cut we caught up with and passed a westbound pushboat with two hopper barge loads of scrap metal. We had heard him on the VHF radio talking to the large eastbound coal tow and he was now talking to another eastbound tow somewhere ahead of us; they were deciding where to meet and safely pass. The tows were using channel 13. When we are driving the GIWW we monitor VHF channels 9 (vessel to vessel hailing), 13 (inter-ship navigation safety) and 16 (hailing and distress, monitored by the United States Coast Guard)–commercial vessels on the waterway general use channel 13 when talking to each other, the bridge tenders in Florida use channel 9, the bridge tenders in Alabama, Mississippi, Louisiana and Texas use channel 13 and lockkeepers are generally on channel 14.

We met the second eastbound tow, two massive LNG (Liquefied Natural Gas) barges, as we were coming out onto Bon Secour Bay, the large shallow bulge on the east side of Mobile Bay. From Bon Secour Bay to the Pass au Herons, The GIWW traces a 22.5-mile course across Bon Secour and Mobile Bays. In Bon Secour Bay, shrimp boats were working the flats both north and south of the dredged channel. As we approached the Mobile Bay shipping channel, we could see three sea going ships in the channel: a container ship and a tanker upbound to Mobile and a heavily loaded bulk carrier down bound to the sea. West of the channel a westbound tow was in the GIWW and to the north, further up Mobile Bay there were several more tows.

The waterway crosses the Mobile Bay shipping channel at GIWW mile 133.6 EHL (30°16.5'N and 88°09'W); 3 miles above Mobile Light (on Mobile Point, the eastern point at the mouth of the bay) and approximately 25.5 miles below Mobile Harbor. Mobile Harbor was ranked 10th on the USACE's list of domestic ports by tonnage in both 2012 and 2016. The Mean Lower Low Water controlling depths for the Mobile Harbor shipping channel are: 47 feet for a width of 600 feet in the Bar Channel, 45 feet for a width of 400 feet in the Lower Bay Channel, 43 feet for a width of 400 feet in the Upper Bay Channel and 42 feet in the Upper Bay Turning Basin. The tidal range in Mobile Bay, from Mean Lower Low Water, is 3 feet.

At the head of Mobile Bay, the Mobile River leads to an extensive network of inland waterways: the Alabama and Coosa Rivers, the Tombigbee River, the Black Warrior River and the Tennessee-Tombigbee Waterway (the Tenn-Tom) which connects the entire system to the Tennessee, Ohio, Cumberland and Mississippi Rivers. The Alabama and Coosa Rivers are no longer used commercially but they do serve pleasure vessels and there is no reason that they could not again carry commercial traffic. The Tenn-Tom was completed on December 12, 1984 and opened to freight on January 10, 1985. On opening day, the *Eddie Waxler* pushed almost three million gallons of petroleum products up the waterway (https://www.history.tenntom.org/.)

It was a clear, almost calm day and from the intersection of the GIWW and the shipping channel, with the help of our binoculars, we could clearly see Fort Morgan on Mobile Point, east of the Inlet and the smaller and lower Fort Gains, on Pelican Point (the tip of Dauphin Island) west of the inlet. Fort Morgan was built as a star fort (an equal sided pentagon with five bastions) between 1818 and 1834. Fort Gains, intended to be a twin of Fort Morgan, was started in 1818 but work on the incomplete fort stopped in 1821 when Congress cancelled funding. Work resumed, on an altered more modern design in 1857. In January 1861, at the start of the Civil

War, both Fort Morgan and the still incomplete Fort Gains were captured by the Alabama State Militia. Fort Gaines was completed, following the USACE's 1857 plans, by Confederate engineers.

By the summer of 1864, Federal forces held the Mississippi River and all but two significant southern ports east of the river. On the Atlantic Coast, Wilmington, North Carolina, on the Cape Fear River and, on the Gulf Coast, Mobile, remained under Confederate control. At sunrise (5:57 a.m.) on August 5, 1864, Admiral David Glasgow Farragut, victor at the battle of New Orleans and naval commander at Vicksburg, led his fleet through the Mobile channel and into Mobile Bay–past the guns of Fort Morgan and Fort Gaines, through the Confederate mine field and past (pre-war friend and rival) Confederate Admiral Franklin Buchanan's powerful ironclad the *CSS Tennessee* and its supporting gun boats. By 8:30 a.m. the federal fleet was anchored across the Mobile channel between three and four miles inside Mobile Bay, about a mile north of where the GIWW now crosses the shipping channel.

Almost as soon as the federal fleet was anchored, Admiral Buchanan took the *Tennessee* out from under the shelter of Fort Morgan's guns and moved north to attack the anchored fleet. After a short, brisk naval battle, a shot from the federal monitor *USS Chickasaw* shattered the *Tennessee's* exposed rudder quadrant and steering chains. Unable to maneuver and under fire from half dozen federal vessels…the *Tennessee* surrendered. The surrender took place on the west side of the channel and just below today's GIWW. Fort Gaines surrendered on August 8th and Fort Morgan on August 23rd.[40]

In the late afternoon we passed under the Dauphine Island Bridge (GIWW mile 127.8 EHL), went through the Pass au Herons and turned south, into the back channel to Dauphin Bay and the Dauphine Island Marina. In the evening we took a long walk around a small part of what was, that evening, a very quiet, very pleasant island.

We had last visited the Dauphin Island Marina on January 6-7, 2011. On that visit it was not quiet. Eight months earlier, on April 20, 2010, forty miles off southeast Louisiana, on the Macondo Prospect oil field, British Petroleum's Deepwater Horizon semi-submersible offshore oil rig had exploded. The cleanup was still in full swing. FEMA, the Federal Emergency Management Agency, had a large crew based on Dauphin Island. Some of their boats were working out of the marina, coming and going at all hours, the marina restaurant was leased to FEMA as a dining hall for their crews and the smell of crude petroleum lingered thickly around piles of blackened, oil soaked floating containment boom and other gear in the parking lot and on some of the boats.

West of Florida, with the exception of a broad shoal that separates the west side of Mobile Bay from Mississippi Sound, a natural, semi-protected, navigable waterway extends along the gulf coast from Bon Secour, on the east side of Mobile Bay, across Mobile Bay and west through Mississippi Sound and Lake Borgne to the dredged channel that leads the GIWW into New Orleans's inner harbor. The shoal, approximately a mile and a half wide at its narrowest point runs north to south across the two and a quarter mile wide gap between Cedar Point on the mainland and Dauphin Island's North Point. This shoal choked gap is the Pass au Herons. At low tide the shoal is covered by barely a foot or two of water and is studded with drying bars and oyster reefs; except for a 2 to 3-foot-deep area approximately a third of a mile wide toward the Dauphin Island side. This slightly deeper, shifting and unstable area, little more than a broad tidal wash over, is the natural channel through the Pass au Herons.

The shoal blocking the Pass au Herons was a serious impediment to safe coastal navigation between Mobile Bay and New Orleans. Unlike Wappoo Creek south of Charleston, here the tide offered little help, the Alabama and Mississippi coasts have a true diurnal tide, one high and one low per day and the mean tidal range is less than 2 feet. Even shoal draft coastal vessels generally had to cross the dangerous bar at the mouth of Mobile Bay and sail west outside the coastal barrier islands. In 1828 Congress appropriated eighteen thousand dollars "For deepening the channel through the Pass au Heron, near the Bay of Mobile." Work ceased and the project was abandoned in 1830 after a major storm erased everything that had been accomplished.

In 1839, the General Assembly of Alabama passed an Act granting Captain John Grant the right to "cut or excavate a channel or canal through the shoal and shell reefs obstructing the inland navigation between Dauphin Island and Cedar Point." The Grant-of-Rights was to run for 25 years (until 1864), during which time Capt. Grant would have exclusive rights to any channel through the Pass au Heron and, to cover costs, would be able to charge vessels using his cut "a toll or tonnage duty at a rate not to exceed 15 cents per registered ton."

Captain Grant began dredging immediately following passage of the Act, and by the fall of 1839, at an estimated cost of $100,000 (entirely his own money) he had dredged a navigable cut with a mean lower low water depth of 6 feet from Mobile Bay to Mississippi Sound. The cut was later deepened to 8½ feet and was

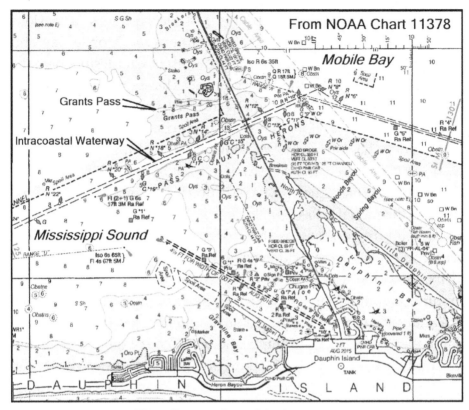

The Pass Aux Herons

maintained at that depth by periodic dredging. Captain Grant's rights to his pass expired in 1864, during the Civil War. The Captain was a strong Union supporter and, on October 23, 1865, the Federal Military Headquarters of the Department of Alabama, in Mobile, under the authority of the Secretary of War, and with the approval of the President, reinstated Captain Grant's rights. The courts upheld the order of reinstatement, and in the final ruling, issued in May 1868, the Supreme Court of Louisiana upheld Captain Grant. The Captain removed obstacles to navigation that Confederate forces had placed in Grants Pass and by 1869 had restored the navigable depth to 8½ feet.

Captain Grant died in New Orleans on April 4, 1887, but maintenance had ceased before his death and Grants Pass had begun to silt in and deteriorate. However as late as 1908 the pass was still in use and was considered by the Corps of Engineers to be private property.[41] Grants Pass still exists and is named and clearly defined on modern nautical charts. In two Bills passed in 1912 and 1913, Congress authorized dredging of a channel through the Pass au Herons or purchasing. Grants Pass. The Corps of Engineers advised against buying the old pass and cut a new channel...the GIWW...through the Pass au Heron shoals 1200-1400 feet south of the old channel.

Wednesday, June 5, 2013, we continued west on Mississippi Sound...glad that we had put in three long days. For several days NOAA had been issuing advisories on Invest 91, a low-pressure system in the Gulf of Mexico that was tracking northeast toward Florida's Big Bend. The system had been getting better organized and stronger and it was now expected to become the first named system of the 2013 Atlantic hurricane season. Westbound on Mississippi Sound we had easterly winds and a low, choppy following sea; possibly the outermost edge of Invest 91.

Mississippi Sound–between the mainland and the barrier islands of the Gulf Islands National Seashore–ranges from 4.5 to 14 miles wide, extends east-west for approximately 80 miles between the Pass au Herons and Lake Borgne, averages 10 feet in depth and has a diurnal tide with an average range of less than 2 feet. Water depths in the bays and bayous along the mainland shore are influenced more by wind than by tide; northerly winds blow the water out, southerlies blow it back in and winds blowing east or west, down the length of the sound can create rough, even dangerous, conditions.

Pirates? Well...sort of. On the north shore of Mississippi Sound, just west of the Pass au Herons, at the end of a long, dredged channel sits Bayou La Batre, the "Seafood Capital of Alabama." Bayou La Batre is a major commercial fishing and shrimping port and a center for building and repairing fishing vessels and work boats. In 2006 Disney Studios had the Steiner Shipyard in Bayou La Batre convert a three-year-old, 106-foot-long modern steel work boat named *Sunset*, into the *Black Pearl*. The ship 'sailed' (there were big diesel engines in that steel hull) by Capt. Jack (Johnny Depp) Sparrow in several of the Pirates of the Caribbean movies. The *Black Pearl* was an elaborate wooden superstructure built on the *Sunset*.

At GIWW mile 104.2 EHL we crossed the dredged ship channel that leads from Horn Island Pass to Pascagoula, Mississippi and the port of Pascagoula Harbor, 24th on the USACE's 2016 list of Domestic Ports by tonnage. There are two sections to the port, the Pascagoula River and, to the east, Bayou Casotte. The dredged channel from the sea buoy out in the gulf to the turning basin in the Pascagoula River is 21.2 miles long and, in 2014, the channels controlling depth was 35.6 feet. The dredged channel to the turning basin in Bayou Casotte was 18.6 miles long and had a controlling depth of 35 feet. Pascagoula, like Biloxi, Gulfport and all the other gulf coastal communities between Mobile Bay and New Orleans was badly damaged by Hurricane Katrina in 2005.

Fifteen miles further west we passed the GIWW end of the 9.5-foot-deep by 150 feet wide dredged channel to Biloxi, Mississippi. The Port of Biloxi Harbor was ranked 144th on the USACE's 2016 list of domestic ports by tonnage and the freight handled was all barge tonnage. Biloxi may not be a deep-water port, but it is a major shrimping center and the self-proclaimed shrimp capital of the gulf coast and/or the United States (a title also claimed by several other gulf coast fishing ports.) In the early mornings the commercial fishing docks morph into a seafood market–gulf shrimp and whatever else the boats brought in is sold, fresh, often still alive, right off the boats.

Biloxi is an interesting and enjoyable place to visit. With nine casinos in or close, Biloxi rivals Lake Charles, Louisiana, for the dubious honor of being the Las Vegas of the gulf coast. In addition to the casinos there is good shopping and dining and there are three good museums: the Ohr-O'keefe Museum of Art, designed by noted architect Frank Gehrey, the Maritime and Seafood Industry Museum and Beauvoir, the final home of Jefferson Davis–U.S. Military Officer, U.S. Senator, first and only President of the Confederacy.

The Ohr-O'Keefe Museum of Arts' primary exhibit is works by the master American Potter George Ohr (1857-1918). But the museum also mounts excellent traveling exhibits and exhibits by good local artists and it has a very pleasant small cafe and a gift shop. The Maritime and Seafood Industry Museum, housed in a new three-story building at 115 E. 1st Street, in Gulf Marine Park on Point Cadet, pays homage to Biloxi's long, rich maritime and fishing/shrimping history. Beauvoir includes Jefferson Davis's nicely restored home, the Jefferson Davis Presidential Library, a museum and a large gift shop. The gift shop was interesting, in addition to a surprisingly good collection of civil war literature and the inevitable confederate iconographic hagiography, there were a few paintings, at least one of which was on velvet, of…Elvis Presley? Gift shops have to sell what sells.

Pre Katrina, we visited and enjoyed Gulfport, Mississippi several times but we had not stopped there since Katrina. When we reached the dredged ship channel to Gulfport (GIWW mile 72.8 EHL,) we cut the day short and stayed for the night. After the boat was tucked in, we walked through several blocks of streets, sidewalks, foundations, parking lots and scrubby grass that pre-Katrina, had been part of Gulfport's historic district. In the part of old downtown Gulfport that had been restored...or spared...we ate dinner in the bar at the Half Shell Oyster House. There was a TV at the end of the bar and half way through dinner an announcer broke into whatever game was on and said that Invest 91 was now Tropical Storm Andrea, the first named Atlantic Basin storm of 2013.

Pre-Katrina a restaurant, partially built on pilings, sat on the end of the seawall that protected the east and south sides of the Gulfport small craft basin. The restaurant's shrimp, fish and oysters came right off the boat, no middle men. The first time we ate there, after we were seated, Betty asked our waitress if the restaurant served wine. The waitress leaned over and said "honey, we got any kind of wine y'all want...we got red, we got pink and we got white." That restaurant fell to Katrina and there was little left of the once large commercial fishing fleet that formerly crowded the basin.

The deep-water port of Gulfport Harbor was ranked 115th on the USACE's 2016 list of domestic ports by tonnage. The channel from deep water in the gulf to the port facilities runs through the pass between Ship Island and Cat Island and is almost 21 miles long. A USACE survey in July of 2015 put the controlling depth at 36 feet. Gulfport Harbor is totally man made, there is: no natural shelter, no coastal island, no bayou or river mouth, not even a natural coastal indentation. The stone, concrete and earth quays and seawalls stick straight out into the open sound. With the larger and better protected ports of Mobile and Pascagoula to the east and the huge complex of port facilities on the Mississippi River to the west, there would seem to be little justification for spending scarce resources on the dredged deep-water channel to, and on the big ship facilities in, Gulfport Harbor. Except, of course, politics.

7. New Orleans and the Mississippi River

Thursday, June 6, leaving Gulfport our goal for the day was to park *Nauset* at the Seabrook Harbor Marina–on the Inner Harbor Navigation Canal and just 4 miles from the Inner Harbor Navigation Canal Lock and the Mississippi River–and then go into New Orleans for a good dinner. At mile 39.8 EHL, we passed the Pearl River and entered Louisiana and at mile 35 EHL, we entered the Rigolets-New Orleans Cut and continued on the GIWW rather than taking the old waterway route through the Rigolets and across Lake Pontchartrain to New Orleans and the Inner Harbor Navigation Canal. Two miles further west we passed the Blind Rigolets and a major piece of oil patch industrial detritus, an old, abandoned oil platform slowly rusting away, returning to nature in the marsh. I had taking several pictures of the thing on past trips, so I took another one; a 15-year record of rusting decay.

At mile 22.5 the waterway crossed Chef Menteur Pass, a natural deep-water connection between Lake Pontchartrain, to our north, and Lake Borgne, to our south. Across Lake Borgne from Chef Menteur, the Lake Borgne Canal Company built a 6-mile-long toll canal between the west side of Lake Borgne and the village of Violet, on the Mississippi River (10 miles below Canal Street.) The

An abandoned oil platform in Louisiana

canal, completed in 1884 and in operation until World War 1, had a depth of 5½-6 feet and a 40-foot-wide by 280-foot-long lock in the Mississippi levee at Violet. In 1908 the toll was 30 cents per gross registered ton, which included passage through the canal and lockage."[42] The old canal, now called The Violet Canal, is still shown on nautical charts, is still navigable and is still in use, although the lock that connected the canal to the Mississippi is closed and largely buried under the levee (the remains of the canal end gate are visible). In Violet, at the river end of the canal, there are two launch ramps, a few docks, a small barge terminal and several other marine related businesses.

In the early afternoon, as we were approaching Flood Gate H just east of the Michoud Canal, the Captain of a passing push boat called

"*Nauset*, you headed west?"

"Yes, Houston."

"Do you know that Algiers is closed?"

He added that he did not think they were letting pleasure boats through, said we had a cute boat, wished us a good day and continued east.

At mile 13.8 EHL we passed the Michoud Slip, on our right, and, on our left, to the south, the former Mississippi River Gulf Outlet Canal (the MRGO.) Political pressure from the State of Louisiana, New Orleans and Gulf Coast business interests for a shorter and safer route from the Port of New Orleans to the Gulf of Mexico began as early as 1852. In 1944 the Louisiana Legislature empowered the governor to "aid and assist the federal government" in building a canal from the eastern side of the Mississippi River at New Orleans to the Gulf of Mexico. The Mississippi River Gulf Outlet was authorized by Congress in the Rivers and Harbors Act of March 29, 1956 (Public Law 84-455.) The canal opened to navigation in 1965 and was completed to project specifications–a depth of 36 feet for a bottom width of 500 feet and a surface width of 650 feet–in 1968.

The MRGO was cut through easily eroded marshes and swamps and within twenty years of completion the surface width of the canal was estimated to have more than doubled, to have eroded to…been washed away to…an average width of 1,500 feet. In 1998, aboard our sailboat with its 5½ foot draft, we left the Orleans Marina on Lake Pontchartrain, went through the Inner Harbor Navigation Canal and down the MRGO. At the FL Red 98 Channel Marker we left the dredged channel, turned toward the marsh grass and, 100 yards past the marker, we anchored…safely…in 8-10 feet of water where less than 30 years earlier tall green marsh grass grew.[43] Waves and the wakes of ships and boats had eroded the marsh to a depth of 8-10 feet for hundreds of feet past the edges of the channel.

In 2005 the wide, washed out swath of open water along the MRGO funneled Hurricane Katrina's surge into the Inner Harbor; probably contributing significantly to the failure of the seawalls and levees along the Inner Harbor Canal and the subsequent flooding. In June 2006, Congress directed the Secretary of the Army, acting through the Chief of Engineers, to plan for the de-authorization and closure of the MRGO. In January 2008 the Chief of Engineers submitted a closure and environmental restoration plan to Congress, which was returned approved on June 5, 2008. Work on a broad earth and rock dam across the MRGO at Bayou La Loutre (29°49.3'N 89°35.7'W) began almost immediately and the closure structure was completed in July 2009.[44] Part of the new levee/seawall system around New Orleans was later run straight across the MRGO a mile and a half below its former junction with the GIWW...a second closure.

We continued on to the Seabrook Harbor Marina. When we were tied-up, I walked up to the office, checked in and asked about the Algiers Lock.

It was closed until further notice, a key piece in the old locks gate control mechanism had failed. Complicating the situation, there had been weeks of heavy rain in parts of the upper Mississippi basin and the river was high, full of debris and running at a fast five to seven knots. When locking through to or from the river, the difference between the river's level and the level of the water behind the levees, expressed in feet, is called the "head." It's the feet a vessel will rise or drop in the lock. In New Orleans Phase 1 Flood Restrictions go into effect when the head reaches +11 feet–when the Mississippi reaches eleven feet higher than the surface of the water behind the levee. The day we arrived the head at the Inner Harbor Navigation Canal Lock was +12.5 feet.

The Algiers Lock was completed in 1956 and it is the larger of the two locks that pass vessels through the Mississippi's west bank levee in New Orleans–the lock chamber is 75 feet wide, 760 feet long and the depth over the sills is 13 feet. In 2011 11,522 vessels carrying 25 million plus tons of assorted commodities passed through the Algiers Lock. The older, shorter and slower Harvey Lock–with a lock chamber 75-feet wide, 415-feet long with a depth over the sills of 12-feet–was completed in 1934. In 2011 the Harvey Lock handled 7,431 vessels, but barely 2 million tons of cargo. Multi-barge tows and larger vessels use the Algiers lock, while the Harvey Lock and the congested narrow Harvey Canal are used by: single barge tows, light boats (push boats with no barges), crew boats, fishing vessels and most pleasure vessels.

With the Algiers lock out of commission, multi-barge tows that would normally have used the larger lock were forced to use the Harvey Lock and Canal. To go through the shorter Harvey Lock and navigate the narrow Harvey Canal, the large tows had to break down, go through a few barges at a time and re-assemble past the narrow section of the canal. A slow process. The afternoon we reached New Orleans the wait time for commercial vessels at the Harvey Lock was 86 hours.

The push boat Captain had been correct. Private pleasure vessels were not being allowed through the locks or on the river.

Over dinner in the French Quarter, we considered our options. While we were enjoying dinner, Tropical Storm Andrea made its landfall near Steinhatchee, Florida. At landfall Andrea's strongest winds were 55 miles per hour, down from a peak of approximately 65 miles per hour. As a named storm Andrea lasted little more than 24 hours.

We had four options:

- We could just sit and wait for an unknown but possibly extended period of time.
- We could leave the boat in New Orleans, rent a car, drive home and return when the Algiers Lock had reopened and the river had settled down.

- The boat could be trucked. It is approximately 340 miles by road from the Seabrook Marina in New Orleans to Clear Lake, Texas, outside Houston.
- We could backtrack to Pass Christian or Gulfport and then continue west on the coastal route–south and west around most of the Louisiana Delta via Bayou Baptist Collette, Venice, Tiger Pass and points west. It's a long trip with few good stopping places. And we would have had to stay out on the coast to at least Vermilion Bay. To help decrease pressure on the New Orleans area levees the Corps of Engineers had increased the amount of water (normally 30% of the Mississippi's volume) diverted into the Atchafalaya through the Old River Control Structure–up the Mississippi, above Baton Rouge–so the Atchafalaya was running high too. At Morgan City where the GIWW crosses the Atchafalaya, the public dock was under water and the Floodgates were closed.

Tuesday, June 25, *Nauset* reached Clear Lake, Texas, on a large hydraulic trailer.

The Algiers Lock re-opened on July 18, 2013.

The Mississippi

The Mississippi River, the longest river in North America, flows 2,340 miles through the mid-continent from its source in Minnesota's Lake Itasca to the Louisiana Delta and the Gulf of Mexico. The Mississippi's watershed, the area drained by the Mississippi, covers 1.85 million square miles, more than one eighth of the entire North American Continent. An area that takes in all or part of 31 states (40 percent of the contiguous United States) and 2 Canadian provinces.[45]

The Louisiana Delta, roughly the 4,700 square miles of coastal plain and wetlands between what is left of the Chandeleur Islands on the east and Vermillion Bay on the west, is the post Late Wisconsin Glaciation active part of the Mississippi Delta–the geologically new low, flat and fragile land where the Mississippi flows into the Gulf of Mexico. This is the delta of Nouvellé Orleans, of: oysters, shrimp, crayfish and red fish, rice and beans, boudin and tabasco, the petroleum and petro-chemical industries, the Gulf Intracoastal Waterway, the great seaports of the lower Mississippi River and of vanishing wetlands and disappearing barrier islands. This part of the greater Mississippi Delta is both geologically and geographically separate and distinct from the older, upper delta; the Mississippi River and Yazoo River alluvial plain in Mississippi and the adjoining parts of southeastern Arkansas and northeastern Louisiana. This older, upper delta is the area that most people associate with the term Mississippi Delta.

At the Head of Passes near the bottom of the youngest, most recent, part of the Louisiana Delta, three of the passes, or mouths of the Mississippi converge–the shallow Pass a Loutre, the deeper South Pass and Southwest Pass, the main shipping channel. The Head of Passes East Jetty Light, the Junction Light, a Flashing Red/Green that flashes once every six seconds and is visible for five miles stands on the end of a jetty on the east side of Southwest Pass at the junction of South and Southwest Passes (at 29°09′N 89°15′W.) Mileage along the Mississippi River upstream from the Head of Passes to Cairo, Illinois, is Above Head of Passes, or AHP[46] and is measured in statute miles from the junction light...the Zero mileage marker. Points along the channel between the junction light and the open Gulf of Mexico are Below Head of Passes, or

201

BHP and are charted in nautical miles with Zero at the junction light.

The federal project depth for the lower Mississippi's deep-water ship channel is 45 feet from the Southwest Pass Entrance buoy (28°52.6'N, 89°25.9'W) to the fixed 65-foot-high U.S. Highway 190 Bridge in Baton Rouge just a few hundred yards downstream from mile 234 AHP. The last big ship terminal, the dock at the Formosa Plastics petrochemical plant on the east bank, is literally just downstream from the U.S. 190 Bridge. At night the lights on the upper works of chemical tankers at the dock seem dangerously close to the bridge and passengers in the cars on the eastbound lanes of the bridge (the south side) can see into the ships brightly lit bridge deck windows.

On the tide gage at Pilottown, 2 miles above the Head of Passes junction light, the Zero is Mean Sea Level. On the tide gage at the river end of the Inner Harbor Navigation Canal Lock, mile 92.7 AHP, the 0 mark is also Mean Sea Level. For 90 plus statute miles there is no gradient, the bottom of the 45-foot-deep navigation channel is 45 or more feet below Mean Sea Level. Only the large volume and strong current of the channelized and walled in Mississippi keeps its water fresh. In periods of drought, the river's reduced flow and weaker current allow sea water ingress, a wedge of brackish to sea salty water creeps up the deep channel under the fresh river water. The water intakes through which Plaquemines Parish draws its freshwater are not far below New Orleans and the intakes were in brackish water in 2012.

When Jean Baptiste le Moyne, Sieur de Bienville, founded Nouvellé-Orleans in 1718 the new city to be and future[47] capital of French Louisiana was built along the Mississippi's natural levee[48] in today's French Quarter. Even though the settlement was on the relatively higher levee, it still suffered from periodic flooding and

Sieur de la Tour, the French engineer who laid out the settlement, almost immediately ordered the construction of drainage ditches and a low earth levee in front of the settlement…a levee on a levee. By 1728 New Orleans is believed to have had a man-made levee along the settlements river side that was 3-4 feet high, 18 feet wide and almost a mile long. By 1735 low earthen levees extended from Caernarvon (mile 82 AHP) upstream to Bonnet Carre (mile 127.5 AHP) on both sides of the river. By the Louisiana Purchase and the acquisition of French Louisiana by the United States, almost continuous man-made levees extended from Caernarvon to Baton Rouge (mile 228 AHP) on the east bank and to somewhere in the vicinity of the Atchafalaya, the south side of Turnbull's Bend, on the west bank. Since then levee building and maintenance have never ceased.

Woldenberg Park runs along the Mississippi River Levee in New Orleans's historic French Quarter, from the French Market and the Café du Monde upstream past the steamboat *Natchez's* dock to the Audubon Aquarium and the Canal Street Ferry Terminal. There are pedestrian walkways on top of the levee for the length of the park and people on the walkways have an excellent view up and down the river, they can see a large part of the Port of New Orleans and, when the river is high, they can clearly see that the land behind the levee is below the level of the river. New Orleans is essentially a shallow depression rimmed by levees and cross cut by river and canal levees. Within the levees large areas are below sea level. While elevations in New Orleans range from 7 feet below to 20 feet above mean gulf sea level, the average elevation is approximately 1.5 feet below mean gulf sea level. On any clear, calm summer day, without floods, high water on the Mississippi or storm surges, if breeches magically appeared in the levees, water would flow in and much of the city would flood. That's today. For the future...the land is sinking...sea level is rising.

Strung out along the river from the Ergon tanker and barge facility at mile 2.4 AHP to the Formosa Plastics dock at the head of deep water navigation in Baton Rouge and on upstream to mile 253 AHP, the upstream limit of the Port of Baton Rouge, are hundreds of barge and deep water port facilities of all types: tanker terminals, container terminals, bulk docks for coal, grain and other commodities, roll-on/roll-off docks, a cruise ship terminal and barge facilities of every possible description. For administrative and political purposes all of these facilities...250 miles of the Mississippi...have been aggregated into four "ports" which, statistically, are among the largest ports in the United States. In upstream order on the USACE's list of domestic ports by tonnage:

- The Port of Plaquemines, 11th on the list, embraces all port facilities on both sides of the river between mile 0 at the Head of Passes and mile 81.2 AHP.

- The Port of New Orleans, 4th on the list, includes: the facilities on both sides of the river from mile 81.2 to mile 114.9 AHP, the facilities on the Harvey Canal, on the Inner Harbor Navigation Canal and on the GIWW between the Michaud Canal and the Inner Harbor Navigation Canal.

- The Port of South Louisiana, 1st on the list and the largest port in the United States in tonnage (and one of the largest in the world) includes all port facilities on both sides of the river between miles 114.9 and 168.5 AHP.

- The Port of Baton Rouge, 8th on the list, includes: all port facilities on both sides of the river between miles 168.5 and the head of deep-water navigation, the barge facilities on both sides of the river from the head of deep-water navigation to mile 253 AHP and the port facilities along the Baton Rouge Barge Canal (mile 235 AHP.)

Three locks pierce the levees in the Port of New Orleans: the Algiers Lock, the primary commercial route to the GIWW west of the Mississippi, is at mile 88.3 AHP; the Harvey Lock, mile Zero on the GIWW and the route west used by most pleasure vessels, is at mile 98.2 AHP; the Inner Harbor Navigation Canal Lock, which leads to the Inner Harbor, Lake Pontchartrain and the GIWW east of the Mississippi, is at mile 92.7 AHP. The Rivers and Harbors Act of March 29, 1956 authorized the replacement of the Inner Harbor Navigation Canal Lock "when economically justified by obsolescence or by increased traffic." In 1986 Congress reauthorized the project and established cost sharing requirements. Following reauthorization, the Port of New Orleans agreed to become the non-federal sponsor and by 2002 the Port had completed purchase of all necessary real estate. Upon completion of real estate acquisition by the Port of New Orleans, the USACE awarded the lock design contact. As of 2016 the project was on hold pending court action on a seemingly endless series of law suits. Should the badly needed replacement lock be built it would have a lock chamber 110-feet wide and 1200 feet long with a depth over the sills of 31.5 feet.

At mile 228.1 AHP the Port Allen Lock–84 feet wide, 1,200 feet long and 13.7 feet deep over the gate sills–connects the Port of Baton Rouge and the Mississippi River to the Atchafalaya River. The Port Allen Lock was completed in 1961 and with its opening, the GIWW Alternate Route, Port Allen to Morgan City was open. The Alternate Route cuts 160 miles off the distance between the GIWW at Morgan City and ports on the Ohio and Mississippi River and diverts through traffic (to Lake Charles, Houston, etc.) away from the congested New Orleans area.

Between river mile 311.8 and 316.5 AHP, approximately 60 river miles upstream from the Port of Baton Rouge, at a complex of levees, dams, channels, sluice gates and a navigation lock collectively called the Old River Control Structure, the Mississippi's largest distributary, the geologically new Atchafalaya River, begins its 142-mile journey south through the Atchafalaya Basin to Morgan City and the Gulf of Mexico. The control complex was built to maintain the existing deep-water channel of the Mississippi and the existing economic infrastructure of south Louisiana by controlling and limiting the portion of the river allowed to follow its natural tendency to shorten its path to the sea...the rivers desire to divert west into the Atchafalaya.

As deltas build at the seaward end of meandering lowland rivers, the rivers course to the sea grows longer and the rivers gradient, its slope from higher land to the sea, decreases. If a delta extends seaward far enough that its length significantly exceeds its width, distributaries, lateral flood channels or adjacent streams may offer a shorter route, with a steeper gradient, to the sea and in a process called avulsion, the river changes channels and begins a new phase of delta building. In the seven millenniums since the lower Mississippi Delta began its modern development, the Mississippi has changed course, avulsed, at least six times: bayous Cocodrie, Teche and Lafourche are all former main channels of the Mississippi.

Prior to the fifteenth century the Red River and the Mississippi flowed, parallel and unconnected, to the Gulf of Mexico. At some point during the fifteenth century a westward meander of the Mississippi, later named Turnbull's Bend, intersected and captured both the Red River and the Atchafalaya, a minor distributary of the Red River. When the first Europeans settled in the area the Red River entered the Mississippi in the northwest curve of Turnbull's Bend and, several miles further south at the bottom of the bend, the Atchafalaya, by then a well-developed distributary of the Mississippi flowed south to the gulf.

In the early years of steamboats on the Mississippi the tight radiuses of the curves in Turnbull's Bend and the current and sand bars where the Red River entered and the Atchafalaya departed, were a problem. In 1831 Capt. Henry M. Shreve, the Steamboat Captain and entrepreneur after whom Shreveport, Louisiana is named, solved the problem…at least from a steamboat captain's point of view. He straightened the mighty Mississippi. He dug a channel through the narrow neck of Turnbull's Bend. A meandering river seeks the steepest gradient and shortest route to the sea, the Mississippi abandoned Turnbull's Bend and diverted into Shreve's cut which became the channel.

Over the next century: the upper arm of the cut off meander silted in, the Red River became tributary to the Atchafalaya (its former distributary) and the lower arm of the bend (now called the Old River) became the head of the Atchafalaya. With every passing decade the shorter steeper path to the gulf offered by the Atchafalaya–half as long with a gradient twice as steep–grew broader and deeper and took evermore of the Mississippi. By the early 1950s thirty percent of the Mississippi River's volume was taking the shorter path to the sea and it was apparent that a few more decades or one catastrophic flood like the devastating 1927 flood, and the Mississippi would again avulse.

The Atchafalaya would be the new Mississippi.

But in the 230 or so years since Jean Baptiste le Moyne founded Nouvellé-Orleans the United States had grown up, the controlled lower Mississippi had become the gateway to the North American heartland and one of the most heavily developed industrial and port areas in the country. Industry, drawn by the rivers freshwater and the confluence of the inland navigation system, the national rail and highway networks, gulf coast petroleum and easy access to the world through the ports of the lower river, had invested billions upon billions of dollars. And the densely populated cities and towns along the lower river depended on the river for most of their freshwater. Avulsion would be catastrophic...politically and economically unacceptable.

A 1953 report by the Mississippi River Commission recommended that the diversion of the Mississippi into the Atchafalaya should be controlled by a complex of structures to be built at the Old River. The report recommended that the proposed Old River control structures be built and operated so as to maintain the distribution of flow and sediments between the lower Mississippi River and the Atchafalaya River in approximately the same proportions as were occurring naturally in 1950 and that a lock to facilitate continued navigation between the Mississippi, the Atchafalaya and the Red Rivers be part of the project. Congress authorized the Old River Control Project on September 3, 1954, construction began the next year and the project was completed in 1962. Over the winter of 1972-73 heavy flooding on the Mississippi damaged the control complex and one wing wall was washed out. The damage was repaired and the complex strengthened. The control complex was able to contain the major floods of 1975 and 1979, and since then the complex has again been strengthened and secondary, auxiliary support structures have been constructed.[49]

During the construction of the Old River Control Complex, the Old River itself, the former south arm of Turnbull's Bend, was dammed and a 2.6-mile-long 12-foot-deep navigation channel was dredged from the Mississippi to a point approximately 1.5 miles

208

west of the dam and the Old River Lock was constructed in the new channel. The lock, completed in 1963, allows commercial and recreational traffic to pass between the Mississippi River and the Atchafalaya and Red Rivers. The lock has a chamber 75-feet wide by 1,185-feet long with a minimum depth over the sills of 11 feet. Except during periods of flooding when the Mississippi River is closed to navigation, the lock is manned, and operates 24 hours a day. There is a fair amount of commercial traffic between the Mississippi and the Atchafalaya and Red River systems. In 2016 3,336 vessels and 7,091,000 tons of commercial commodities locked through at the Old River lock and 7,823 vessels and 21,829,000 tons of commercial commodities locked through at Port Allen (Baton Rouge).

In the half century since completion of the Old River control complex, development along the lower river has continued unabated. Today a trip up the Mississippi terminal by terminal, wharf by wharf from Head of Passes to the Port of Baton Rouge through the pages of United States Coast Pilot 5 and then back down river through the overhead lens of Google Earth shows the billions upon billions of dollars of industrial development lining the lower river. Every significant petroleum, petrochemical and bulk commodity corporation in the United States is there–Shell, Exxon, Conoco-Phillips, Chevron, Marathon, Valero, Dow, Cargill, Archer Daniels Midland, Monsanto, Bunge, Domino Sugar, etc.– most with multiple facilities. Both conventional and nuclear power plants use the rivers freshwater for cooling. And, even with the loss of population in New Orleans following hurricanes Katrina and Rita, the population of the lower river parishes has doubled. What was politically and economically unacceptable in the middle of the twentieth century is unthinkable in the second decade of the twenty-first.

The USACE has been able to control the Mississippi Rivers urge to divert and as long as Congress has the political will and continues to provide the financial resources, the Corps can probably keep the situation under control. But a 1980 study by Kazmann and Johnson, of Louisiana State University, concluded that "in the long run the Atchafalaya will become the principle distributary of the Mississippi River and the current main-stream will become an estuary of the Gulf of Mexico...the final outcome is only a matter of time."[50] Other papers written since then have reached the same conclusion.

8. The Mississippi to the Calcasieu

In Louisiana west of the Mississippi, early settlers dug canals for transportation between the Mississippi and the out-outlying farms, plantations and settlements along the major bayous west of the river. The first well documented canal was a 25-foot-wide canal built between 1736 and 1740 by Claude Dubreuil de Villars who owned a plantation along the Bayou Fatma[51] branch of the Bayou Barataria. There were no locks on the canal, the connection to the Mississippi was dependent on seasonal high water. The canal was an important trade route until at least the late 1830s and it may have been the route the privateer and pirate brothers Pierre and Jean Lafitte, used to smuggle contraband from their base on Barataria Bay to New Orleans. Barthélémy Lafon, a respected Creole architect, engineer, surveyor, businessman and investor in New Orleans—he laid out the initial plan for the Lower Garden District—owned land that adjoined Dubreuil's, and Lafon was an associate of the Lafitte brothers. After the Battle of New Orleans, at the end of the War of 1812, Lafon turned completely to piracy and smuggling. The Gardere canal in Harvey, just south of the Harvey Canal, is what remains of Dubreuil's canal.

Another early canal was dug on the Petit Desert Plantation–later known as the Seven Oaks Plantation. The earliest mention of the canal is a bill of sale in which Alexandre Harang sold 10 arpents[52] of the plantation to his son-in-law Michel Zeringue. The bill of sale stipulated that the owner of an adjacent plantation had the right to use the canal. In 1830 the canal was sold to the Barataria and Lafourche Canal Company and by 1838 steamboats were using Bayou Barataria. In 1847 the canal reached Longueville (today Lockport) on Bayou Lafourche. It was 1903 before a lock was completed at the Mississippi River end of the canal. The lock and part of the canal were badly damaged in the 1927 flood and were abandoned soon after the flood. In 1956 the west bank levee was extended across the area of the lock and the canal was permanently closed.

Between 1839 and 1845 Nicolas Noel Destrehan dug a canal from the Mississippi River Levee to the Bayou Barataria. Destrehan's daughter, who was married to Joseph Hale Harvey, acquired the canal and the adjacent property following her father's death. In 1882, shortly after Joseph Harvey's death, the canal was sold to the Harvey Canal Land and Improvement Company which, in 1924 sold the canal to the federal government for $425,000 and it was incorporated into the Intracoastal Waterway.

The first significant federal legislation pertaining directly to a navigable inland waterway west of the Mississippi was an order for a survey "For connecting the inland waters along the margin of the Gulf of Mexico, from Donaldsonville, Louisiana, to the Rio Grande River, in Texas, by cuts and canals..." included in the Rivers and Harbors Act of March 3, 1873. Donaldsonville, on the west bank of the Mississippi, approximately 65 river miles upstream from New Orleans, is where the Bayou Lafourche, a natural distributary of the Mississippi, departed the main channel before the modern levees were built.

In 1923 Congress directed the Secretary of War to have the Corps of Engineers examine and survey the Intracoastal Waterway

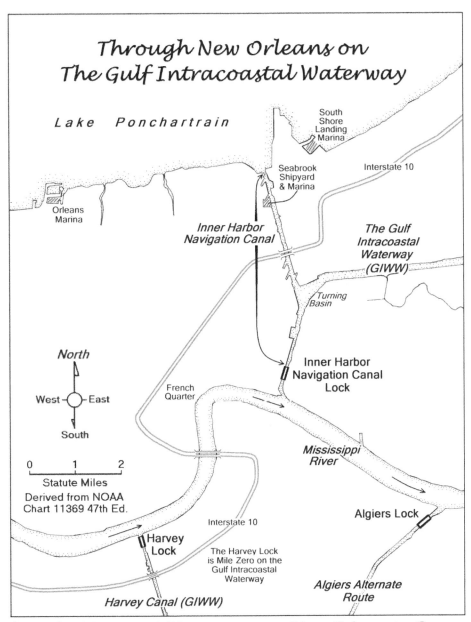

Through New Orleans on The Gulf Intracoastal Waterway

Lake Ponchartrain

South Shore Landing Marina

Interstate 10

Seabrook Shipyard & Marina

Orleans Marina

Inner Harbor Navigation Canal

The Gulf Intracoastal Waterway (GIWW)

Turning Basin

North

West — East

South

French Quarter

Inner Harbor Navigation Canal Lock

0   1   2
Statute Miles
Derived from NOAA
Chart 11369 47th Ed.

Mississippi River

Algiers Lock

Interstate 10

Harvey Lock

The Harvey Lock is Mile Zero on the Gulf Intracoastal Waterway

Algiers Alternate Route

Harvey Canal (GIWW)

from the Mississippi River at or near New Orleans to Corpus
Christi, Texas. Then in the Rivers and Harbors Act of March 3,
1925, Congress authorized and funded a 9-foot-deep by 100-foot-

wide "Louisiana and Texas Intracoastal Waterway, from the Mississippi River, at or near New Orleans, to Galveston, Texas," with several restrictions, the last of which was the usual one "...that no expense shall be incurred by the United States for acquiring any lands required for the purpose of this improvement." And in 1942, as a national defense requirement, Congress authorized the expansion of the gulf waterway from its original 9 feet deep by 100 feet wide to 12 feet deep by 125 feet wide.

At the Inner Harbor Navigation Canal Lock (GIWW mile 5.8 EHL) the waterway enters the Mississippi River and divides into the main and Algiers Alternate routes. The main route runs upstream in the river for 5.5 miles–past Bywater, Marigny, the French Quarter and the cruise ship terminal, and under the high twin spans of the Crescent City Connector (Interstate 10 and U.S. 90 Business)–and leaves the river via the Harvey Lock (GIWW mile Zero.) From the Harvey Lock the main route follows the Harvey Canal southwest for 6.5 miles to the Bayou Barataria. The Algiers Alternate route runs downstream in the river for 4.4 miles, leaves the river via the Algiers Lock (Algiers Alternate mile Zero) and continues west for 8.9 miles to GIWW mile 6.5 WHL where it rejoins the main route. In good weather and good river conditions...the river near normal level and not running too fast...the short river trip is interesting and enjoyable.

Mile 10 WHL to the Atchafalaya River and Morgan City

Land subsidence is often thought of as human caused; for example, as the result of pumping ground water from shallow aquifers in unconsolidated sediments at a rate faster than the aquifers rate of recharge. But the soft, unconsolidated sediments that built the low, fragile lands of the newest parts of the Louisiana delta (and many other coastal and inland depositional wetlands) contain large amounts of organic material which naturally decays and breaks down. As the organic material breaks down the land settles…subsides…and consolidates. To maintain their level, and build higher, the subsiding, consolidating marshes and swamps need infusions of new building material…new sediment. And in this part of the delta the only significant source of new sediment is the walled off, leveed Mississippi. The rivers annual floods and the heavy loads of sediment they carry, no longer spread over the delta. In addition to subsidence, the soft sediments erode easily and constantly; washed and moved by currents, waves and boat wakes. The winter winds accompanying strong cold fronts and hurricane season cyclonic storms can cause large changes. Between 2004 and 2008, hurricanes Katrina, Rita, Gustav and Ike washed out, transformed into open water, approximately 328 square miles of gulf coast marsh–more than the estimated national total wetland loss between 1978 and 2004.[53][54]

The cutting of drainage canals and the oil and gas industry's largely unregulated canal cutting chops the marshes and swamps into smaller patches, provides ingress routes for saltwater and allows increased erosion. The encroaching saltwater changes freshwater marshes to salt and kills the cypress, oak, willow and other vegetation in the freshwater swamps. The long, wide, straight navigation canals between the Gulf of Mexico and inland shipping and fishing ports are generally dredged to depths of 9 or more feet. Because the marshes and swamps through which the canals are cut are barely above mean sea level, a depth of 9 feet means 9 or almost 9 feet below mean gulf sea level. The navigation canals allow the ingress of large amounts of ocean water and can potentially serve as storm surge highways…remember Katrina and the MRGO. And the wakes of boats on the navigation canals, particularly the wakes of large work boats, crew boats and rig service vessels, which tend to run fast, are a major factor in channel bank erosion.

Coastal Louisiana's wetlands, the composite lower Mississippi Delta, form the 7th largest delta on earth. According to a recent U.S. Geological Survey study,[55] this area–which contains almost 40 percent of the estuarine marshes in, and supports the largest commercial fishery in, the contiguous 48 states–has decreased in size by approximately 2,000 square miles since 1932. A loss of about 25 percent of the 1932 land area within the lifetime of the oldest delta residents. The 2000 or so square miles of the Louisiana Delta lost since 1932 represents approximately 90 percent of the coastal wetlands lost over the period in the lower 48 states. A part of the U.S.G.S.'s study was a loss trend analyses of the 25 years from 1985 to 2010. During this short period the trend analyses found an average wetland loss rate of 16.57 square miles, or 10,604.8 square acres, per year (one square mile equals 640 square acres.) If the loss rate was constant, Louisiana would be losing 29.05 square acres of land per day. To put 29.05 square acres per day into an urban or suburban perspective, according to the United States Bureau of the Census the average lot size of new suburban homes in 2013 was 8,596 square feet or two tenths of a square acre. Allowing for roads and sidewalks, a suburban neighborhood of 90-100 homes is being washed out, lost, every day.

Eastbound, in the fall of 2011, aboard *Nauset's* predecessor, a Cape Dory named *Walkabout*, we passed through Houma, Louisiana on November 7th and reached the Barataria Waterway, at mile 15 WHL in the early afternoon. The Barataria extends south from the GIWW for 34 miles, through the towns of Barataria and Lafitte and several canals and bayous to Barataria Bay, Grand Isle and the Gulf of Mexico. The federal project specifications for the Barataria call for a channel 12-feet deep for a width of 125 feet throughout. However, the 2014 (42nd Edition) of <u>United States Coast Pilot 5, Gulf of Mexico</u>, gives a controlling depth of 12 feet from the Gulf into Barataria Bay, 2 feet from the bay to the Bayou Rigolettes and 4 feet from there to the GIWW, and NOAA Chart 11367, <u>Intracoastal Waterway, Waveland to Catahoula Bay</u> (1:40,000), 36th Edition, April 2010, gives a controlling depth of 7 feet from the Bayou Rigolettes to the GIWW. But in the fall of 2011, large shrimp and work boats, including two very large Jack-up Drilling Rigs, were docked along the waterway in Barataria and Lafitte and pushboats with barges…loaded barges…were using the waterway.

By the time we reached the Barataria there was not enough time left in the day for us to reach a marina in New Orleans. So, we turned hard right and took a seven mile drive down the Barataria Waterway to the Laffite Harbor Marina, the last parking spot before land dry enough to build on peters out. The Lafitte Harbor Marina has diesel and gas (C&M Bayou Fuel), a laundry, usable heads and showers, a good hardware/marine store and, for a night off the boat, several nice rooms and cabins for rent. Fisherman, and in the fall duck hunters, who have towed their small boats down from all over the midcontinent fill the rooms. For a good dinner off the boat, Voleo's Restaurant "The Best Food on the Bayou" will pick you up and bring you back. The chef at Voleo's cooked in New Orleans for many years, then came home to the bayou and opened his own place. The food is good, the seafood as fresh as it gets.

The Lafitte Harbor Marina is only 22 miles from Harvey Lock. Our plan was to spend the night, enjoy dinner at Voleo's, get an early start in the morning and have plenty of daylight to get through the Harvey Lock, down the Mississippi, through the Inner

Harbor Navigation Canal Lock and through the Inner harbor Navigation Canal and its restricted bridges. The early start was a success. When we reached the old, in poor condition, and chronically under repair Barataria Swing Bridge, a mile south of the GIWW, I radioed a request for an opening.

"Barataria Swing Bridge, *Walkabout* inbound requesting an opening please."

"Bridge is closed to marine traffic."

"Will you be opening in the next hour or two?"

"No...two, three days...maybe."

Two hard hats coming from the bridge in a John Boat stopped and told us that there was a way to return to the GIWW via Bayou Perot but they did not know the details. I called the Lafitte Harbor Marina and asked about the alternate route and was told to leave the Barataria Waterway and enter the Bayou Rigolettes through the marked cut at 29°40'N 90°6.7'W and then to just follow the barge channel to Bayou Perot and the GIWW "tugs and barges do it all the time, plenty of water."

We happily went down the rabbit hole and into Alice's wonderland. The cut that gave access to the Bayou Rigolettes was clearly marked. Beyond that well marked cut? No buoys, no pilings, no signs, not even any sticks standing up in the water...nothing. We gave up and started back to the Barataria, thinking we'd be going down the waterway to Grand Isle, Tiger Pass and Venice. And then on to Gulfport or Biloxi...taking the coastal route. Half a mile from the cut, a pushboat with two barges came through from the Barataria. As soon as we could see that pushboat's name and hailing port...M/V *Lorina*, NO-LA [motor vessel *Lorina*, hailing port New Orleans, Louisiana.] I got on the radio.

"*Lorina, Walkabout*"

"Lorina"

"You going through to the waterway?"

"Yes."

"Walkabout will be right behind you."

We followed the *Lorina* through a twisting, turning, and utterly unmarked "barge channel" to the GIWW and never saw less than 9 feet on our depth sounder. On the waterway *Lorina* turned east toward New Orleans and we sped up and passed him. Betty was driving and waved as we passed. When we were safely in front of him

"Walkabout, Lorina"

"Walkabout here"

"How far you going?"

"New Orleans for a couple days, then on to the Florida Keys."

"Dam...have a good trip, be safe...*Lorina* clear."

"Thank you, *Walkabout* clear."

Older editions of NOAA's nautical charts, and some that are still in use,[56] show an extensive marsh area south of the waterway between Bayou Rigolettes and Bayou Perot. The Bayous are much wider than charted, the marsh area largely washed out. Early aerial photographs of this area, relative to today, show: narrower bayous, extensive marshes, patches of cypress swamp, very few oil company canals and much less open water. Historic charts and maps in NOAA's collection depict a very different landscape. Landsat imagery from 1975 is noticeably different from imagery obtained in 2014.

Ideally a chart or map is an accurate rendering of selected aspects of a portion of the earth's surface at a specific moment in time. The charted rendering of this area, and of a large part of the rest of the lower delta, excepting the marked and surveyed waterways, is little more than a fairy tale depiction of an ancient dreamscape. And the area is changing so fast that NOAA's underfunded chart makers cannot keep up...have no hope of keeping up. Over the next half century as sea levels inevitably rise, perhaps a foot or more, and subsidence, erosion and storms alter the land, NOAA will need to collect a lot of data and redraw a lot of coastlines. And not just in Louisiana.

Between miles 34.5 and 36 WHL, the waterway passes through Larose and crosses the Bayou Lafourche. The Bayou Lafourche runs southeast for 93 miles, from the Mississippi River at Donaldsonville–174 miles AHP (70 river miles above Canal Street, New Orleans)–through Napoleonville, Thibodaux, Lockport, Larose and Golden Meadow to Port Fourchon, Belle Pass and the deep waters of the Gulf of Mexico. The Bayou Lafourche was a natural distributary of the Mississippi before the modern levees were built, in the nineteenth century, during periods of higher water, steamboats entered the Bayou from the Mississippi at Donaldsonville. And for 1200-1300 years, from approximately the beginning of the Christian era to an avulsion around 1300 AD that diverted the Mississippi into its present channel, the Bayou Lafourche was the Mississippi.

Because the Bayou Lafourche was formerly the Mississippi and was, until recently, an active distributary, it has broad, relatively high natural levees. In 1756 Acadian French–who had been expelled from Canada by the British in 1755–began to settle along the bayou. The natural levees offered higher, dryer land and rich soil for farming and the bayou provided access and a transportation route.

The Acadians brought the French Canadian 'Long Lot' land holding pattern from Canada with them and, as they settled along the Bayou Lafourche and other bayous, long narrow lots that ran from the bayous back onto or even across the levees were laid out.

The lots had a width to length ratio of 1:10 or more and houses and farm buildings were generally built at the bayou end. As settlement progressed and the waterfront filled in, the bayou became Main Street for a long linear community. Brochures published by the Louisiana State Tourist Office and by the Lafourche Parish Chamber of Commerce call Bayou Lafourche "the World's Longest Main Street." The long lot settlement pattern is clearly visible from the air (see Google Earth) and Bayou Lafourche is one of the places where it is most distinct.

Thirty-four miles above its mouth at Belle Pass, the Bayou Lafourche crosses the GIWW. The town of Lockport, originally named Longueville, 15 miles up the bayou from the Intracoastal, was linked to the Mississippi at New Orleans a century and a half ago by the Barataria and Lafourche Canal Company. From the GIWW up to Lockport the bayou is used by barges, shrimp boats and large work boats. Bollinger Shipyards, Inc. and Thoma-Sea Marine operate shipyards in Lockport that are capable of building and servicing large vessels. Bollinger's Lockport yard has built patrol vessels and gunboats ranging from 87 to 170 feet in length for the U.S. Coast Guard and Navy. Above Lockport the bayou is navigable by small craft to Thibodaux where, at about mile 64 above Bell Pass a dam at the Thibodaux Water Plant blocks further travel.

From Larose and the GIWW down the bayou to Port Fourchon, Belle Pass and the Gulf of Mexico the bayou is heavily utilized by the oil industry and by a large fishing fleet. Two Floodgates, one just below the GIWW with a depth over the sill of 10 feet at Mean Low Water and the other about half way to Port Fourchon with a depth over the sill of 9 feet at Mean Low Water set the controlling depth for the bayou. From the lower flood gate to Belle Pass the bayou is deeper and Port Fourchon, just above Belle Pass, has dockside depths as deep as 27 feet and is a major base for offshore oil exploration and production. The Louisiana Offshore Oil Port (LOOP), a deep-water tanker loading and offloading terminal is supported from Port Fourchon and in 2016 Port Fourchon (includes the LOOP) was 57th on the USACE's list of domestic ports by tonnage.

At mile 49 WHL the GIWW crosses the Company Canal. The Company Canal was built in the first half of the nineteenth century by the Barataria and Lafourche Canal Company, which received a charter from the State of Louisiana in 1829 for the stated purpose of enlarging an older canal that connected the west bank of the Mississippi at New Orleans to the Bayou Barataria and extending that canal to the Bayou Lafourche. In 1847 the company's canal reached Longueville (today Lockport) on Bayou Lafourche and it was eventually extended to Bourg, on the Bayou Terrebonne, up the Terrebonne to Houma and, through several bayous and cuts, to Morgan City and the Atchafalaya River. The Mississippi River end of the canal was permanently closed in 1956, but the short section from Lockport south to the GIWW and on to Bourg and Bayou Terrebonne is navigable and still in use.

In downtown Houma, between GIWW miles 55.6 & 55.7 WHL, the waterway passes under the Park Avenue Bridge, crosses Bayou Terrebonne and passes under the Main Street Bridge. Houma, the seat of Terrebonne Parish, was first settled by Europeans, primarily Cajun French, in the early 1830s, on the site of a Houma Indian settlement. Originally an agricultural community (sugar cane, rice, cotton) with a strong secondary economy in natural resources exploitation (fishing, trapping, timber), Houma was incorporated in 1848 and re-incorporated in 1898. Oil was discovered in Terrebonne Parish in 1929 when the Texas Company (Texaco) drilled two successful wells.[57] Today Houma is a thriving, prosperous town with an economy primarily based on petroleum: coastal, nearshore and wetland exploration, oilfield development, oil and gas production, oilfield services and the building and repair of vessels used in the coastal and nearshore petroleum industry. Houma (Port of Terrebonne) was 87th on the USACE's 2016 list of domestic ports by tonnage. Agriculture and fishing, particularly for shrimp, are still economically important and tourism is rapidly developing.

At GIWW mile 59.5 WHL, two miles west of the Park Avenue and Main Street Bridges, the 31-mile-long Houma Navigation Canal links Houma (the Port of Terrebonne) and the GIWW to the Gulf of Mexico. The canal, a federal project maintained by the USACE and classified as a deep draft waterway (14+ feet deep), has an authorized project depth of 15 feet and a width of 150 feet. But despite being dredged, in whole or in part 10 times between 1991 and 2014, the Houma Navigation Canal note (Note C) on the May 2015 edition of NOAA Chart 11355 Catahoula Bay to Wax Lake Outlet Including the Houma Navigation Canal gives a controlling depth of just 10 feet through Terrebonne Bay to Bayou Petit Caillou and 12 feet from there to the GIWW. The shipyards in Houma can handle ships and barges to 300+ feet long with a draft of up to 16 feet…if they can get there.

The Bayou Boeuf Lock, at GIWW mile 93 WHL, is built into the flood control levee on the east side of the Atchafalaya River and permits navigation through the levee. The lock, completed in 1954, has a chamber 1,156-feet long (1,148 usable), 75 feet wide, with a depth of 13 feet over the sills and it can lift/lower vessels up to 11 feet during periods of high water on the Atchafalaya. When the Atchafalaya's water level is at or marginally higher than the water level in the GIWW, the lock gates stand open and the lockmaster instructs vessels to "float the lock." This saves wear and tear on the lock, speeds up traffic through the lock and permits the flow of Atchafalaya River water and its suspended sediments into and east along the GIWW.

The Atchafalaya River is the largest distributary of the Mississippi, the Corps of Engineers normally allows 30 percent of the Mississippi's flow to divert into the Atchafalaya at the Old River Control Structure but during floods on the Mississippi a much larger volume of water can be diverted into and down the Atchafalaya. The Atchafalaya is also the Gulf of Mexico outlet for the water and suspended sediments of the Red River, Black River, Little River, Ouachita River, Tensas River and the other streams that are tributary to it. Depending on the level and current strength of the Atchafalaya's outflow, varying amounts of river water and sediments are pushed east and west along the GIWW as far as 30 to 50 miles east of the Atchafalaya and west of the Wax Lake Outlet Canal. In effect the man-made GIWW has become a possibly significant distributary of the river, feeding river water and sediments to the marshes to the east and west.[58]

GIWW Mile 95.7 WHL, is the confluence of the GIWW, the Morgan City to Port Allen Alternate Route (a part of the GIWW) and the Atchafalaya River Route which extends inland commercial navigation to the Red River and north to Shreveport, Louisiana and Camden, Arkansas. Approximately 60,000 vessels of all types pass through the confluence of the three routes annually. The authorized dimensions for both the Morgan City to Port Allen Alternate Route and for the Atchafalaya River Route, from its confluence with the GIWW upstream to the head of commercial navigation, are a depth of 12 feet for a width of 125 feet, the same as the authorized dimensions for the GIWW. Downstream, from Morgan City to the Gulf of Mexico, the Atchafalaya is the shipping channel for the Port of Morgan City and the dimensions for the channel in this section of the river are a depth of 20 feet for a width of 400 feet. The Port of Morgan City, 116th on the USACE's 2012 list of domestic ports by tonnage. In 2016 Morgan City, although still an active seaport, was unranked on the USACE's list of ports because heavy silting in the Atchafalaya channel seaward of Morgan City hindered the ports use by all but the smallest ocean capable vessels.

Morgan City, occupies a leveed and sea-walled island between Bayou Boeuf, Lake Palourde, Flat Lake, Berwick Bay and the Atchafalaya River. The cities tall seawall looms over the docks and the river front like the battlements of some medieval city. Through the massive concrete and steel flood gate, behind the seawall, the small, compact, walkable city is enjoyable and has an old Louisiana, New Orleans, Cajun French feel: blocks of shot gun houses, beautiful old homes and nineteenth century store fronts…some restored, some not. The International Petroleum Museum is at the foot of First Street, looking out over the junction of the GIWW and the Atchafalaya. The museum highlights Morgan City's role in the coastal and offshore oil industry and the exhibit that draws the tourists is Mr. Charlie, the world's first movable and semi-submersible drilling rig.

European settlement in the Morgan City area began in the 1760s when the Acadian French started settling along Bayou Teche northwest of Morgan City. In the mid-1780s Thomas Berwick established a sugar plantation on land that is today most of the town of Berwick and part of Morgan City. The town remained primarily an agricultural (sugar and rice) center until the first decade of the twentieth century when logging became important. In the early 1930s, with most of the usable timber cut out and the regional logging industry collapsing, large, rich shrimping grounds were discovered in the gulf off Morgan City and until after World War II Morgan City was the shrimp capital of the world. There are no longer any active seafood processors in Morgan City but shrimping, now a carefully regulated and sustainable fishery, remains an important part of the local economy. The petroleum industry arrived in Morgan City with the discovery of the Jeanerette field[59] in 1935[60] and today the city's economy is primarily based on oil and gas. The annual five-day extravaganza of the Louisiana Shrimp and Petroleum Festival is Louisiana's largest and oldest harvest festival and it is generally considered second only to New Orleans's Mardi Gras among state events.

The network of navigable waterways radiating from Morgan City has made it a center for wetland, nearshore, coastal and offshore oil and gas exploration and development. Offshore drilling in the United States began from piers built out from the beach in Summerland, California in 1897, but it was 1949 before a successful production well was drilled out of sight of land. On November 14, 1949, Kerr-McGee (Anadarko Petroleum) operating from Morgan City brought in the Kermac 16 well in the Ship Shoal salt dome field off Louisiana. Although the well was drilled from a fixed platform and was in just 20 feet of water, it was ten miles from land and 43 miles southwest of Morgan City. By the time it was capped in 1984, the Kermac 16 well had produced 1.3 million barrels of oil and 307 million cubic feet of gas.[61]

Morgan City to the Calcasieu and Lake Charles

At GIWW mile 108 WHL the waterway crosses the Wax Lake Outlet Canal–the Atchafalaya Flood Control Diversion Canal. The USACE cut the canal in 1941 and diverted almost half of the Atchafalaya's flow into it to reduce the severity of floods in

Morgan City. Both the Atchafalaya River and the canal carry heavy loads of sediment and both are building small deltas in Atchafalaya Bay. Geologists first noticed mud building up in the bay off both the river and the canal in the 1950s. Land first appeared above the water line in both of the new deltas following a major flood in 1973. Since then both deltas have grown considerably and they are now well enough established that large areas support vegetation. Both deltas are within Louisiana's Atchafalaya Delta Wildlife Management area and the Louisiana Department of Wildlife and Fisheries estimates the vegetated (mostly marsh and willow scrub) land area at 15,000 acres in the Atchafalaya delta and 12,000 acres in the Wax Lake Outlet delta.[62]

Twenty-eight miles west of the Wax Lake Outlet, the waterway cuts through the north edge of Cote Blanche Island, eight miles further west it shaves the south side of Weeks Island. Neither Cote Blanche nor Weeks is a true island. They are patches of higher land surrounded by and rising over a sea of marsh and swamp. Two of a line of five such islands, referred to in the geological literature and in tourist brochures as "the five islands," that are the highest and driest structural terrain features in Louisiana's coastal delta. From east to west, the islands and their elevations above mean sea level are: Belle Isle, southwest of Morgan City (80 feet); Cote Blanche, at mile 129 WHL (97 feet); Weeks Island, mile 137.5 WHL (the highest at 171 feet); Avery Island, nine miles up Bayou Petite Anse, mile 145.8 WHL (163 feet); and Jefferson Island, on the east side of Lake Peigneur, 1.2 miles north of Delcambre (at 35 feet, the lowest.)

The islands are salt domes, low mounds created by the upward deformation of thousands of feet of sedimentary rock caused by columns and masses of salt squeezed up from deep below the surface. Rock salt under uniform pressure, squeezed from all sides, is mechanically stable but under uneven pressure it becomes plastic and flows toward areas of lesser pressure. Under the intense pressure of thousands of feet of overlying rock, salt can flow laterally and be extruded upward with sufficient force to penetrate through thinner or weaker areas in the overlying rock or to force passage through structural weak points such as faults or fractures. Salt structures are of deep interest to the petroleum industry and are frequently surrounded by a field of oil and/or gas wells. This is because salt, although structurally weak and plastic under pressure, is impervious to natural hydrocarbons. It's a trap layer, or wall, for oil and natural gas, and the deformed sedimentary layers above, around or along the flanks of the salt columns and masses frequently contain multiple reservoirs of oil and/or gas. Sometimes a whole series of layered reservoirs at sequentially deeper depths.

The salt in the five island domes originates in the Louann Salt,[63] a thick evaporate formation deep beneath the Gulf Coast and a large part of the adjacent Continental Shelf from the Florida Panhandle to Matagorda Bay, Texas…an area known as the Gulf Coast Salt Basin. Within the basin there are at least 500 and possibly well over 600 salt structures, columns and masses of salt rising from the Louann. The Flower Garden Banks 120 miles off Galveston, the site on the Ship Shoal near Morgan City where the first out of sight of land production well was drilled and the Spindle Top Dome near Beaumont, Texas are Louann Salt structures. The great majority of the salt structures, either because they have not risen close enough to the surface to have any visible or map-able surface expression or because they are out on the continental shelf, can be detected only by sub-surface mapping technics such as seismic and gravity surveys.

There are also several prominent salt dome islands along the GIWW in Texas; notably High Island at mile 320 WHL and Bryan Mound at mile 400 WHL. High Island, rising to 38 feet above mean sea level fronts directly on the Gulf of Mexico and is the highest land directly on the gulf between the Florida Panhandle and Mexico's Yucatan Peninsula. Bryan Mound, in Freeport, Texas, is one of the four salt structures used as storage facilities for the United States strategic petroleum reserve.[64]

At mile 140.1 the GIWW crosses the Acadia Navigation Canal which provides gulf and waterway access for the Port of Iberia, 110th on the USACE's 2016 list of domestic ports by tonnage handled. And at mile 145.8 the Waterway crosses Bayou Petite Anse which leads north to Avery Island, the home of Tabasco Sauce, and to Bayou Carlin, which gives access to: the Delcambre Canal, the town of Delcambre (the fishing center of Iberia Parish), Lake Peigneur and Jefferson Island. On the south side of the waterway, immediately opposite Bayou Petite Anse, the Avery Canal gives the large fishing fleet based in Delcambre access to Vermilion Bay and the Gulf of Mexico.

Avery Island, originally Ile Petite Anse, was purchased in 1818 by John Marsh, a transplant from New Jersey, who established a sugar plantation on the island. In 1837 Marsh's daughter Sarah married Daniel Avery, a lawyer from Baton Rouge. Daniel and Sarah Avery inherited the sugar plantation in 1855 and shortly after that their daughter married Edmund McIlhenny, a banker. Edmund McIlhenny began experimenting with pepper sauces during the Civil War. In 1868 he founded the McIlhenny Company and began manufacturing Tabasco Pepper Sauce. In 1870 he patented both the name and his method of making Tabasco Sauce. Exactly when salt was discovered on Avery Island is debated, but a rock salt mine, producing salt for the confederacy was in production by mid-1861. Oil was discovered at Avery Island in 1942 and production began with the discovery well. Today Tabasco Sauce–exactly the same as and produced by the method described in the 1870 patent–oil, gas and rock salt are all produced at Avery Island. And the Island's Spanish moss draped live oaks, world famous gardens, bird sanctuary[65] and Tabasco Museum are a major tourist destination.[66]

Between miles 159 and 163 WHL, the GIWW passes the Vermilion River (also called Bayou Vermilion), the Four Mile Cutoff, Intracoastal City and the Freshwater Bayou Canal. Both the Four Mile Cutoff and the Freshwater Bayou Canal provide access to the coastal bays and the Gulf of Mexico, consequently this area has developed into another center for the wetland, nearshore and coastal exploration, production and well service industries. There are also several seafood packing and processing plants and a large number of fishing vessels operate from or visit the area.

Just west of Intracoastal City the Freshwater Bayou Canal leads south to the Gulf of Mexico. The canal, authorized in the Rivers and Harbors Act of July 14, 1960 and completed in 1968, has an authorized depth of 12 feet for a width of 125 feet...the same dimensions as the GIWW. The junction of the GIWW and the Freshwater Bayou Canal marks the eastern edge of the Corps of Engineer's Mermentau Basin Project.[67] The waterway crosses the western edge of the project at the Louisiana State Route 27 Bridge in Gibbstown, mile 219.8 WHL. The low-lying freshwater marshes, swamps and agricultural lands (primarily rice) of the lower Mermentau River drainage basin–roughly the wetlands in Cameron and Vermilion Parishes between the southern edge of Louisiana's coastal prairie and the Gulf of Mexico[68]–are threatened by, and in periods of low water on the Mermentau River are subject to, saltwater intrusion through drainage, oil company and navigation canals. The Mermentau Basin Project's navigation structures, dams, dikes and levees: retain freshwater in the basin, control saltwater intrusion from the Gulf of Mexico and permit marine traffic to enter and pass through the basin with minimal saltwater intrusion. The target freshwater level in the basin is 2.0 feet above mean low gulf sea level. The navigation structures included in the saltwater intrusion control project are:

- The Leland Bowman Lock, on the GIWW at mile 163 WHL–chamber 110 feet wide, 1,200 feet long, with a depth over the sills of 13 feet and a lift of 4 feet–was completed in 1985. The lock was a replacement for the old Vermilion Lock (completed in 1933) and controls the intrusion of saltwater from Vermillion Bay via the GIWW.

- The Calcasieu Lock, on the GIWW at mile 238.2 WHL–chamber 75 feet wide, 1,200 feet long, with a depth over the sills of 13 feet and a lift of 4 feet–was completed in 1950 and controls saltwater intrusion from the deep Calcasieu Ship Channel via the GIWW. Although it lies outside the Mermentau Basin, this lock provides protection to the freshwater marshes within the northwest portion of the basin.

- The Freshwater Bayou Lock–chamber 75 feet wide, 600 feet long, with a depth over the sills of 16 feet–is a part of the Freshwater Bayou Canal, completed in 1968, which provides a navigation channel from Intracoastal City to the Gulf of Mexico. The lock is at the Gulf of Mexico end of the canal and controls the intrusion of saltwater from the gulf but, because the head of the Freshwater Bayou Canal lies east of (outside of) the Leland Bowman Lock, some saltwater from Vermilion Bay enters.

- The Catfish Point Control Structure (a flood gate)–width 56 feet and depth over the sill 13 feet–is located at the Mermentau River's exit from Grand Lake and was completed in 1951. The flood gate controls salt water intrusion from the Gulf of Mexico into the lower Mermentau River, Grand Lake and White Lake.

- The Schooner Bayou Control Structure (a flood gate)–width 75 feet, depth over the sill 13 feet–was completed in 1951 as a replacement for the old Schooner Bayou Lock, built in 1913. The flood gate controls saltwater intrusion from Vermilion Bay via the Schooner Bayou Channel. The Schooner Bayou Channel was a part of the original "Inland Waterway Channel from Franklin to Mermentau, Louisiana," authorized in the March 2, 1907 Rivers and Harbors Act. The original Schooner Bayou Channel was 5 feet deep for a width of 40 feet. It was later enlarged to a depth of 9 feet for a width of 90 feet. The channel is still used for navigation.

In the Mermentau Basin, between the Leland Bowman (east side) and Calcasieu (west side) locks, the feel of the waterway changes. Its' not that the area is natural, like most of the Gulf Coast from the Florida Panhandle to Texas it's been heavily modified for drainage, irrigation, navigation and oil. The only thing not here is beach and suburban development. But this part of the waterway looks and feels more old-South, pre-petroleum and pre-USACE. The miles of salt marsh with a few patches of willow scrub and long dead trees, drowned or salt killed to the east and west give way to fresh (or slightly brackish) water with freshwater marshes, Cyprus swamps, patches of oak and in places rice fields, often dotted by rows of crayfish trap floats when flooded. Crayfish are a crop, raised in the seasonally flooded rice fields.

The waterway crosses the short Mermentau River at mile 202 WHL, about 35 miles above the river's mouth on the Gulf of Mexico and 37.5 miles below its head. A meandering navigation channel follows the Mermentau upstream from the waterway through Lake Arthur and past the lovely old town of Lake Arthur, to the ship building, oil service and grain facilities at the Port of Jennings just below the river's head–where the Bayou Nezpique and the Bayou des Cannes merge and become the Mermentau. The town of Jennings, the Parish seat of Jefferson Davis Parish, is where oil was discovered in Louisiana in 1901. The discovery was the impetus for the Port of Jennings, on the river four miles east of Jennings, and the improved Mermentau channel above Lake Arthur. Upstream from Jennings, both the Bayous are navigable to the Interstate 10 bridges.

The Calcasieu Lock at mile 238.2 WHL, one of the busiest locks in the country–in 2016 it handled 38,689,000 tons of commercial commodities–serves as both a saltwater intrusion barrier, protecting the freshwaters of the Mermentau Basin during times of low water in the basin and as a flood water drain during periods of high water. Long navigation delays are common during high water events in the Mermentau Basin when the lock is being used solely to relieve flooding. The Corps of Engineers, New Orleans District is currently studying various options for solving this problem. Two and a half miles west of the Calcasieu Lock the waterway crosses the Calcasieu River Channel, the 68-mile-long, deep draft, dredged channel that connects the Port of Lake Charles, 12th on the USACE's 2016 list of domestic ports by tonnage handled, to the Gulf of Mexico.

Lake Charles was a port of call for coasting vessels well before the Civil War but shifting sand and mud bars in Lake Calcasieu and at the mouth of the Calcasieu River limited commerce to shoal draft vessels. In 1910 Congress authorized a 5-foot-deep by 40-foot-wide Intracoastal Waterway from the Mermentau River to the Sabine River (the Louisiana-Texas state line) and construction of the section between the Calcasieu and Sabine Rivers was completed in 1915. In 1921 the Louisiana State Legislature authorized Calcasieu Parish to raise and use local funds to enlarge the Calcasieu to the Sabine section of the waterway and the Calcasieu River Channel from its junction with the Intracoastal Waterway to the town of Lake Charles, to a depth of 30 feet for a bottom width of 125 feet in order to provide deep water access from the Gulf of Mexico to Lake Charles. In 1922 the voters of Calcasieu Parish approved a $2.75 million bond issue for the project. The project–known variously as the Lake Charles Deep Water Project, the Lake Charles Deep Water Canal or the Lake Charles Channel–was completed in 1926. Additionally, between 1922 and 1926 the Lake Charles Harbor and Terminal District was created by the Louisiana State Legislature and new port facilities were built. The final cost of the channel and port projects was $5 million, paid entirely with locally raised funds.

In legislation passed in 1926 Congress made the new Port of Lake Charles an official Port of Entry and on April 2, 1926 the *SS Sewalls* Point, the first ocean going freighter to call at the new port offloaded 8,205 tons of mixed cargo. The formal ceremony opening the new port was held on November 30 1926 and the *USS Cleveland C-19*, a Denver class protected light cruiser with an overall length of 304 ft., a beam of 44 ft. and a draft of 15 ft., 8 inches (built in 1901 and scrapped in 1930) was docked at the new wharves for the ceremony.[69] In the Rivers and Harbors Acts of August 30, 1935 and August 25, 1937 Congress authorized the federal government to assume the costs of maintaining the 30 foot channel and assigned the project to the Corps of Engineers. In the Chief of Engineers Annual Report for 1940 (Part 1, Vol. 1, page 904) the channel was reported to be in good condition with a controlling depth of 30 feet at mid channel throughout. For a brief period, the section of the

GIWW between the Calcasieu and Sabine Rivers was a big ship canal.

The first federal project involving the entire Calcasieu River from deep water in the Gulf of Mexico to the Port of Lake Charles was authorized in the Omnibus Rivers and Harbors Act of 1938, which included $1 million for the "Calcasieu River Deep Waterway Project." The Act specified a channel from deep water in the gulf to the Port of Lake Charles with a depth of 33 feet for a bottom width of 250 feet and with jetties at the river mouth. The project was completed in early 1941, at a final cost of $9.2 million, and the opening ceremony was held on July 12, 1941. When the river channel was open and operating, maintenance of the 30-foot channel from the Sabine to the Calcasieu ceased. Since then the waterway between the Sabine and the Calcasieu has been maintained at the GIWW dimensions, a depth of 12 feet for a width of 125 feet.

The Calcasieu River Channel, as it exists today, was authorized in the Rivers and Harbors Act of July 14, 1960. That Act directed the USACE to enlarge the Calcasieu River Channel to a depth of 42 feet for a width of 800 feet from deep water 32 miles out in the Gulf of Mexico to the jetties at the mouth of the river and a depth of 40 feet for a width of 400 feet from the jetties upstream for 36 miles, to just below the Interstate 10 bridge in the Port of Lake Charles. To maintain authorized project depths, portions of the channel in the gulf off the jetties must be dredged twice annually and, above the jetties, mile 5 to mile 28 must be dredged every other year.

9. The Calcasieu to Brownsville, Texas

In 1841 the Republic of Texas[70] granted the Brazos Canal Company a charter to build a toll canal between West Galveston Bay and the mouth of the Brazos River. The company began digging in 1847 using a labor force of slaves rented from local slave owners (the canal was called the slave canal.) The first mile took two years to dig and the project was abandoned. On February 8, 1850, a successor company, the Galveston and Brazos Navigation Company received a State charter for a canal to connect West Galveston Bay to the Brazos River. A detailed (1:20,000 scale) U.S. Coast Survey chart of the Texas coast between the Brazos River and West Galveston Bay inshore of the barrier islands, derived from surveys carried out during February, March and April 1852, shows "New Canal(s)" at three points and a line of probable spoil islands between Christmas Point and a natural tidal channel through Mud Island that connected Oyster Bay (todays Bastrop Bay) Bay to West Galveston Bay.

By 1855 the Galveston and Brazos Navigation Company had completed a navigable 50-foot-wide by (believed to have been) three-foot-deep channel between West Galveston Bay and the Brazos River and small stern wheel steam boats and other small craft were transporting manufactured goods and agricultural products, primarily cotton, between the Port of Galveston and the Brazos. Beginning in 1859 and apparently working through the Civil War, the State of Texas improved the connection between the Brazos and Galveston Canal Company's canal and Galveston by dredging a channel through West Galveston Bay between the Port of Galveston and Mud Island and after the Civil War the canal company carried out some widening and deepening of the channel from Mud Island west to the Brazos. In 1892 Congress authorized the enlarging and straightening of the channel between Galveston and the Brazos and between 1893 and 1895 the USACE dredged the channel, from west of Galveston to and through Mud Island to Christmas Point.

On June 16, 1896 Major A. M. Miller USACE, in a survey report to Congress described the Galveston and Brazos Navigation Company's canal as being about 11 miles in length, with a width varying from 40 to 80 feet and a depth varying from 2 to 7 feet at low tide. Major Miller went on to state that the canal was used by fishing boats, market craft and, during the cotton season, stern-wheel steamers and that the company was entitled to and did collect a toll from all passing vessels. At the end of the report Major Miller said "the canal company has done very little of late years to improve or deepen the canal; the property is not valuable as a private investment...and in view of the high estimate of value placed upon it is not worthy of improvement by the United States. If these works could be purchased at a reasonable price, I think the Government would be justified in keeping the route open." [71] On February 11, 1897 the company offered to sell the canal to the federal government and the purchase was completed in December of 1902.

Chapter 9

In the Rivers and Harbors Act of January 21, 1927 Congress authorized the extension from Galveston to Corpus Christi of the 9-foot-deep by 100-foot-wide Louisiana and Texas Intracoastal Waterway. The 1933 edition (corrected to May 1934) of U.S. Coast and Geodetic Survey Chart 1283 still shows and names the 11.5-mile-long Galveston and Brazos Navigation Company's canal between West Galveston Bay and the Brazos River and carries a note that "The controlling depth in the canal was 3½ feet in February 1934." The 9 foot by 100-foot waterway from Galveston to Corpus Christi was not completed until 1942. That year, on July 23, as a national defense requirement–brought about by German submarine activity in the Gulf of Mexico–Congress authorized the expansion of the entire Gulf Intracoastal Waterway from 9 feet by 100 feet to 12 feet deep by 125 feet wide. The Corpus Christi to Brownsville section of the 9 by 100-foot waterway had not yet been authorized, so that section was initially dredged at the enlarged dimensions. The project was completed, and the final segment of the GIWW opened, on June 18, 1949.

Between the Calcasieu River and its western terminus in the turning basin at the head of the Port of Brownsville, the GIWW is a dredged channel cut through marshes, shallow bays, lagoons and low, flat sandy land. Very little of the waterway follows natural rivers, tidal creeks or bayous that are 12 feet deep or deeper, all of the large bays and lagoons through which the waterway runs have average depths of less than 12 feet and some have half that, or less. The numerous land cuts are dredged through marshes and land that is often barely above the reach of the highest tides and in wind driven higher water coastal flooding is common.

The tide is essentially diurnal, but some of the tide gages–for example: the gages at Port Arthur, High Island and East Matagorda–show a mixed pattern with a deep lower low followed

239

by a high and then a nominal, barely noticeable low followed by another high. This can cause apparent high water for three quarters of the 24-hour tide cycle. Inshore, along the GIWW the tide ranges from nominal to 1-2 feet, on the ocean side of the barrier islands and in the passes the range is greater. Both inshore and alongshore strong or prolonged winds can raise the water level to as much as 4 feet above tidal Mean High Water or lower it to 3-3.5 feet below tidal Mean Low Water.

Currents are generally weak, but the large bays, lagoons and marshes, although shallow, contain a lot of water and the larger rivers drain vast areas. The passes through which water enters and exits with the tide are few, narrow and, unless improved, generally constricted by bars. So, where the waterway crosses an inlet, at the larger river crossings and where the waterway enters a large bay (particularly Matagorda Bay) currents can be strong: in Sabine Pass and the lower Sabine Neches Waterway currents reach 2.2 mph; at the Galveston Inlet crossing 2.5 mph, at the Galveston Causeway Bridges 1.7 mph and at the Matagorda Bay Inlet crossing 2.8 mph. As with water levels, the winds augment or decrease currents–strong northers can create dangerous currents–and wind can create a noticeable current in places where there is normally little, if any.

The prevailing coastal wind direction is southeasterly and the wind averages 9-11 knots. Off Galveston the prevailing winds are N in January, SE from February through June, S in July, SE in August, E in September and October and SE in November and December. In the Coastal Bend, off Aransas Pass, the wind is northerly in December and January and SE throughout the rest of the year. And off Port Isabel, the dominant wind throughout the year is SE. In the early morning the wind speed ranges from calm to 5 knots, in the afternoon, as the land warms and the sea breeze kicks in, the wind speed increases to 15+ knots and often remains high until midnight or 2:00 a.m. In the large, shallow bays along the Texas coast, the sea breeze reinforced winds often create choppy to rough conditions and salt haze–a smoky appearing haze created by salt particles thrown into the air by waves and choppy water–limits visibility.

The GIWW is the most heavily commercial section of the entire Boston to Brownsville Waterway and the short 159-mile segment between the Calcasieu Lock (mile 238.2 WHL) and Freeport (mile

A mobile drilling rig on the GIWW

395 WHL) is the most heavily utilized portion of the GIWW. Along this section of the waterway there are 8 deep water commercial ports, among them the 2nd, 5th, 12th and 15th largest ports in the United States (by tonnage handled in 2016) and Houston, the second largest port in the United States overall, is the largest for foreign export tonnage. Waterway traffic is intense and constant. Westbound in January 2011, in the 56.7 miles between the Calcasieu Lock and the Texas Route 87 Bridge (mile 288.8 WHL)

where the waterway parts from the Sabine-Neches Waterway, we met, passed or were passed by: twenty-seven pushboats with barges, most with multiple barges, 3 ocean going ships, a barge mounted mobile drilling rig that was being both pushed and pulled, a large drilling rig service vessel with a deck load of drill pipe and a light boat...roughly one non-fishing commercial vessel every two miles. At the Route 87 Bridge I quit counting. If I had continued all the way to Freeport the vessel count would have been much, much higher.

From the Calcasieu River, the GIWW runs south to the impressive Ellender Lift Bridge (mile 243.8 WHL) which clears 50 feet when down and 135 feet raised. Beyond the bridge, the waterway runs almost straight west to the Sabine River (the Louisiana-Texas state line) and the Sabin-Neches Waterway–the 79-mile-long deep draft ship channel that makes the inland east Texas cities of Port Arthur, Beaumont and Orange sea ports. The GIWW follows the Sabine River and the Sabine-Neches Canal, a section of the Sabine Neches Waterway, to the mouth of Taylor Bayou.

Prior to improvement maritime commerce through Sabine Pass–the gulf outlet for the Angelina, Neches and Sabine River basins and the Sabine Lake Estuary–was limited to shoal draft vessels by oyster reefs and shifting mud and sand bars. The shallowest area, the Blue Buck Bar off Blue Buck Point, Louisiana, at the south end of Sabine Lake was reported to have only 3.5 feet of water over it at low tide. In 1875 Congress appropriated $20,000 for "the improvement of Sabine Pass." Between the 1875 appropriation and 1896, thirteen Rivers and Harbors Acts authorized and appropriated funds for improving some or all of: Sabine Pass, Sabine Pass Harbor, Sabine Lake, the Blue Buck Bar and the mouths of the Sabine and/or Neches Rivers. By the 1890s Sabine

Pass was being maintained at a depth of 20-25 feet and the town of Sabine Pass (founded in the 1830s, incorporated 1861) was a sea port and a customs port of entry. But upstream navigation to the Neches and Sabine Rivers was still limited to barges and shoal draft vessels. The USACE's channel ran up the middle of Sabine Lake and rapid re-siltation was a chronic problem.

Port Arthur, Texas (incorporated 1898) was founded by Arthur E. Stilwell in 1895 as the southern, Gulf of Mexico, terminus for his Kansas City, Pittsburg and Gulf Railroad Company. On February 8, 1897 Stilwell and others associated with the Kansas City, Pittsburg and Gulf Railroad, along with the Missouri, Kansas and Texas Trust Company and the Texarkana & Fort Smith Railway Company incorporated the Port Arthur Channel & Dock Company. In the two years following its incorporation, the Port Arthur Channel & Dock Company dredged a 7.1-mile-long canal with a surface width of approximately 180 feet and a depth of 25 feet, along the western shore of Sabine Lake from deep water in Sabine Pass to the mouth of Taylor Bayou. To help prevent the re-siltation that plagued the USACE's mid-lake channel, dredged material was piled in a berm between the canal and the lake. In addition to the canal, the company built: a turning basin in Taylor Bayou, docking slips, wharves, a lumber dock, a grain elevator, a railyard and a rail line connecting the complex to an existing Texarkana & Fort Smith Railway Company track.

On September 10, 1900 the Port Arthur Channel & Dock Company went into receivership and, on January 7, 1902, they were sold to The Kansas City Southern Railway Company which transferred them to a newly created corporation...the Port Arthur Canal & Dock Company.[72] In early 1906 the assets of the Port Arthur Canal & Dock Company were offered to the federal government, free of charge, in exchange for Port Arthur being made a customs port of entry and on June 19, 1906 Congress passed an Act accepting the transfer.[73]

The January 10, 1901 Spindletop well[74] and the resulting east Texas oil boom led to rapid local economic growth throughout the Beaumont, Port Arthur, Orange area. Pipelines quickly connected Port Arthur and its deep-water canal to the emerging oil fields. Gulf Oil and Texaco (chartered in Beaumont) were founded in 1901, during the first year of the boom and both immediately built large refineries in Port Arthur. By 1909 Port Arthur was the 12th largest port in the United States in the value of its exports and by 1914 it was the largest petroleum refining center in the nation. Port Arthur was ranked 20th on the USACE's 2016 list of domestic ports by tonnage and it was still primarily a petroleum port. Significantly more than half of the tonnage handled was petroleum or petroleum products and Port Arthur was home to three refineries, among them Motiva Enterprises, the nation's largest.

Political pressure to extend the deep draft Port Arthur Canal to the Neches and Sabine Rivers (and to develop deep water facilities in Lake Charles, Louisiana) began as soon as the oil began to flow. By the end of 1908, the USACE had dredged a 100-foot-wide by 9-foot-deep barge channel...designated the Sabin-Neches Canal...that connected Taylor Bayou and the deep draft Port Arthur Canal to the Neches and Sabine Rivers. The Corps had also cleared and dredged navigable barge channels 100 feet wide by 9 feet deep up the Neches River to Beaumont and up the Sabine River to Orange. By May 1916, the Sabine-Neches Canal was a ship canal. Over the next 90 years the Sabine-Neches Channel was progressively enlarged and by 2014, the project depths for the channel, now called the Sabine-Neches Waterway, were:[75]

- 42 feet for a width of 800 feet in the Outer Bar Channel
- 40 feet for a width of 800-500 feet in the Jetty Channel

- 40 feet for a width of 500-1150 feet in the pass channel
- 40 feet for a width of 500 feet in the Port Arthur Canal
- 40 feet for a width of 400 feet in the Sabine-Neches Canal from the Port Arthur Canal to the mouth of the Neches River and 30 feet for a width of 200 feet from the mouth of the Neches River to the mouth of the Sabine River
- 40 feet for a width of 400-1306 feet in the Neches River from its mouth to Beaumont and then 30 feet for a width of 200 feet to the Bethlehem Shipyards
- 30 feet for a width of 200-1400 feet in the Sabine River from its mouth to 30°05′N, 93°43′W (where the old highway bridge crossed the Sabine) in Orange and 25 feet for a width of 100-200 feet in the channel around Orange Harbor Island.

The minor Port of Orange, on the Sabine River at the junction of the Sabine River Channel and the GIWW (mile 266.3 WHL) was first incorporated in 1852 and is the county seat of Orange County. The Port of Orange is primarily a ship building, servicing, maintenance and lay (storage) port.

Beaumont, founded in 1835, incorporated in 1881 and the county seat of Jefferson County, is 18.5 miles up the Neches River from GIWW mile 277 WHL. Beaumont was ranked 5th on the USACE's 2016 list of domestic ports by tonnage handled. Beaumont is, like Port Arthur, primarily a petroleum port. Of the total tonnage handled in 2016, almost 60% was petroleum or petroleum products.[76] Beaumont is also a part of the National Port Readiness Network and is the nation's largest military staging, shipping and receiving port.[77]

At mile 288.6 WHL the GIWW leaves the Sabine-Neches Waterway and continues west for approximately 61 miles through a series of marsh and land cuts, skirting the High Island Salt Dome and its associated oil fields and following the East Galveston Bay side of the Bolivar Peninsula to its tip at mile 349.3 WHL...Galveston Inlet.

The eye of category two hurricane Ike crossed the east end of Galveston Island between 2:00 and 3:00 a.m. the morning of September 13, 2008 and then tracked north up the eastern side of Galveston bay. The stronger winds and higher storm surge east of the eye swept the Bolivar Peninsula. In January 2011 we brought our boat from Mobile, Alabama to Texas and between High Island and Freeport, Ike was still very evident. In January 2015, there was little evidence of Ike remaining, new construction, denser than pre-Ike, was everywhere and the HGTV show Beachfront Bargain Hunt was touting the Bolivar Peninsula and West Galveston...and, at least on screen, saying nothing about hurricanes.

The beaches of the upper Texas Coast, from Sabine Pass to the Brazos River–the Bolivar Peninsula, Galveston Island and Follets Island–like most of the east and gulf coast beaches are lined with: condos, hotels, motels, houses, surf shops, restaurants and everything else that goes with beach resort and residential development. In an attempt to protect these investments, portions of the beaches have been stabilized with groins, geo-tubes and other structures. And sections, including the entire length of the beach in front of the Galveston Seawall, must be nourished to replace sand eroded and washed away in spite of, or perhaps because of, the stabilization structures. In the half century between 1960 and 2010, nine hurricanes have made landfall along this part of the coast, roughly one every five and a half years.

Early surveys and plans for the Intracoastal Waterway's route from Sabine Lake to the Brazos River, had the waterway running down the middle of East Bay, across Galveston Bay and then down the middle of West Bay to the existing Galveston and Brazos Navigation Company canal (acquired by the federal government in 1902.) In 1923 the Gulf Division Engineer, Col. George M. Hoffman, rerouted the proposed waterway from the open bays to marsh and land cuts along the shore stating: "This route, while a little longer and requiring more excavation will cost less for maintenance than other routes previously proposed through the bays...boats using this route will be less exposed to storm conditions in the open bay."[78] In East Bay the waterway follows the Bolivar Peninsula, in West Bay it follows the north, mainland, side because of existing development on the Galveston Island side.

The 27-mile-long Bolivar Peninsula, 3¼ miles wide at its widest point, separates East Bay, the eastern arm of Galveston Bay, from the Gulf of Mexico. The first successful, settlers arrived on the Bolivar Peninsula in 1838 and by 1850 15 families were farming and ranching along the peninsula. The community on the tip of the peninsula that became Port Bolivar, was first settled before and during the Civil War but it did not really develop until after the federal government improved the Galveston Entrance Channel, Bolivar Roads and the Port of Galveston in order to make them usable by ocean going ships.

On May 9, 1894 the Gulf and Inter-State Railway Company was chartered. The company planned to build a rail line from Port Bolivar to the Southern Pacific rail line in Liberty County, north of Galveston Bay. Four months after being chartered, the company was reorganized, the name was changed to The Gulf and Inter-State Railway Company of Texas and the proposed route was changed to Port Bolivar to a bridge over the Red River, east of Dallas, in either Fannin or Grayson County. Only the 70 miles between Port Bolivar and Beaumont were built and that section was in use by the end of 1896. In 1898, L. P. Featherstone and Fox Winnie, contractors for the Gulf and Inter-State Railway, who intended to develop a deep-water port at Port Bolivar, acquired the railway. In conjunction with Featherstone and Winnie, the Santa Fe Railway organized the Santa Fe Dock and Channel Company to build docks and a railyard in Port Bolivar. In 1908 the Atchison, Topeka and Santa Fe Railway Company acquired the rail line and railyard and in 1914 they leased the line and yard to the Gulf Colorado and Santa Fe Railway Company.[79]

The 1900 Galveston Hurricane nearly destroyed Port Bolivar and recovery was slow; it was June 9, 1909 before the first ocean going vessel docked in the new port and later that year another hurricane washed out the rail line. By 1915 the port was in full operation and the U.S. Coast Pilot's description said that:

> "Port Bolivar, at the southwestern extremity of Bolivar Peninsula and 3½ miles north of Galveston, is the terminus of a line of the Gulf, Colorado and Santa Fe Railway from Beaumont and the Interior of the State. It has good terminal facilities and car ferry service to Galveston. Lumber and cotton are the principal articles of commerce. A channel 200-feet wide and 24 feet deep (project depth 30 feet) has been dredged from Bolivar Roads to a turning basin 1,000-feet wide in front of the wharves."[80]

On August 17, 1915, another major hurricane hit Galveston Island and the Bolivar Peninsula. The storm made landfall with sustained winds of 145 mph and a storm surge estimated at 21 feet. Galveston was largely protected by its new seawall but, on the low-lying Bolivar Peninsula, the rail line was again washed out and Port Bolivar and its port facilities were badly damaged. World War I brought a boom in shipping but the storm damaged port facilities were never fully rebuilt and the dredging of the Houston Ship Channel to 30 feet (completed in 1925) along with the post war shipping downturn and the great depression ended Port Bolivars days as a deep-water commercial port. The 27 miles of track between Port Bolivar and High Island was abandoned in 1942 and the ports channel, turning basin and wharf area silted in and were filled with dredge spoil.[81] Today Port Bolivar is a beach community and home to a large commercial fishing and shrimping fleet.

The Galveston Entrance lies between the tip of the Bolivar Peninsula and Galveston Island. The Entrance is both the navigable inlet from the Gulf of Mexico to Galveston Bay and the primary outlet for the drainage basins of the San Jacinto River, the Trinity River, Buffalo Bayou and the whole of the Galveston Estuary. Prior to dredging the Galveston Entrance, like all of the entrances, inlets and passes along the gulf coast, was obstructed by a bar and was suitable for navigation by shoal draft vessels only. A United States Coast Survey[82] chart of the Galveston Entrance published in 1853–based on hydrographic surveys carried out in 1851 and 1852–shows 12 feet over the entrance bar, 24-36 feet in Bolivar Roads,[83] 12-13 feet over the bar between Bolivar Roads and Galveston Harbor, 19-30 feet in Galveston Harbor and less than 10 feet in the small section of Galveston Bay shown.

Small scale federal dredging of the Galveston Entrance Bar began in 1870. A series of projects over the next 30 years progressively enlarged and deepened the inlet until by 1910 the Galveston jetties were as they are today–converging stone jetties 4½ miles long and 1¼ miles apart at the seaward end–and the entrance channel had a least depth of 30 feet. Since 1910, as ships grew larger, the channels depth and width have increased.[84] In 2015 the Galveston Entrance channel had an authorized project depth of 45 feet for a width of 800-1,000 feet in the Entrance Channel (seaward of the jetties) and 45 feet for a width of 800 feet through the Outer Bar Channel (between the jetties), Bolivar Roads and the Inner Bar Channel.

Galveston, both Bay and Island, were named after Bernardo de Galvez, Spanish Viceroy of New Spain (1785-1786) by Spanish Naval Captain and Cartographer Jose Antonio de Evia (or Hevia) during his 1785-1786 surveying and mapping expedition along the gulf coast between the Florida Keys and Tampico, Mexico. The Port of Galveston was formally established, by the government of Mexico, on October 17, 1825 and the City of Galveston was incorporated in 1836 with the establishment of Galveston County immediately following Texas's independence from Mexico.[85] The Galveston Harbor channel leaves the entrance channel at the junction of the Inner Bar Channel and the Bolivar Channel. In 1912 the Galveston Harbor Channel had a depth of 30 feet for a width of 1,200 feet from Bolivar Roads to the head of the harbor. By 2015 the channel had a depth of 40-45 feet throughout[86] and Galveston was 52nd on the USACE's 2016 list of domestic ports by tonnage handled.

The Houston and Texas City channels begin in Bolivar Roads a mile in from the Galveston Harbor Channel.

Texas City, 15th on the USACE's 2016 list of domestic ports by tonnage handled, began in 1893 when the Texas City Improvement Company received permission from the State of Texas and the federal government to dredge a 6.8-mile-long channel from Shoal Point, on the mainland opposite Galveston, to Bolivar Roads. By 1896 the privately dredged channel had a minimum depth of 16 feet. The tide flowing into and out of West Bay from Galveston Bay caused constant channel shoaling and the company turned to Congress, and the Corps of Engineers for channel dredging and maintenance.[87] In 1899 Congress authorized and funded deepening the channel to 25 feet, with the usual provision that the company's interest in and rights to the channel be transferred, free of cost, to the federal government. By May of 1916 the channel had a controlling depth of 30 feet and the 5.3-mile-long Texas City Dike had been completed. The dike limited channel silting and offered some protection to the channel and port from storm surges on Galveston Bay. At the end of 2014 the Texas City Channel had a project depth of 45 feet for a width of 400 feet from Bolivar Roads to the turning basin and the 1,200-foot-wide by 4,320-foot-long turning basin also had a project depth of 45 feet. In both the channel and the turning basin, the controlling depth exceeded project depth.

In 2016 the Port of Houston was the 2nd largest port in the United States exceeded only, and narrowly, by the Port of South Louisiana, and Houston was 1st in foreign trade tonnage. The Port of Houston was created by the City of Houston on June 10, 1841 and 41 years later, on July 14, 1870, the port was made an official port of entry. In December 1909, in order to secure a deep-water channel to Houston, the city offered to assume half the cost of dredging a 25-foot-deep channel from Bolivar Roads to the turning basin at the head of the port. The offer was accepted and little more than a year later Houston's voters approved the creation of the Harris County Houston Ship Channel Navigation District (now the Port of Houston Authority) and authorized $1,250,000 in bonds–fifty percent of the Corps of Engineers estimated cost. Work on the project began in June 1912. The Corps had estimated that the project would take three and a half years, it was completed on September 7, 1914 and the channel was officially opened on November 10, 1914.[88] By 1925 the channel had been deepened to 30 feet from Bolivar Roads to the turning basin. In February 2015 the Houston Ship Channel's project dimensions were: 45 feet deep for a width of 530 feet from Bolivar Roads to Carpenter Bayou, 40 feet deep for a width of 300-700 feet from Carpenter Bayou to Clinton Island and then 36 feet deep for varying widths to the upper turning basin. Two outlying parts of the Port of Houston, the Bayport Terminal and the Barbours Cut Terminal, both on the west side of the upper part of Galveston Bay, also had project depths of 45 feet in the federal portion of their channels.[89]

Galveston Bay–the aggregate of Galveston Bay, Trinity Bay, East Galveston Bay and West Galveston Bay–is approximately 35 miles long, with a maximum width of 19 miles, an average depth of just over 7 feet, an open water surface area of almost 600 square miles and more than 170 square miles of salt and brackish marsh rim the bay. The bay and its related marshes are the largest bay and estuary on the Texas Coast and the seventh largest estuary in the United States. The bay and estuary lie entirely within the Houston Standard Metropolitan Statistical area and, according to the U.S. Bureau of the Census, the five counties surrounding the bay–Harris, Brazoria, Galveston, Liberty and Chambers Counties–had an estimated population of 4,991,794 people in 2012.[90] A population that equaled approximately 19.2% of Texas's total population and 78% of the state's coastal population.

Despite the high population and heavy, primarily petrochemical, industrial development around Galveston bay, the bay and estuary have historically been a major source of seafood, particularly oysters, brown and pink shrimp and blue crabs. Shrimp and blue crabs remain important and productive fisheries but the oyster harvest has declined. In 2007, prior to Hurricane Ike (2008) the oyster harvest in Galveston Bay equaled approximately eighty percent of the Texas oyster harvest and had a value of more than $30 million. As Ike tracked across the bay its storm surge and turbulence deposited from 2 to more than 12 inches of sediment on the oyster reefs, smothering the oysters and killing more than half of the reefs. The year after Ike less than $7 million worth of oysters were harvested in the bay.[91] Because of the value of oysters, both as seafood and in filtering and cleaning the bays waters,[92] the state and the regional counties are working to restore the oyster reefs.

Around Galveston Bay, land subsidence is a serious, widespread and ongoing problem. While there is some natural subsidence caused by the settling and compaction of the deep layers of unconsolidated, organic rich sediments in and around the bay and oil and gas extraction has caused localized subsidence, the primary cause…the overwhelmingly dominant cause…is ground water pumping to meet the needs of the sprawling densely inhabited urban area that has grown up along the west and north west of the bay. Significant subsidence was noted as early as the first decade of the twentieth century and by World War II subsidence was affecting much of the Houston area. By the mid-1970s a broad swath along the Houston Ship Channel and Buffalo Bayou, from Baytown to Houston had subsided more than 6 feet. By 1995 parts of Pasadena had subsided more than 10 feet and almost 3,200 square miles of the greater Houston urban area had subsided a foot or more.[93] Coastal flooding and submerged sections of marsh and shore are now the norm.

In 1975, the Texas Legislature created the Harris-Galveston Coastal Subsidence District: to control ground water pumping, aid the development of alternative water sources and promote water conservation and education. Although a large part of the urban areas water needs are now being met by surface water, pumping is still a significant source of fresh water and subsidence is ongoing. Subsidence lags behind pumping and once the water is gone the slow compression of the aquifer(s) cannot be controlled, stopped or altered.

According to the United States Geological Survey and the National Atmospheric and Oceanic Administration, tide gage records indicate that average global sea level has risen 19 centimeters (7.5 inches) over the last century and that the rate of rise is increasing. In the Galveston Bay area, tide gage records show that sea level rise has significantly exceeded the global average. When the effects of land subsidence are combined with an inexorably rising sea...raising and/or sea walling the shore where infrastructure cannot be moved and a retreat from the sea in other areas seems inevitable.

Galveston to Brownsville

From the tip of the Bolivar Peninsula, the GIWW crosses Bolivar Roads, the Houston Ship Channel and the Texas City Channel to the Pelican Island Cut, approximately Mile 351 WHL, where it enters West Galveston Bay. From Pelican Island cut to its terminus in the Brownsville turning basin, except for short segments in Matagorda Bay, Aransas Bay and Corpus Christi Bay, the waterway follows dredged channels and land cuts.

At miles 357.2 & 357.3 WHL the GIWW passes under the Galveston Causeway RR Bridge and the twin spans of the Gulf Freeway (I-45) Bridge. Just west of the bridges, broad and deep Offatts Bayou cuts into Galveston Island. In the 19th century, prior to the Great Galveston Hurricane of 1900 (landfall on September 8, 1900), Offatts Bayou was a narrow but apparently fairly deep tidal marsh creek. In 1827 some of the first American (Anglo) settlers on Galveston Island settled along and near Offatts Bayou.[94] Following the 1900 hurricane, Galveston's elevation above mean sea level was raised by between 6 and 17 feet. Offatts Bayou's current size, shape and depth are a result of the bayou and its surrounding marsh having been used as one of the sources for the fill that elevated Galveston. Today the bayou's shores are heavily developed and the bayou is the most popular recreational boat anchorage in the entire Houston-Galveston area.

Off the mouth of Offatts Bayou the GIWW turns north, passes between North Deer Island and Tiki Island–a residential development built on salt marsh and dredge spoil that was largely destroyed by Hurricane Ike–and continues west to the Corpus Christi ship channel following the alignment of the original (1927) 9-foot-deep by 100-foot-wide waterway.

At Mile 390 WHL the GIWW intersects the Galveston and Brazos Navigation Company's Canal, dredged between 1851 and 1855. It then follows the old canal for 4 miles, to Freeport and the Freeport Inlet–the original, natural mouth of the Brazos River. The old canal's entire 11.5-mile route–from West Galveston Bay through Mud Cut (Mud Island), across Bastrop Bay to Christmas Point, around Christmas Point and across Christmas Bay to Rattlesnake Point, across Drum bay to Drum Point, through a land cut to Oyster Creek and from Oyster Creek to the Brazos–can still be traced on modern nautical charts.[95]

Freeport, like Texas City, began life as a company town. The Freeport Sulphur Company (today Freeport McMoRan), was incorporated on July 12, 1912 for the purpose of mining Sulphur and salt at, and drilling for oil and gas in the vicinity of, the Bryan Mound salt dome. The town was established in 1912 on the west side of the Brazos River, across from the historic town and port of Velasco. The Sulphur operation at Bryan Mound was closed in 1935 and the mine is now part of the National Petroleum Reserve. On March 7, 1940 Dow Chemical bought 800 harbor side acres in Freeport and by January 1941 their first plants were in operation and the company was producing magnesium and bromine from seawater. Today Dow Texas Operations sprawls over 7,000 acres, is the largest integrated chemical manufacturing complex in the

The GIWW near Freeport, Texas

western hemisphere and the Freeport areas largest employer. Which probably explains why Freeport is sometimes called Port Dow.[96]

256

Chapter 9

The Brazos River, unlike any other significant Texas stream that flows to the Gulf of Mexico, flows directly into the gulf without an intervening bay, lagoon or tidal basin. Prior to engineering intervention, the mouth of the river was obstructed by both a fluctuating nearshore inner bar that was frequently covered by as little as 4 feet of water and a deeper, more stable outer bar. Despite the bars, small schooners and coastal vessels used the port at Velasco and, as early as 1834 small sternwheel steam boats were ascending the Brazos as far as Washington on the Brazos. The danger in crossing the inner bar and the volume and value of the cotton and other agricultural commodities shipped from the Brazos River to Galveston spurred the building of the Galveston and Brazos Navigation Company's canal.

If there was a physical mile marker present, the marker for GIWW mile 395 WHL would be in the middle of the intersection of the Freeport Harbor Channel and the GIWW and directly off the entrance to the privately built and maintained Dow Barge Canal. Port Freeport was 33rd on the 2016 list of domestic ports by tonnage handled. Federal work on the mouth of the Brazos River and Freeport Harbor began in 1880, but little was accomplished until the first decade of the twentieth century. By 1911 the Corps of Engineers had constructed substantial jetties at the mouth of the river and had dredged an 18-foot-deep by 150-foot-wide channel from the outer end of the jetties to the port area. Flooding on the Brazos and sediment brought down by the river hampered port operations and in 1929 the river was dammed above Freeport and was diverted into a by-pass canal which reached the coast more than 6 miles west of the natural river mouth.[97] A Corps of Engineers survey carried out in February 2015 showed controlling depths of 44 feet in the Outer Bar (the approach) Channel, 43-44 feet in the Jetty Channel, 42-43 feet to and in the Lower Turning

Basin and 44-48 feet from the Lower Turning Basin to and in the Upper Turning Basin. The authorized project depths are 47 feet in the Outer Bar Channel and 45 feet from the Jetty Channel to and in the Upper Turning Basin.

Freeport may become one of the first gulf coast ports to be deepened for the larger New Panamax class ships. Port Freeport is on the mainland, behind the barrier islands, has good road, rail and water transportation links, has a large amount of vacant developable land close to the city and harbor and has a short channel that–because the Brazos River was diverted west of the town and harbor–has a low rate of siltation and is relatively easy to maintain. Port Freeport and local business interests would like to extend the Outer Bar Channel, deepen it to 55-58 feet and widen it to 600 feet, deepen the Jetty Channel and the lower harbor to 56 feet and deepen the channel to and the Upper Turning Basin to 51 feet.[98]

From June 25, 2013 when *Nauset* arrived in Texas through early 2014, we kept the boat at the Seabrook Marina and Shipyard, in Seabrook, Texas. During that time, we made several short trips to various places around Galveston Bay and along the gulf coast. In Freeport we stayed at a Marina in Surfside Beach on Follets Island– the ocean side of the waterway and a mile east of the Freeport Inlet. Texas Route 232 carries beach goers across the GIWW from Freeport to Surfside Beach. In 1967 the Texas Historical Commission placed a roadside marker with information about the Gulf Intracoastal Waterway near the junction of Route 232 and the Blue Water Highway, Texas Route 257. The information given is, and was in 1967, slightly less than historically accurate.

In full the marker reads:

"Gulf Intracoastal Waterway

This complex of barge canals and natural channels–most valuable waterway in America–stretches 1,116 mi. from Brownsville, Texas, to St. Marks, Florida. Is longer and carries more tonnage than Suez and Panama Canals. Is a vital link in economy of Texas and has been one of main causes of rapid development of Gulf Coast area.

The Canal system was begun in 1854 when a short canal was built from Galveston Bay to mouth of Brazos River as aid to Texas trade; it was 50 ft. wide 3½ ft. deep and dug by hand labor and mule teams. Later projects widened, lengthened canal along the coast.

Most important period in growth of the waterway system was result of determined efforts by two Texas businessmen, Clarence S. E. Holland and Roy Miller. In 1905-1907 these men organized the initial financial support, arranged construction and won congressional backing for canal improvements. By 1966 annual total tonnage on the waterway exceeded 78,500,000 tons.

Hundreds of Companies now have plants and warehouses along the canal; its impact on growth of Gulf Coast has been immense. Several inland cities have become seaports; canal helped to make Houston nation's third largest port. Low shipping costs created by waterway have brought prosperity to entire Texas Gulf Coast." (1967.)

The section of the Gulf Intracoastal Waterway between West Galveston Bay and the Brazos River is the oldest portion of the Waterway within Texas. But the GIWW's deepest historical roots lie in the New Orleans area and further east. In 2012 the GIWW carried 113,800,000 tons of commercial commodities (up 1.1% from 2011)[99] and the GIWW was the third most valuable waterway within in the United States ranking behind only the main stems of the Ohio and Mississippi Rivers. In 2012, the Panama Canal carried

333,700,000 tons[100] and the Suez Canal carried 928,472,000 tons.[101] In 1967, the GIWW was also third in value among domestic waterways and it carried far less tonnage than either the Panama Canal or the Suez Canal.

Between the Brazos Floodgates (mile 400.5-400.8 WHL) the waterway crosses the diverted and canalized Brazos River. Both the 1925 legislation that authorized the 9-foot-deep by 100-foot-wide waterway between New Orleans and Galveston and the 1927 legislation that extended the waterway to Corpus Christi, contained a provision authorizing the construction of locks and other structures, subject to funding, along the waterway where necessary. In Texas the Brazos and Colorado Rivers, during periods of high water, had strong enough currents and carried enough sediment and debris that control structures were deemed necessary. Funding for Floodgates on the GIWW at both rivers was included in the 1942 legislation that authorized enlarging the waterway and extended the waterway from Corpus Christi to the Brazos Santiago Pass, Port Isabell and Brownsville. The Brazos River Floodgates were completed in September 1943.

Under normal conditions the Brazos River has a current of about one-half mile per hour, but during periods of high water the current can reach 2.5 mph, or more. When the head differential, the difference between the water level in the river and the water level of the GIWW, reaches .7 feet, navigation restrictions go into effect and at a differential of 1.8 feet the gates are closed to navigation.

The Brazos Floodgates have a width, of 75 feet, wide enough that, current and river stage permitting, standard barges can be pushed through two abreast. Even fairly large tows can go through without having to break apart and go through in sections. But the gates are only .3 miles…1,584 feet…apart and they do not line up in a straight line, tows going through must make a 60 degree turn in the short distance between the gates. When the head differential reaches .7 feet and navigation restrictions go into effect, tows must break down and push through one barge at a time. Entering the river, they are pushing against the current surging from the river into the waterway, leaving the river the current is behind them. And, because of that between-the-gates bend the current hits them at an angle both entering and leaving. The Corps of Engineers has studied converting the Brazos Floodgates to locks. But it would be a major and expensive project that might require realigning the GIWW to eliminate the 60-degree bend. At this time the political will to authorize and fund such a project does not exist.

The 862-mile-long Colorado River–the 18th longest river in the United States and the longest entirely within one state–enters Matagorda Bay and the Gulf of Mexico at GIWW mile 442 WHL, near the town of Matagorda. Prior to the mid-1930s the Colorado River did not reach the Gulf of Mexico, it flowed into Matagorda Bay. Historically, both geologically and since the beginning of local written history, the lower Colorado has been plagued by the formation of massive log jams or rafts. There are references to a log raft, or rafts, in the lower Colorado from 1824, 1831, 1837 and many subsequent years. In the 1920s, the most recent log raft extended 46 miles upstream from just above the town of Matagorda. In 1923 the Texas Legislature passed legislation authorizing the hiring of General George Goethals (Corps of Engineers, Retired) to break up the Colorado raft. The general planned to slowly and carefully remove key logs along the east side of the raft and allow the river current to clear a channel. But a major flood in 1929 broke up the weakened raft before much had been accomplished. When the raft broke up the whole mess, logs, debris and impounded sediment, surged into and began building a delta in Matagorda Bay.

The 1934 Edition of U.S. Coast and Geodetic Survey Chart 1234, Matagorda Bay and Approaches, shows the building Colorado Delta extending approximately two thirds of the way across Matagorda Bay. On the 1934 chart, the delta is mostly broad mud flats but on the pro-grading face there is a small, well defined crow foot delta. The mouth of the Colorado is still in Matagorda Bay, the Matagorda Peninsula across from the building delta is unbroken and between the delta and the peninsula an area of 3 to 5-foot deep open water still connects East Matagorda Bay to the main bay.

By 1935 the delta had reached the Matagorda Peninsula, forming a land bridge from the mainland to the peninsula and cutting East Matagorda Bay off from the main body of the bay. During periods of high water, the mass of heavier debris close to the mainland and in the river mouth, backed up the river causing flooding around the mouth of the river and the town of Matagorda. In an attempt to control the flooding, Matagorda County cut a channel (now called the Colorado Navigation Channel) from the old river mouth on the mainland side of Matagorda Bay through the new delta and through the Matagorda Peninsula to the Gulf of Mexico. The flood relief channel was completed in 1936.

When the GIWW reached the Colorado the strong currents and frequently high water in the confined river were a problem. To protect the waterway and control the turbulence, strong currents and high water, floodgates were constructed on each side of the Colorado. The floodgates, completed in September 1944, were not as successful as the Brazos River floodgates. The high flow volume and frequent high water–at times the head differential reached 12 feet–caused excessive navigation delays and waterway closures. In May 1951 the USACE issued a contract for conversion of the Colorado floodgates to locks and the locks were in operation in

Looking west at the GIWW and the Colorado River Locks from the Matagorda bridge

April 1954. The lock chambers are 1200 feet long and the gates have a width of 75 feet and a depth over the sills of 15 feet.

At 352 square miles, Matagorda Bay is the second largest bay/estuarine system on the Texas coast. Before the construction of the flood relief/navigation channel in 1935/36 the Colorado River was the largest source of fresh water inflow into the estuary. While the channel brought relief from all but the worst floods, it also hustled essentially 100% of the Colorado's fresh water straight through to the Gulf of Mexico. Fresh Colorado River water no longer flowed into Matagorda Bay, the salt/fresh ratio changed and the estuarine system suffered. In 1990 the USACE agreed to dredge a channel from the river, at the locks, that would divert most of the rivers flow back into Matagorda Bay.

Unfortunately for Matagorda Bay...for the estuary...the Colorado River's drainage basin lies in a semiarid climatic region that is characterized by periods of moderate rainfall alternating with sometimes extended periods of moderate to severe drought. While the climate and the alternating periods of moderate rain and drought have not changed in the decades since the original drainage/navigation channel was built, the cultural geography of the basin has. On its way to the bay and estuary the Colorado flows through and provides the water for the Austin Metropolitan Statistical Area. The Austin SMSA is the second fastest growing urban area in the United States. In 1950 the population of the five counties within the Austin SMSA was 160,980, by 2015 the population had grown to 2,020,452 (estimated).[102] While the population and the need for water was growing, the Colorado River's rate of flow was not. Today, according to the Lower Colorado River Authority (LCRA), during dry years little of the Colorado River's water reaches the bay, in severe drought almost none and the bays' salinity can rise to hypersaline levels (>30-35 parts per thousand dissolved salt).

The Colorado River navigation channel, between the waterway and the gulf, is used by local recreational fisherman and shrimp boats. Upstream from the locks there is a navigable barge channel to the Port of Bay City. The USACE does not provide figures for the Port of Bay City, but the Texas Department of Transportation[103] says that the 15-mile-long channel to Bay City is 12 feet deep for a width of 100 feet and that Bay City handled 2,000,000 tons of commercial commodities in 2016.

West of the Colorado River the waterway follows a land cut to mile 455.6 where it enters Matagorda Bay. On the west side of the Bay, it crosses the historic Pass Cavallo channel, passes between the Port O'Connor[104] jetties and enters the 67 miles of land cuts and dredged channels that lead it west to Corpus Christi Bay. Pass Cavallo, the natural entrance to Matagorda Bay, lies between Decros Point at the tip of the Matagorda Peninsula and Matagorda

Island. Pass Cavallo was among the first inlets on the Texas coast to be used for navigation and, among Texas's natural inlets it was considered second only to Galveston. Depths over the outer bar and in the pass were relatively stable. Nautical charts produced in 1858, 1872, 1882, 1909 and 1934 show 9-11 feet over the outer bar and deep water (20 plus feet) in the pass.

The opening of the Colorado River flood channel decreased the amount of water flowing through Pass Cavallo and it began to shoal in. By 1949 the outer bar carried less than 6 feet at Mean Low Water. As an emergency measure the Corps cut a 3,000-foot-long, 17-foot-deep by 135-foot-wide channel through the outer bar. The project was completed in September 1949. Just in time for the strong category 2 (modern scale) hurricane that made landfall near Bay City and Matagorda on October 3, 1949. A month after the hurricane the newly dredged channel had been reduced to a depth of 10 feet and by 1952 it had shoaled to 8 feet. There has been no further attempt to dredge Pass Cavallo.

In 1958 Congress authorized a deep draft channel through Pass Cavallo, across Matagorda and Lavaca Bays to Point Comfort, on the east side of Lavaca Bay opposite Port Lavaca. Alcoa had established a facility at Point Comfort in 1948 and Union Carbide in 1954; both these firms, and developing oil interests, wanted deep water access.[105] Following hydrological studies, the shipping channels entrance was moved from Pass Cavallo to a cut across the Matagorda Peninsula approximately 4.5 miles east of Decros Point. Work on the channel began in 1962 and the first ocean going ships docked at Point Comfort in 1965.

The channel extends from deep water in the Gulf of Mexico, through the Matagorda Peninsula land cut and across Matagorda and Lavaca Bays for 22 miles to a turning basin at the port facilities on Point Comfort. Point Comfort was 76th on the USACE's 2016 list of domestic ports by tonnage (down from 48th in 2012.) In April 2015 the Matagorda Ship Channel's controlling depths were 40 feet for a width of 300 feet to and through the Jetty Channel, 35-37 feet for a width of 200-300 feet from the peninsula to Flashing Red 48, near the head of Matagorda Bay and from there 26-32 feet for a width of 200 feet to Point Comfort and 38 feet in the turning basin.

From Pass Cavallo to Aransas Pass the modern Intracoastal Waterway parallels an old steamboat and flat boat route composed of fairly short 4 to 5-foot deep cuts dredged through sand and oyster bars that connect the deeper bays. The steamboat route was built between the late 1840s and 1858, in part pursuant to the River Bill passed by the Texas State Legislature on August 13, 1856 [106] which, among other things, directed the Texas State Engineer to contract for the dredging of selected coastal channels and the cutting of oyster and sand bars. An 1858 chart titled Reconnaissance of the Coast of Texas Between Matagorda and Corpus Christi Bays, published by the U.S. Coast Survey, clearly shows the steamboat route.

On the Coast Survey's 1858 chart, the steamboat route runs from the town of Saluria—established in 1847 on the northwest point of Matagorda Island opposite Decros Point and across Saluria Bayou from Bayucos Island—through McHenry Bayou (today Saluria Bayou) to the dredged State Channel, which carried a minimum of 5 feet into Espiritu Santo Bay. The route continued west across Espiritu Santo to dredged Steamboat Pass and into San Antonio Bay. On the west side of San Antonio Bay, it passed through Ayres Dugout (a dredged cut through a bar) entered Mesquite Bay, passed through Belden Dugout and then through Cedar Dugout and into Carlos Bay, and on through the Cape Carlos Dugout to Aransas Bay. At the west end of Aransas Bay, the steamboat route dipped south and continued west to Aransas Pass through todays' Lydia Ann Channel.

In addition to the route between Matagorda Bay and Aransas Pass, the 1858 chart shows defined steamboat routes running up the east and west sides of San Antonio Bay to the mouth of the Guadeloupe River. The names Steamboat Pass, Ayres Dugout, Belden Dugout, Cedar Dugout and Cape Carlos Dugout appear on NOAA's current, detailed Intracoastal Waterway charts and many of the old cuts are still used by small boat recreational fisherman. Todays' Intracoastal Waterway Alternate Route, which leads waterway traffic to Aransas Pass via the western half of Aransas Bay and the Lydia Ann Channel, follows the old steamboat route.

At mile 492 WHL, on the east side of San Antonio Bay, the 34.8-mile-long barge channel to the Port of Victoria leaves the waterway. The Guadalupe River carried limited steamboat traffic from ports on Matagorda and Corpus Christi Bays to the Port of Victoria from the mid-1840s to the 1880s. Prior to the Civil War there was scheduled service between Saluria (Pass Cavallo) and Victoria; the trip was said to take two days.[107]

In 1905, Clarence Holland, a Victoria, Texas banker and President of the Victoria Businessmen's Association called for a meeting of Texas and Louisiana businessmen interested in the construction of a waterway along the gulf coast between Brownsville, Texas and Donaldsonville, Louisiana. The meeting, held in Victoria, Texas in August 1905–without representation from Louisiana, because of a Yellow Fever outbreak–resulted in the creation of the Interstate Inland Waterway League. Over time the League became the Intracoastal Waterway League of Louisiana and Texas and eventually the Gulf Intracoastal Canal Association. The Association has been a strong advocate of and lobbyist for the Gulf Intracoastal Waterway.

The 1945 Act that enlarged the GIWW from 9 feet deep by 100 feet wide to 12 feet by 125 feet included authorization for lateral channels to several ports, one of which was Victoria. Work on building the Victoria Barge Channel began in 1951 and the channel and turning basin were completed in 1965. The federal project dimensions for the channel and for the turning basin in the Port of Victoria are 12 feet deep for a width of 125 feet, but the 33rd Edition (corrected to September 2016) of NOAA Chart 11315 gives a controlling depth of 9.5 feet in the channel and 11 feet in the turning basin. The Port of Victoria was ranked 74th on the USACE's 2016 list of domestic ports by tonnage.

The minor port of Aransas Pass, located on the mainland and directly on the GIWW (mile 533 WHL) opposite the Aransas Pass inlet, was 142nd on the 2012 list and had fallen off the list by 2016. At mile 539.5 WHL, the waterway crosses the deep-water channel to the port of Corpus Christi and a tenth of a mile further west it enters Corpus Christi Bay. A channel from Aransas Pass to Corpus Christi was among the projects funded by the Texas Legislature's 1856 River Bill. By 1860, the channel is reported to have been 8 feet deep for a width of 60 feet from pass to port. This channel, now called the Morris and Cummings Channel[108] followed Corpus Christi Bayou from the southwest corner of Aransas Bay to Corpus Christi Bay. The U.S. Coast Survey's 1858 chart <u>Reconnaissance of the Coast of Texas between Matagorda and Corpus Christi Bays</u> carries a note placed between Aransas Pass and Corpus Christi Bayou that reads "There is 6 feet of water through Corpus Christi Bayou into Corpus Christi Bay and 10-20 feet through the Bay." U.S. Coast and Geodetic Survey chart 209 <u>Aransas Pass, Aransas and Copano Bays</u>, issued in 1884, clearly shows but does not name this channel. The Morris and Cummings Channel is still shown and named on coastal charts, is still navigable and used by local small craft.

The Port of Corpus Christi was 6th on the USACE's 2016 list of domestic ports by tonnage. In the Water Resources Development Act (WRDA) of 2007 Congress authorized, but did not fund, deepening the Corpus Christi Ship Channel to 52 feet. The project was reauthorized, again without funding, in 2014. At that time the project dimensions for the Corpus Christi Ship Channel were: 47 feet for a width of 600-700 feet from deep water in the gulf to the Jetties, 45-47 feet for a width of 600 feet in the Jetty Channel and 45 feet for varying widths throughout the Main and La Quinta Channels and surveys by the USACE showed depths that equaled or exceeded project dimensions. Then in September 2017 the Port of Corpus Christi Authority and the USACE signed a Project Partnership Agreement to improve the shipping channel by: increasing its minimum width to 530 feet, its depth to 54 feet and adding barge channels (barge shelves) along both sides. The estimated cost of the project was $327 million of which the Corps of Engineers…the federal government…would pay $225 million and the Port Authority $102 million. Work was to begin before the end of 2017. Corpus Christi will soon be able to handle the new Panamax ships.

At mile 549 WHL, the GIWW leaves Corpus Christ Bay and enters the Laguna Madre. From there it follows dredged channels and land cuts past the Packery Channel (approximately mile 552 WHL),[109] the Corpus Christi beach resort area on North Padre Island, the Padre Island National Seashore, Port Mansfield and the Mansfield Channel (mile 629 WHL) and the South Padre Island resorts to the Brownsville Shipping Channel (mile 668.4 WHL). The hypersaline Laguna Madre[110] is the least developed large coastal lagoon in the world. The eastern, seaward side is formed by Padre Island, the world's longest barrier island, 70 miles of which is the Padre Island National Seashore and much of the rest is in Nature Conservancy environmental easements. The western, mainland side is largely the King Ranch, several other large ranches and the Laguna Atascosa National Wildlife Refuge.

The lagoon is divided into northern and southern sections by the Saltillo Flats, an approximately 20 mile stretch of normally dry sand and mud flats that, prior to the dredging of the GIWW, formed a land bridge between the mainland and Padre Island. The northern section of the Laguna Madre is approximately 50 miles long and ranges from less than 2 to 4 miles in width while the southern, at approximately 60 miles in length and from less than 2 to 7 miles in width, extends south to within a few miles of the Mexican border. Both sections average about three feet in depth. Prior to cutting the GIWW through the Saltillo Flats and opening the two seawater ingress channels–the Mansfield Channel in 1962 and the Packery Channel in 2006–salinity levels in the lagoon occasionally reached as high as 80 parts per thousand. Opening the GIWW and the ingress channels improved circulation in the lagoon, significantly reduced the salinity levels and changed the bays ecology. A salinity of 70 parts per thousand will kill many fin fish and the reduction in salinity levels led to a boom in sport fishing throughout the lagoon but the reduced salinity also let to a reduction in sea grass acreage, a reduction in the seasonal duck population, an increase in oysters and, possibly, to algal blooms, particularly brown algae.[111]

The waterway crosses the Port Mansfield Channel at mile 629.8 WHL. Port Mansfield was established by the Willacy County Navigation District in 1950 as a safe harbor for vessels traveling the Intracoastal Waterway and as a fishing harbor. The Mansfield Channel was cut by the Willacy County Navigation District between 1955 and 1957. By 1961 the channel had completely silted in. The USACE constructed new jetties and reopened the channel in 1962. Since then maintenance dredging has been necessary roughly every two years. The federal project dimensions for the channel are a depth of 16 feet for a width of 250 feet in the Entrance Channel and a depth of 14 feet for varying widths to the Port Mansfield Turning Basin. Project depths have been difficult to maintain and in 2014 the controlling depth in the Entrance Channel was 8 feet and in the Main Channel just 4 feet. The initial impetus for the Port Mansfield Inlet was gulf access for area fisherman but increased circulation in the Laguna Madre and fish migration are now generally cited as the inlet's primary value.

At the Arroyo Colorado Cutoff, mile 644 WHL, approximately 90 miles south of Corpus Christi, the 25-mile-long barge channel to the town of Rio Hondo and the Port of Harlingen departs from the GIWW. The project dimensions for the barge channel are a depth of 12 feet for a width of 125 feet from the waterway to its head in the turning basin at the Port of Harlingen. A USACE survey carried out in May of 2015 showed channel depths of 11-13 feet and a depth in the turning basin of 14 feet. The Texas Department of Transportation[112] says that the barge facilities in Rio Hondo and the Port of Harlingen handled 900,000 tons in 2014; which included all of the raw sugar produced in the Rio Grande Valley and 90% of the fertilizer used by the region's farmers.

In the lower Laguna Madre, at mile 668.4 WHL, the GIWW intersects and merges into the Brownsville Ship Channel. From there the waterway follows the ship channel to its end at mile 681.8 WHL, approximately in the center of the turning Basin at the head the Port of Brownsville. Statistically counted as a single port, Brownsville and Port Isabel, Texas, were ranked 66th on the 2016 list of domestic ports by tonnage. Brownsville-Port Isabell is also, by far the largest commercial fishing port in Texas–although just 18th nationwide. Seafood landings exceeded $50 million in 2015.

Brazos Santiago Pass is one of the better natural inlets on the Texas Coast. U.S. Coast and Geodetic Survey Chart 212, <u>Latitude 26° 33' to the Rio Grande, Texas</u>, issued in May 1886, shows 6-7 feet over the bar at the mouth of the pass, a narrow but deep channel through the pass and 5 feet from the pass across the Laguna Madre to the railhead at Point Isabel. The first serious improvements to the pass (authorized in 1930) involved construction of stone jetties and dredging the channel to 25 feet deep for a width of 300 feet from deep water in the Gulf of Mexico through the pass and 25 feet deep for a width of 100 feet from the pass to Brownsville. By 1949 the channel from deep water through the pass was 35 feet deep for a width of 300 feet and the channel from the pass to the Brownsville Turning Basin was 32 feet deep for a width of 300 feet. In 2015 the federal project dimensions for the 22.2-mile-long project were 44 feet for a width of 300-400 feet from deep water through the Jetty Channel and 42 feet for varying widths to the Brownsville Turning Basin and 36 feet for a width of 200 feet in the Port Isabell Channel. Controlling depths were approximately four feet below authorized project depths.

Although World War II and military necessity were the justification for enlarging the Gulf Intracoastal Waterway to a depth of 12 feet and a width of 125 feet, work on the final segment, the 130 miles from the Corpus Christi Channel through Corpus Christi Bay and the Laguna Madre to the Brownsville shipping channel, did not begin until the war was over. On December 12, 1945 dredging began at both ends...one crew cutting north from the Brownsville channel, another south from the Corpus Christi channel. The official opening of the final segment of the Gulf Intracoastal Waterway took place in the middle of the Laguna

Madre on June 18, 1949. Following the ceremonial ribbon cutting, the first commercial tow to travel the Corpus Christi to Port Isabell section moved through.

The Intracoastal Waterway never reached the Grand River...the Rio Grande. Flatboat and steamboat traffic on the Rio Grande began in the 1820s and continued into the twentieth century. But in 1904 the St. Louis, Brownsville and Mexico Railroad reached Brownsville and steamboat navigation ended.[113] And by 1910 water withdrawals from the Rio Grande for irrigation and siltation

The Brownsville Texas channel, the turning basin, the west end of the Intracoastal Waterway, is in the Upper right corner.

from agricultural and urban runoff had rendered the river unfit for navigation.[114] In 1949 when the Gulf Intracoastal Waterway reached the existing deep water channel to the Port of Brownsville, the "...continuous waterway, inland where practicable, From Boston, Massachusetts to Point Isabel and thence to the Rio Grande" ended.

Betty & Bill

A professional cartographer, Bill's lifelong infatuation with the sea, ships and boats began in 1961 when, at seventeen, he went to sea on a square-rigged Norwegian school ship. He met Betty, an aerospace engineer, mathematician, pilot and experienced sailor, in a sailing club in Annapolis in 1993. A year later they left the Chesapeake on what was supposed to be a one year-round trip cruise, south to the Florida Keys, over to the Bahamas and back to the Bay. They never returned to their former lives. They lived aboard and cruised full time, power and sail, for fourteen years from Maine and the New York and Canadian canals, south to Florida, the Bahamas, and the Caribbean, west to Texas and through the canals of France. During that time, they renovated, sailed and lived aboard boats ranging from an ocean-going ketch through a trawler and several Down East boats to a large antique, iron hulled Dutch motor barge. They still spend half the year cruising the east and gulf coasts and the Bahamas aboard their retirement from cruising boat, a Nauset 28 down east hardtop power cruiser.

August 2016, back on Cape Cod, at the Kingman Yacht Center: Nauset on a mooring, Betty and Bill on the Chart Room's deck.

Sources

A Connected View of the Whole Internal Navigation of the United States; Natural and Artificial, Present and Perspective, by George Armroyd. Published by George Armroyd and printed by Lydia R. Bailey, Philadelphia, PA 1830.

A History of the Board of Engineers for Rivers and Harbors, published by the Board of Engineers for Rivers and Harbors, Fort Belvoir, VA, June 1980.

A Modal Comparison of Domestic Freight Transportation Effects on the General Public, by C. J. Krusc, Λ. Λ. Protopapas and L. E. Olson. Texas Transportation Institute, The Texas A&M University, College Station Texas, Report # 406391-F, February 2012.

American Association of Port Authorities, http://www.aapa-ports.org

An Overview of the U.S. Inland Waterway System, by Chris Clark, Kevin E. Henrickson and Paul Thoma of the Department of Economics, the University of Oregon. For the Institute of Water Resources, U.S. Army Corps of Engineers. IWR Report 05-NETS-12, November 1, 2005.

A Historical Geography of Southwest Florida Waterways, Volume One, Anna Maria Sound to Lemon Bay and Volume Two, Placida to Marco Island. Both volumes written by: Gustavo A.

Antonini, David A. Fann and Paul Roat. Published by the Florida West Coast Inland Navigation District, 200 E. Miami Ave., Venice, Florida 34285.

Custodians of the Coast, History of the United States Army Engineers at Galveston, by Lynn M. Alperin, Published by the United States Army Corps of Engineers, Galveston District, 1977.

Florida Inland Navigation District http://www.aicw.org/

Florida West Coast Inland Navigation District, http://www.wcind.net/

Freight Facts and Figures 2012 and 2016, Published annually by the U.S. Department of Transportation, Federal Highway Administration, Office of Freight Management Operations,

Geohydrology of the Cross-Florida Barge Canal Area with Special Reference to the Ocala Area, by Glen L. Faulkner. U.S. Geological Survey, Water-Resources Investigations Report I-73, Prepared in Cooperation with the U.S. Army Corps of Engineers, Tallahassee, FL 1973.

History of the Waterways of the Atlantic Coast of the United States; by Aubrey Parkman. Navigation History NWS-83-10, National Waterways Study, U.S. Army Engineer Support Center, Institute for Water Resources, January 1983.

History of the Gulf Intracoastal Waterway, by Lynn M. Alperin. Navigation History NWS-83-9, National Waterways Study, U.S. Army Engineer Support Center, Institute for Water Resources, January 1983.

History of the Offshore Oil and Gas Industry in Southern Louisiana, in 6 volumes, published by the U.S. Department of the Interior, Minerals Management Service, New Orleans, 2008.

- Volume I: Papers on the Evolving Offshore Industry, OCS Study MMS 2008-042, by Diane Austin, Tyler

Priest, Lauren Penney, Joseph Pratt, Allen G. Pulsipher, Joseph Abel and Jennifer Taylor. 264 pages.

- Volume II: <u>Bayou Lafourche – Oral Histories of the Oil and Gas Industry</u>, OCS Study MMS 2008-043, by Tom McGuire. 177 pages.
- Volume III: <u>Morgan City's History in the Era of Oil and Gas – Perspectives of Those Who Were There</u>, OCS Study MMS 2008-044, by Diane E. Austin. 238 pages.
- Volume IV: <u>Terrebonne Parish</u>, OCS Study MMS 2008-045, by James L. Sell and Tom McGuire. 90 pages.
- Volume V: <u>Guide to the Interviews</u>, OCS Study MMS 2008-046, by Diane E. Austin. 1259 pages.
- Volume VI: <u>A Collection of Photographs</u>, OCS Study MMS 2008-047, by Diane E. Austin and Justin Gaines. 165 pages.

<u>Inlets Along the Texas Gulf Coast</u>, U.S. Army Corps of Engineers, Galveston District, August 1992.

<u>Inside Route Pilot, Coast of New Jersey</u>, U.S. Department of Commerce, Coast and Geodetic Survey, published in a number of editions, each of which was accompanied by a folio of charts. The editions used were the first, published in 1915 and the second, published in 1920.

<u>Inside Route Pilot, New York to Key West</u>, U.S. Department of Commerce, Coast and Geodetic Survey, Published in eight editions between 1912 and 1936. Each edition was accompanied by a folio of charts. The editions used were the second, published in 1913, the fifth, published in 1922 (with the August 1926 supplement), and the eighth, published in 1936 (with the May 1938 supplement.)

Land's End, Written and Published by Albert E. Cowdrey, 1977. An extensively documented history of the New Orleans District, U.S. Army Corps of Engineers. Contains numerous historical charts, maps and photographs.

Laws of the United States Relating to the Improvement of Rivers and Harbors; From August 11, 1790 to January 2, 1939, Compiled by the Office of the Chief of Engineers, U.S. Army. Published by the United States Government Printing Office, Washington, DC 1940.

- Volume 1-From 1790 1896,
- Volume 2-From 1897 to 1913,
- Volume 3-From 1913 to 1939.
- General Index (Embraces the Index of the laws published in House Document: No. 1491, 62nd Congress, 3rd Session.)

NOAA, the National Geodetic Survey, http://www.ngs.noaa.gov/

NOAA, the Office of Coast Survey, Historical Map and Chart Collection, http://www.historicalcharts.noaa.gov/

NOAA, the Office of Coast Survey, Interactive Chart Viewer, http://www.charts.noaa.gov/

Preliminary Report of the Inland Waterways Commission, Senate Document 325, 60th Congress, 1st Session, February 26, 1908. Government Printing Office, Washington, DC.

Reaching for the Sea, the Story of the Port of Houston, written by Lee Vela and Maxine Edwards. Published by the Port of Houston Authority, 1989.

Report of the Committee on Traffic of the Proposed Intra-Coastal Canal connecting New York and Delaware Bays, Published by the Atlantic Deeper Waterways Association, Addison B. Burke, Editor of Publications. Philadelphia, 1911.

Salt Dome Locations in the Gulf Coastal Plain, South-Central United States, by Jeffery D. Beckman and Alex K. Williamson. U.S. Geological Survey Water Resources Investigations Report 90-4060. Austin, Texas 1990.

Texas Gulf Intracoastal Waterway Master Plan: Technical Report 0-6807-1, by: C. James Kruse, David Ellis, Annie Protopapas, Nicolas Norboge and Brianne Glover. Texas A&M Transportation Institute, Collage Station, Texas 77843-3135. Prepared in cooperation with the Texas Department of Transportation and the Federal Highway Administration for Project 0-6807. August 2014.

Texas Gulf Intracoastal Waterway Master Plan: Project 0-6807, Texas Department of Transportation, Austin, Texas. Accompanies Technical Report 0-6807-1. June 2014.

The Cape Cod Canal, by Robert H. Farson. Second, revised edition, published by Cape Cod Historical Publications, Yarmouth Port, Massachusetts, 1993.

The Delta Engineers, A History of the United States Army Corps of Engineers in the New Orleans District, by Albert E. Cowdrey, Published by the USACE New Orleans District in 1971

The Great Dismal, A Carolinian's Swamp Memoir, by Bland Simpson. The University of North Carolina Press, Chapel Hill, 1990.

The Gulf of Mexico, by Robert H. Gore. Published by Pineapple Press, Inc., Sarasota, Florida, 1992.

The Handbook of Texas Online, https://www.tshaonline.org/handbook/online/

The Intracoastal Waterway, Part 1 – Atlantic Section, booklet prepared by the U. S. Army Corps of Engineers. Published by the U.S. Government Printing Office, Washington, DC. 1951. Includes 10 charts.

The Intracoastal Waterway, Part 2 – Gulf Section, booklet prepared by the U.S. Army Corps of Engineers. Published by the U.S. Government Printing Office, Washington, DC. 1951. Includes 8 charts.

The National Waterway; a History of the Chesapeake and Delaware Canal, 1769-1965, by Ralph D. Gray. Published by the University of Illinois Press, 1967.

The U.S. Waterway System, Transportation Facts and Information, Navigation and Civil Works Support Center, U.S. Army Corps of Engineers. Editions of November 2011, 2012 and 2013 and 2016.

To Great and Useful Purpose; A History of the Wilmington District, U.S. Army Corps of Engineers, By Ronald B. Hartzer, David A. Clary and Associates. March 1983.

United States Army Corps of Engineers, Jacksonville District, http://www.saj.army.mil/

United States Army Corps of Engineers, Lock Performance Monitoring System (LPMS), http://www.corpslocks.usace.army.mil/

United States Army Corps of Engineers, Navigation Data Center, http://www.navigationdatacenter.us

United States Bureau of the Census, https://www.census.gov

United States Bureau of Ocean Energy Management, http://www.boem.gov/Gulf-of-Mexico-OCS-Region-Publications

United States Coast Guard Navigation Center, http://www.navcen.uscg.gov/

United States Coast Pilot 1; Atlantic Coast, Eastport, ME to Cape Cod, MA, 2014 (44th) Edition, U.S. Department of Commerce, National Oceanic and Atmospheric Administration, National Ocean Service.

United States Coast Pilot 2; Atlantic Coast, Cape Cod, MA to Sandy Hook, NJ, 2015 (44th) Edition, U.S. Department of Commerce, National Oceanic and Atmospheric Administration, National Ocean Service.

United States Coast Pilot 3; Atlantic Coast, Sandy Hook, NJ to Cape Henry, VA, 2015 (48th) Edition, U.S. Department of Commerce, National Oceanic and Atmospheric Administration, National Ocean Service.

United States Coast Pilot 4; Atlantic Coast, Cape Henry, VA to Key West, 2014 (46th) Edition, U.S. Department of Commerce, National Oceanic and Atmospheric Administration, National Ocean Service.

United States Coast Pilot 5; Gulf of Mexico, Puerto Rico and the Virgin Islands, 2014 (42nd) Edition, U.S. Department of Commerce, National Oceanic and Atmospheric Administration, National Ocean Service.

United States Coast Pilot, Section E, Gulf of Mexico from Key West to the Rio Grande, published 1916 (the first standalone edition of Coast Pilot 5), U.S. Department of Commerce, Coast and Geodetic Survey.

Waterborne Commerce of the United State; Calendar Year 2012 and 2016, Part 1 – Waterways and Harbors Atlantic Coast (WR-WCUS-12-1), the Institute for Water Resources, U.S. Army Corps of Engineers.

Waterborne Commerce of the United States; Calendar Year 2012 and 2016, Part 2 – Waterways and Harbors Gulf Coast, Mississippi River System and Antilles (IWR-WCUS-12-2), the Institute for Water Resources, U.S. Army Corps of Engineers.

Waterborne Commerce of the United States Year 2012 and 2016, Part 5-National Summaries, the Institute for Water Resources, U.S. Army Corps of Engineers.

Waterway Guide, Waterway Guide Media, LLC, P.O. Box 1125, Deltaville, VA 23043. Published annually in seven regional editions. https://www.waterwayguide.com

And the detailed Log Books that I kept over five boats and twenty-four years (1993-2017) of coastal and waterway cruising between Maine and Texas.

Endnotes

[1] The amended act of 1972, the Act commonly referred to as the Clean Water Act (CWA) took effect on October 18, 1972 when the House of Representatives, following the lead of the Senate, overcame fierce chemical and petroleum industry opposition and voted to override President Nixon's Veto. The Federal Water Pollution Act of 1948 was, itself, built on a number of earlier laws and regulations including Rivers and Harbors Acts governing disposal and dumping in the inland and coastal navigable waters, the various Refuse Acts and the Oil Pollution Act of 1924 [which

extended dumping and disposal to include oil of any kind or in any form, including (but not limited to): fuels, oily sludge and oily refuse]. The Oil Pollution Act of 1924 also defined the coastal navigable waters of the United States as "all portions of the sea within the territorial jurisdiction of the United States, and all inland waters navigable in fact in which the tide ebbs and flows" and further extended the prohibition on dumping or disposal of oil to include "polluting substances...deposited into the navigable waters of the United States, or into non-navigable waters connecting with navigable waters to such an extent as to endanger or interfere with navigation or commerce upon such navigable waters or the fisheries therein." The Refuse Acts and the Oil Pollution Act are the direct roots of today's clean water regulations.

[2] Cape May Inlet is the commonly used name, but the inlet's official name is Cold Spring Inlet. Cold Spring Inlet is the name sanctioned by the United States Board on Geographic Names and the name that appears: on most nautical charts, on other government produced maps and in most official documents. Discrepancies between local, common use names and official names are fairly common and often the common use name becomes the official name.

[3] Edition 1 of the <u>Inside Route Pilot</u> was issued by the U.S. Coast and Geodetic Survey in 1912 and the Pilot was issued intermittently until 1936, when the eighth and final edition came out. The eight charts in an envelope inside the rear cover of editions 1 through 5 have what may be the first version of the "magenta line" that is shown on current Intracoastal Waterway charts.

[4] As it is in the Port of New York and New Jersey and along the lower Mississippi River.

[5] Page 162, <u>A Connected View of the Whole Internal Navigation of the United States</u>, by George Armroyd. Printed in Philadelphia, PA by Lydia R. Bailey, 1830.

[6] The information on the C&D Canal was obtained from the Corps of Engineers Philadelphia District Office and at the USACE's excellent Chesapeake and Delaware Canal Museum and Visitors Center in Chesapeake City, Maryland.

[7] Information, facts and figures for the Chesapeake Bay were obtained from: the U.S. Army Corps of Engineers, the Chesapeake Bay Foundation, the National Oceanic and Atmospheric Administration, the States of Maryland and Virginia, and (used by permission) the Chesapeake Bay Edition of <u>The Waterway Guide</u>.

[8] The inflation rate in the United States between 1880 and 2016 averaged 2.31%. At that rate $86,138.99 in 1880 would equal approximately $1,920,069 in 2016.

[9] For the canal company's creditors and shareholders, it was probably a very profitable deal. $500,000 in 2013 would be the equivalent of $12,121,565 in 2016.

[10] A 1:200,000 scale chart, *Coast of North Carolina and Virginia,* compiled by the U.S. Coast Survey in February 1862, shows the "Washington Canal" extending NNW from Lake Drummond to the edge of the Great Dismal Swamp south of Suffolk, Virginia.

[11] <u>The Great Dismal, A Carolinian's Swamp Memoir,</u> Bland Simpson, The University of North Carolina Press, 1990, and <u>Cruising Into History,</u> a United States Army Corps of Engineers (Norfolk District) brochure, published July 2007.

[12] National Oceanic and Atmospheric Administration, National Climatic Data Center, Ashville, North Carolina.

[13] At AICW mile 111.8 the Alligator-Pungo Canal crosses a still older canal about which little is known. This canal parallels the Fairfield Canal and runs from a natural bend in the Alligator River to Lake Mattamuskeet. In the late nineteenth and the early twentieth centuries it was known locally as the "Carter Canal." The canal is believed to have been dug just prior to the Civil War, possibly by slave labor and the builder may have been the Fairfield Canal and Turnpike Company. During the 1880s Col. William S. Carter (of Fairfield) was president of the Fairfield Canal and Turnpike Company.

[14] Boat Wakes and Their Influence on Erosion in the Atlantic Intracoastal Waterway, North Carolina, M. S. Fonseca and A. Malhotra, NOAA Technical Memorandum NOS NCCOS #143, March 2012.

[15] The Federal Gasoline Tax at a Glance: A History. A 23-page booklet by James Strouder Sweet, published by Bybee House, 1993.

[16] Page 2155, Volume III, Laws of the United States Relating to the Improvement of Rivers and Harbors. Compiled by the Office of the Chief of Engineers, U.S. Army. Published by the United States Government Printing Office, Washington, DC 1940. I believe that this Act is still applicable, if Congress has amended it, or deleted it, I have been unable to find the change.

[17] There were attempts at Tiger Prawn aquaculture on the east coast of the United States, in the Carolinas and Florida. The last known attempt, in Florida, closed in 2004. In 1988 at least 2000 Tiger Prawns escaped from an aquaculture facility in South

Carolina. USGS Asian Tiger Shrimp Fact Sheet
https://nas.er.usgs.gov/queries/factsheet.aspx?SpeciesID=1209

[18] Down East is an old, possibly very old, term with a convoluted etymology that migrated into nautical and common usage, particularly in the United States, as a reference to sailing or traveling east, down the degrees of longitude, or to running east—sailing down wind—in an area of prevailing westerly winds. Today in the United States, Down East is most commonly used as a geographic/cultural area designation for coastal New England east of Boston, coastal Maine or, more specifically Maine between Searsport and the Canadian border. But the term was also used and is still in common use in North Carolina and, I believe, it was also used on Long Island Sound in the days of commercial sail. Boats sailing from Beaufort/Morehead City to the outlying coastal communities on Core and Pamlico Sounds, sailed Down East, down wind and down longitude. The residents of the area were (and are) called down easters. Today in North Carolina the term is general limited to the Carteret County coastal communities on Core Sound east of Beaufort. In the past the term probably referred to all of the small boat building and fishing communities on the Inner Banks behind the Outer Banks and on the Outer Banks as far up as Hatteras and Frisco (Trent prior to 1898). North of Cape Hatteras the sailing directions change from predominantly east-west to north-south.

[19] Originally compiled and drawn by Adolph Lindenkohl in 1855 at the Coast Survey, Washington, DC.

[20] This chart also shows a dashed course line, hi-lighted in magenta and labeled "Course of the Inland Navigation." The magenta hi-lighted course line is an early antecedent of the

Endnotes

Magenta Line shown on Inside Route and Intracoastal Waterway charts since 1912.

[21] The tidal waters of Myrtle Grove Sound and of the Cape Fear River are out of phase by approximately an hour and a half, as a result there is a water level difference between the sound and river that generates swift currents. To overcome the water level difference and the currents, the original specifications for Snow's Cut called for a tide lock in the cut. The tide lock proved to be unnecessary. It was never built and it was de-authorized in Section 12 of PL 93-251, September 23, 1986.

[22] From the Georgetown Chamber of Commerce, the Rice Museum and www. seaportgeorgetown.com.

[23] *James Island and Johns Island Historical and Architectural Inventory*, by Preservation Consultants, Inc. for the South Carolina Dept. of Archives and History, City of Charleston and Charleston County, 1989.

[24] *The Siege of Charleston – 1780*, by Gen. Wilmot G. DeSaussure, in the (Charleston) City Year Book - 1884.

[25] Jekyll Island Museum, 100 Stable Road, Jekyll Island, Georgia 31527; (912) 635-4036.

[26] Florida Inland Navigation District – Our History, http://aicw.org/history.jsp

[27] Florida Inland Navigation District – Our History, http://aicw.org/history.jsp

[28] *Poleward Expansion of Mangroves is a Threshold Response to Decreased Frequency of Extreme Cold Events*, by: Cavanaugh, K.C., Kellner, J.R., Ford, A.J., Gruner, D.S., Parker, J.D., Rodriguez, W. and Feller, I.C.; Proceedings of the National Academy of Sciences; 2013.

[29] https://www.gao.gov/key_issues/disaster_assistance/national-flood-insurance-program and https://www.fema.gov/statistics-calendar-year

[30] According to a probably apocryphal tale, King Cnut of England (1016-1035), in order to demonstrate the limits of royal power, had the throne placed on a beach at low tide and, from the throne, he commanded the tide, the sea, not to rise…and he was ignored. Congress directed the Corps of Engineers to prevent the sea from damaging the value of coastal property…structures appeared…but the damage continues.

[31] History of the Gulf Intracoastal Waterway, by Lynn M. Alperin. Page 41.

[32] *Monthly Weather Review, December 1947*, NOAA, National Weather Service Archives.

[33] USACE LPMS Summaries by River Basin, January – December 2013 and January – December 2016.

[34] Chapter 12, *Intracoastal Waterway* in U.S. Coast Pilot 4, Atlantic Coast, Cape Henry to Key West, 2014 and http://www.saj.usace.army.mil/Missions/CivilWorks

[35] *Venice did not welcome Intracoastal Waterway*, by Dale White, April 7, 2014 on http://www.heraldtribune.com (web site of the Sarasota Herald Tribune.)

[36] In July 1914, the Louisiana State Legislature authorized the Port of New Orleans to build a deep-water canal between Lake Pontchartrain and the Mississippi River. The project specifications called for a canal with a surface width of 300 feet, a bottom width of 150 feet, a depth of 30 feet and a lock through the levee at the Mississippi River end. The lock was to have a chamber 640-feet long, 74 feet wide and with a depth over the

gate sills of 30 feet. The lock was to have a minimum lift/drop of 20 feet. Work began on June 6, 1918 and the official opening ceremony was held on May 5, 1923. The Port of New Orleans charged commercial vessels transiting the canal a fee of $.05 per gross ton.

[37] The Gulf County Canal was built by Gulf County in 1937 and 1938 in an attempt to revive the local economy. The six-mile-long, 9-foot-deep by 100-foot-wide canal, completed at the end of 1938, was financed with $200,000 in bonds issued by Gulf County which were to be repaid by tolls on commercial traffic. The volume of tolls anticipated did not materialize and the canal was incorporated into the federal GIWW project in 1944, without financial compensation to Gulf County or the bond holders. The canal was subsequently enlarged to, and has been maintained at, prevailing GIWW dimensions by the USACE. There has been no commercial freight traffic reported for the canal since 2006, but the canal is heavily used by commercial fishing and private vessels.

[38] In May 2015, the channel through East Pass had a controlling depth of 11.5 feet and a width of 80 feet and the U.S. Highway 98 fixed bridge across the pass had a Mean High-Water clearance of 49 feet. NOAA Chart 11385.

[39] The Congressionally authorized depth for the channel from the Gulf of Mexico, through Pensacola Pass to Pensacola Harbor is 35 feet for a width of 500 feet. To meet naval requirements, the U.S. Navy maintains the channel from deep water to the Naval Turning Basin at a depth of 44 feet for a width of 800 feet. The USACE maintained civil channel departs from the from the U.S. Navy channels at the junction of the Barrancas and Pickens

Channels and from there to Pensacola Harbor had a controlling depth of 33 feet in 2015.

[40] https://www.civilwar.org/mobilebay, https://www.historynet.com/battle-of-mobile-bay/, and https://www/nps.gov/ (the National Park Service.)

[41] Annual Report of the Chief Engineers, House Documents, 60th Congress, 1st Session, December 2, 1907-May 30, 1908.

[42] Preliminary Report of the Inland Waterways Commission, February 26, 1908, and the United States Coast Pilot, Atlantic Coast, Section E, 1916 Edition, Page 96.

[43] From *S/V Walkabout's* Log Book Number Two (20 May 1997-26 May 1999.)

[44] USACE, New Orleans District, History of MRGO http://www.mvn.usace.army.mil/Missions/Environmental/MRGO EcosystemRestoration/History

[45] DRAGON (Delta Research and Global Observation Network), U.S. Department of the Interior, U.S. Geological Survey, http://www.deltas.usgs.gov/

[46] In some documents and publications miles Above Head of Passes are referred to as LMR miles. LMR means Lower Mississippi River, the river downstream from the intersection of the thalwegs of the Ohio and Mississippi Rivers near Cairo, Illinois. Regardless of what it's called, the mileage is still counted upstream from a zero point at the Junction Light.

[47] The capital was moved to New Orleans from Biloxi in 1722. Fort Maurapas, the initial French settlement on Biloxi Bay was established by Pierre le Moyne, Sieur de Iberville, Jean Baptiste le Moyne's older brother, in 1699.

[48] Natural Levee. As a river carrying a heavy load of suspended sediment descends from higher ground onto lower, flatter ground, the force, or speed, of the river's current decreases, which decreases the amount of sediment that can remain suspended in the water and heavier particles such as sand and small pebbles settle out in the river channel, creating sand bars and shoals and raising the river bed, which makes flooding more likely. When the river floods and the water spreads out in a relatively thin layer over the lands adjacent to the river, the current decreases further and more of the rivers suspended sediment is deposited; heaviest particles and largest quantities closest to the river. Over long periods of time and many annual flooding cycles, the sediments deposited near the river build up, layer by layer into a natural levee. In time the natural levees become broad ribbons of land that are significantly higher than the land further from the river. The natural levees, high dryer land with good river access, were a preferred location for early settlements.

At its mouth, where the river flows into the sea, the rivers current slows and dissipates in the ocean and any suspended sediment is deposited. At first the sediment forms subsurface mud banks and sand bars. With time and more sediment, the mud banks and sand bars become marshes, beaches and barrier islands, the natural levees creep seaward and new land appears…the living, growing face of the river's delta.

[49] Old River Control Complex information obtained from the USACE New Orleans District's Public Affairs Office and on line at http://www.mvn,usace.army.mil/portals/56/docs/PAC

[50] If the Old River Control Structure Fails? (the Physical and Economic Consequences) By Raphael G. Kazmann and David B.

Johnson, with technical addenda by John R. Harris and David B. Johnson, Louisiana Water Research Institute, Bulletin 12. Louisiana State University, Baton Rouge, September 1980.

[51] The Bayou Fatma branch of the Bayou Barataria flows into the Barataria very close to the junction of the Harvey Canal and the Algiers Alternate Route.

[52] Arpent: a royalist French unit of measurement that in France was equal to 220 French Feet. In North America (Quebec and Louisiana) an arpent equaled 180 French feet or 192 English feet. In Louisiana, Mississippi, Alabama and Florida, one square arpent equals 0.84628 of an acre. In general usage a square arpent is considered to equal 0.845 of a square acre.

[53] Land Area Change and Overview of Hurricane Impacts in Coastal Louisiana, 2004-2008, by J. A. Barras. U.S. Geological Survey Scientific Investigations Map 3080, scale 1:250,000 with 6 pages of text. Published 2009.

[54] Land Area Change in Coastal Louisiana–A Multidecadal Perspective, by J. A. Barras, J. C. Bernier and R. A. Morton. U.S. Geological Survey Scientific Investigations Map 3019, scale 1:250,000 with 14 pages of text. Published 2008.

[55] Land Area Change in Coastal Louisiana from 1932 to 2010, by: R. R. Couvillion, J. A. Barras, G. D. Steyer, W. Sleavin, M. Fisher, H. Beck, N. Trahan, B. Griffin and D. Heckman. U. S. Geological Survey Scientific Investigations Map 3164, scale 1:265,000, with 12 pages of text.

[56] Aids to navigation, marked channel surveys, powerlines, bridges and anything else that effects navigation are updated regularly. The underlying charts–hydrographic data outside the

marked channels, the depiction of coastlines, marsh, terrain, urban areas, etc.–frequently go years between updates.

[57] History of the Offshore Oil and Gas Industry in Southern Louisiana: Volume IV, Terrebonne Parish, by James Sell and Tom McGuire. Published by the U.S. Department of the Interior, Minerals Management Service. New Orleans, Louisiana 2008.

[58] The Gulf Intracoastal Waterway as a Distributary of Mississippi River Water to Coastal Louisiana Wetlands, by Christopher M. Swarzenski. U.S. Geological Survey, Louisiana Water Resource Center, Baton Rouge, Louisiana.

[59] Along the Atchafalaya River in St. Mary Parish, between the towns of Jeanerette and Charenton, northwest of Morgan City

[60] History of the Offshore Oil and Gas Industry in Southern Louisiana: Volume III,

[61] American Oil and Gas Historical Society, http://www.aoghs.org/offshore-history/

[62] Growing Deltas in Atchafalaya Bay, http://earthobservatory.nasa.gov/Features/WorldOfChange/, History of Wax Lake Delta, Department of Oceanography and Coastal Sciences, by Robert Twilley, The University of Louisiana, Baton Rouge, http://www.oceanography.lsu.edu.twilleylab/, and the Louisiana Department of Wildlife and Fisheries, http://www.wlf.louisiana.gov/wma/32639/

[63] The Louann Salt, along the northern margin of the gulf, and the Campeche Salt along the southern margin, formed during the Middle Jurassic, 161-176 million years ago, when the separation and spreading apart of the North and South American tectonic plates created the Gulf of Mexico. For tens of thousands of years during the early stages of separation shallow, subsidence

depressions in and hyper-saline lagoons on the periphery of the proto-Gulf repeatedly filled with saltwater, which evaporated, precipitating salt. Over thousands upon thousands of evaporative cycles, the salt built into a thick layer. Over geologic time as formation of the gulf progressed, the depressions and lagoons deepened and stabilized and the salt bed was slowly covered by thousands of feet of layered sediment which compressed and hardened into rock.

[64] The others are: Big Hill in Winnie, Texas, West Hackberry in Lake Charles, Louisiana and Bayou Choctaw near Baton Rouge, Louisiana.

[65] Plume hunters, seeking feathers for ladies hats, slaughtered millions of egrets and herons along the gulf coast between the Everglades and south Texas. In 1895 Edward McIlhenny made Avery Island a bird sanctuary. He gathered 8 baby egrets, the remnant few his men could find, raised them in captivity and released them as adults at the start of the annual fall migration across the gulf to Mexico. In the spring they returned, leading others and today thousands of egrets and herons of every variety found in North America live on and around Avery Island.

[66] Information obtained at the Avery Island Tabasco Museum and from http://www.tabasco.com/avery-island/

[67] The Mermentau Basin Project http://www.mvn.usace.army.mil/Portals/56/docs/PAO/Brochures/mermentau.pdf/

[68] Paradise Lost? The Coastal Prairie of Louisiana and Texas http://www.nwrc.usgs.gov/prairie/paradise_lost.pdf

[69] Port of Lake Charles http://www.portlc.com/about/history/

[70] Texas was an independent Republic from March 2, 1836, when it declared its independence from Mexico, through December 29, 1845 when it was admitted to the Union as the 28th State.

[71] <u>Annual Reports of the War Department, Fiscal Year Ended June 30, 1897</u>, Report of the Chief of Engineers, Part 2, Washington, Government Printing Office, 1897.

[72] https://en.wikipedia.org/<u>Trains/ICC/valuations/PortArthur/</u>

[73] Chap. 3436, Vol. 34, p. 302 [H.R. 10715], "An Act To establish an additional collection district in the State of Texas, and for other purposes." Passed June 19, 1906.

[74] On January 10, 1901 Anthony F. Lucas brought in the Lucas Gusher at the Spindletop salt dome oilfield, south of Beaumont, Texas. When the gusher blew in a crude oil geyser shot over 100 feet into the air. The oil flowed under natural pressure at a rate estimated at 100,000 barrels per day for the nine days it took to cap the well. The great East Texas Oil Boom was underway. In 1902 the Spindletop field yielded 17,500,000 barrels of oil and all that oil had to be moved and refined.

[75] <u>U.S. Coast Pilot 5, Gulf of Mexico, Puerto Rico and Virgin Islands</u>, 42nd Edition. Published in February 2015. Chapter 10, pages 391-400.

[76] <u>Waterborne Commerce of the United States</u>, Calendar Year 2016, Part 2-Waterways and Harbors Gulf Coast, Mississippi River System and Antilles, Department of the Army, Corps of Engineers, Institute for Water Resources publication IWR-WCUS-12-2.

[77] Overview of Texas Ports and Waterways, prepared by the Texas Department of Transportation for testimony before the Senate Select Committee on Texas Ports, May 4, 2016.

[78] History of the Gulf Intracoastal Waterway, Lynn M. Alperin. Page 30.

[79] Gulf and Inter-State Railway by Robert Wooster, https://www.tshaonline/handbook/articles/eqg20

[80] U.S. Coast Pilot, Section E, Gulf of Mexico. 1916 Edition.

[81] http://www.co.galveston.tx.us/Port_Bolivar_History/ and Bolivar Peninsula, by A. Pat Daniels https://www.tshaonline.org/handbook/articles/rrb06

[82] The United States Coast Survey, known as the Coast and Geodetic Survey since 1878, was established in 1807 and is the oldest U.S. Government scientific organization.

[83] Bolivar Roads is the naturally deep area, scoured out by tidal currents, between the Bolivar Peninsula and Galveston Island. The Galveston Entrance Bar lay seaward of the Peninsula and Island, in the area now named the Outer Bar Channel, between and just outside of the jetties.

[84] Pages 12-13 in Inlets along the Texas Gulf Coast, U.S. Army Corps of Engineers, Galveston District, August 1992.

[85] https://tshaonline.org/handbook/online/articles/hcg02 Galveston County by Diana Kleiner and http://www.galveston.com/history/

[86] USACE surveys carried out between August 2014 and January 2015.

[87] http://www.texascity-library.org/history/

[88] Pages 46-47 in Reaching for the Sea, the Story of the Port of Houston, published by the Port of Houston Authority in 1989.

[89] Pages 412-418 in U.S. Coast Pilot 5, Chapter 10. Edition of February 22, 2015.

[90] U.S. Bureau of the Census, 2012 estimates: State of Texas 26,059,203; all 19 coastal counties 6,402,703; the five Galveston Bay coastal counties 4,991,794 (Harris County 4,253,963; Brazoria County 324,295; Galveston County 301,092; Liberty County 76,349; Chambers County 36,095.) The five Galveston Bay counties had 78% of the population of Texas's coastal counties.

[91] Texas Department of Parks and Wildlife and the Texas A&M University AgriLife Extension Service.

[92] The Chesapeake Bay Foundation estimates that each adult eastern oyster (*Crassostrea Virginica*, the oyster common to the Atlantic and Gulf coasts) filters and cleans up to 50 gallons of water per day—eating the algae and removing nitrogen and other pollutants.

[93] USGS Fact Sheet 110-02, https://pubs.usgs.gov/fs/FS_110-02/Fact%20Sheet%20110-02.htm

[94] https://tshaonline.org/handbook/online/articles/hcg02 *Galveston County* by Diana Kleiner

[95] See NOAA Nautical Chart 11322, 1:40,000, Intracoastal Waterway, Texas, Galveston Bay to Cedar Lakes.

[96] https://www.dow.com/locations/texas/freeport/about and the History of Freeport-McMoRan Copper & Gold Inc. http://www/fundinguniverse.com

[97] Pages 17-19 in Inlets along the Texas Gulf Coast, U.S. Army Corps of Engineers, Galveston District, August 1992.

[98] USACE, Galveston District, *Freeport Harbor, TX Fact Sheet, February 21, 2012* and *Freeport Harbor, Texas Channel Improvement*

Project, USACE Galveston District Civil Works Review Board Briefing, June 2011.

[99] In Short Tons, calendar years 2011 and 2012, USACE, *Domestic Traffic for Selected U.S. Inland Waterways.*

[100] In Net Tons, fiscal year 2012 (October 2011 through September 2012.) http://panama-guide.com/article.php/20121010120839381

[101] In Net Tons, calendar year 2012. http://www.suezcanal.gov.eg/TRstatHistory.aspx?reportid=4

[102] U.S. Bureau of the Census.

[103] Overview of Texas Ports and Waterways, Texas Department of Transportation, produced for the (Texas) Senate Select Committee on Texas Ports, May 2016.

[104] The small fishing, tourism and retirement town of Port O'Connor was established in 1909 by the Calhoun Cattle Company on the 70,000-acre Alligator Head Ranch, formerly owned by Thomas M. O'Connor.

[105] https://www.calhounport.com

[106] *Texas's Internal Improvement Crisis of 1856: Four Remedial Plans Considered*, by Earl F. Woodward (1975), East Texas Historical Journal: Vol. 13: Issue 1, Article 6.

[107] *Kate Ward*, by Mike Cox, http://www.texasescapes.com/

[108] The channel is named for August Morris and James Cummings who cleaned out, deepened and widened the channel between 1871 and 1874.

[109] The natural pass between Mustang Island and Padre Island, originally called Corpus Christi Pass and, formerly the main entrance to Corpus Christi Bay. In its natural state the pass was a 2 to 4-mile wide area with multiple ephemeral, shifting channels

and openings to the Gulf of Mexico. U.S. Coast and Geodetic Survey Chart 210 <u>Aransas Pass and Corpus Christi Bay</u>, issued in February 1887, shows the pass as a well-defined channel named "Corpus Christi Pass" and having: 4-6 feet over the bar at its seaward end, 8-15+ feet in the channel but only a foot and a half over the channels inshore end. On charts issued in 1928 and 1933, the pass was open and the 1928 chart shows two gulf entrances. The State of Texas and the Corps of Engineers, with some help from Hurricane Emily, reopened the channel between 2003 and 2006 and named it the "Packery Channel" after post-Civil War packing plants that operated along one of the pass's channels. The pass was reopened primarily to increase seawater circulation in the Laguna Madre and, secondarily for use by local small craft.

[110] By definition, a hypersaline lagoon must as its normal state contain more dissolved salt than standard seawater. On average seawater contains 35 parts per thousand, or 35 grams of salt, per liter of water. There are five large hypersaline lagoons in the world. The Texas Laguna Madre and the Laguna Madre de Tamaulipas, on the Mexican gulf coast immediately south of the Rio Grande Delta, a single system, are one. The other four are: the Laguna Ojo de Liebre, on the Pacific coast of Baja California, the Syvash, on the east side of the Crimean Peninsula (Sea of Azov), Spencer Gulf, on the south coast of Australia (off the Great Australian Bight) and Shark Bay, on the west coast of Australia. There are a lot of small hypersaline lagoons and coastal ponds and the semi-enclosed bays along the coast of Texas can reach minimal hyper salinity during periods of drought.

[111] *Laguna Madre*, Christopher P. Onuf, https://pubs.usgs.gov/sir/2006/5287/pdf, *USGS Fact Sheet 167-98*

https://pubs.usgs.gov/fs/fs-167-98 and *The Big Laguna*, Texas Parks and Wildlife Magazine, July 2008.

[112] Overview of Texas Ports and Waterways, Texas Department of Transportation, produced for the (Texas) Senate Select Committee on Texas Ports, May 2016.

[113] *Steamboats big part of Valleys Start*, by Mel Huff, in The Brownsville Herald, May 25, 2003.

[114] *Navigation on the Rio Grande*, by M.G. Pat Kelley, http://www.tshaonline.org/handbook/online/articles/etno1

Made in the USA
Columbia, SC
14 March 2019